Office 2007

Top 100

W9-AAV-867

Simplified®

TIPS & TRICKS

by Kate Shoup

Visual™

Wiley Publishing, Inc.

Office 2007: Top 100 Simplified® Tips & Tricks

Published by
Wiley Publishing, Inc.
10475 Crosspoint Boulevard
Indianapolis, IN 46256
www.wiley.com

Published simultaneously in Canada

Library of Congress Control Number: 2007939640

ISBN: 978-0-470-11870-2

Manufactured in the United States of America

10 9 8 7 6 5 4 3 2 1

Trademark Acknowledgments

Contact Us

For general information on our other products and services contact our Customer Care Department within the U.S. at 800-762-2974, outside the U.S. at 317-572-3993 or fax 317-572-4002.

For technical support please visit www.wiley.com/techsupport.

Wiley Publishing, Inc.

U.S. Sales

Contact Wiley at (800) 762-2974 or fax (317) 572-4002.

PRAISE FOR VISUAL BOOKS

"I have to praise you and your company on the fine products you turn out. I have twelve Visual books in my house. They were instrumental in helping me pass a difficult computer course. Thank you for creating books that are easy to follow. Keep turning out those quality books."
Gordon Justin (Brielle, NJ)

"What fantastic teaching books you have produced! Congratulations to you and your staff. You deserve the Nobel prize in Education. Thanks for helping me understand computers."
Bruno Tonon (Melbourne, Australia)

"A Picture Is Worth A Thousand Words! If your learning method is by observing or hands-on training, this is the book for you!"
Lorri Pegan-Durastante (Wickliffe, OH)

"Over time, I have bought a number of your 'Read Less - Learn More' books. For me, they are THE way to learn anything easily. I learn easiest using your method of teaching."
José A. Mazón (Cuba, NY)

"You've got a fan for life!! Thanks so much!!"
Kevin P. Quinn (Oakland, CA)

"I have several books from the Visual series and have always found them to be valuable resources."
Stephen P. Miller (Ballston Spa, NY)

"I have several of your Visual books and they are the best I have ever used."
Stanley Clark (Crawfordville, FL)

"Like a lot of other people, I understand things best when I see them visually. Your books really make learning easy and life more fun."
John T. Frey (Cadillac, MI)

"I have quite a few of your Visual books and have been very pleased with all of them. I love the way the lessons are presented!"
Mary Jane Newman (Yorba Linda, CA)

"Thank you, thank you, thank you...for making it so easy for me to break into this high-tech world."
Gay O'Donnell (Calgary, Alberta,Canada)

"I write to extend my thanks and appreciation for your books. They are clear, easy to follow, and straight to the point. Keep up the good work! I bought several of your books and they are just right! No regrets! I will always buy your books because they are the best."
Seward Kollie (Dakar, Senegal)

"I would like to take this time to thank you and your company for producing great and easy-to-learn products. I bought two of your books from a local bookstore, and it was the best investment I've ever made! Thank you for thinking of us ordinary people."
Jeff Eastman (West Des Moines, IA)

"Compliments to the chef!! Your books are extraordinary! Or, simply put, extra-ordinary, meaning way above the rest! THANKYOU THANKYOU THANKYOU! I buy them for friends, family, and colleagues."
Christine J. Manfrin (Castle Rock, CO)

CREDITS

Project Editor
Tim Borek

Acquisitions Editor
Jody Lefevere

Copy Editor
Lauren Kennedy

Technical Editor
Lee Musick

Editorial Manager
Robyn Siesky

Business Manager
Amy Knies

Sr. Marketing Manager
Sandy Smith

Editorial Assistant
Laura Sinise

Manufacturing
Allan Conley
Linda Cook
Paul Gilchrist
Jennifer Guynn

Special Help
Alissa Birkel

Book Design
Kathie Rickard

Production Coordinator
Erin Smith

Layout & Graphics
Joyce Haughey
Andrea Hornberger
Jennifer Mayberry
Amanda Spagnuolo
Christine Williams

Screen Artist
Jill Proll

Cover Design
Anthony Bunyan

Proofreader
Laura Bowman

Quality Control
Melanie Hoffman

Indexer
Slivoskey Indexing Services

**Vice President and Executive
Group Publisher**
Richard Swadley

Vice President and Publisher
Barry Pruett

Composition Director
Debbie Stailey

ABOUT THE AUTHOR

Kate Shoup has written more than a dozen books, including *The Agassi Story, iPhone VISUAL Quick Tips, Windows Vista VISUAL Encyclopedia, Webster's New World English Grammar Handbook,* and more. She has also co-written a screenplay, and worked as the Sports Editor for *NUVO Newsweekly*. When not writing, Kate loves to ski (she was once nationally ranked), ride her motorcycle, and play video poker — and she plays a mean game of 9-ball. Kate lives in Indianapolis with her daughter and their dog.

How To Use This Book

Office 2007: Top 100 Simplified® Tips & Tricks includes 100 tasks that reveal cool secrets, teach timesaving tricks, and explain great tips guaranteed to make you more productive with Microsoft® Office 2007. The easy-to-use layout lets you work through all the tasks from beginning to end or jump in at random.

Who is this book for?

You already know Microsoft Office basics. Now you'd like to go beyond, with shortcuts, tricks and tips that let you work smarter and faster. And because you learn more easily when someone *shows* you how, this is the book for you.

Conventions Used In This Book

❶ Steps

This book uses step-by-step instructions to guide you easily through each task. Numbered callouts on every screen shot show you exactly how to perform each task, step by step.

❷ Tips

Practical tips provide insights to save you time and trouble, caution you about hazards to avoid, and reveal how to do things in Office 2007 that you never thought possible!

❸ Task Numbers

Task numbers from 1 to 100 indicate which lesson you are working on.

❹ Difficulty Levels

For quick reference, the symbols below mark the difficulty level of each task.

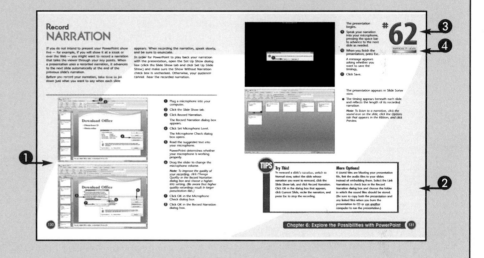

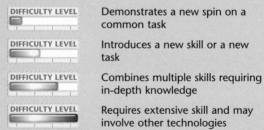

DIFFICULTY LEVEL	
	Demonstrates a new spin on a common task
	Introduces a new skill or a new task
	Combines multiple skills requiring in-depth knowledge
	Requires extensive skill and may involve other technologies

Table of Contents

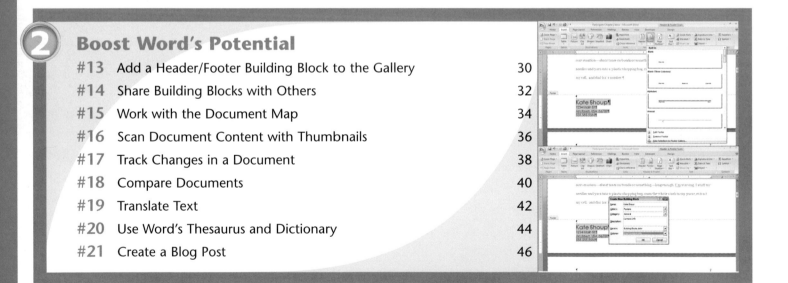

3 Jazz Up Your Work with Word

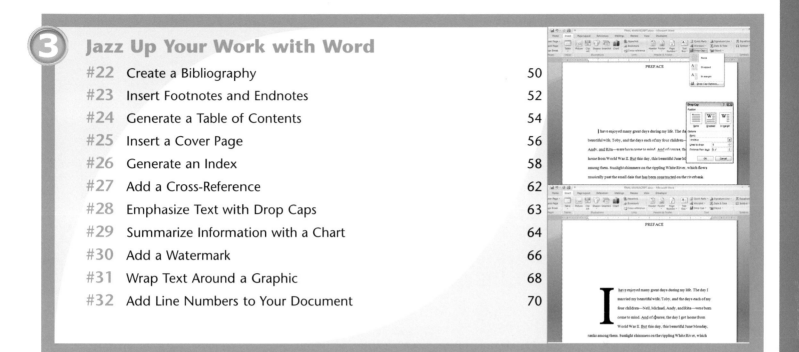

4 Optimize Excel

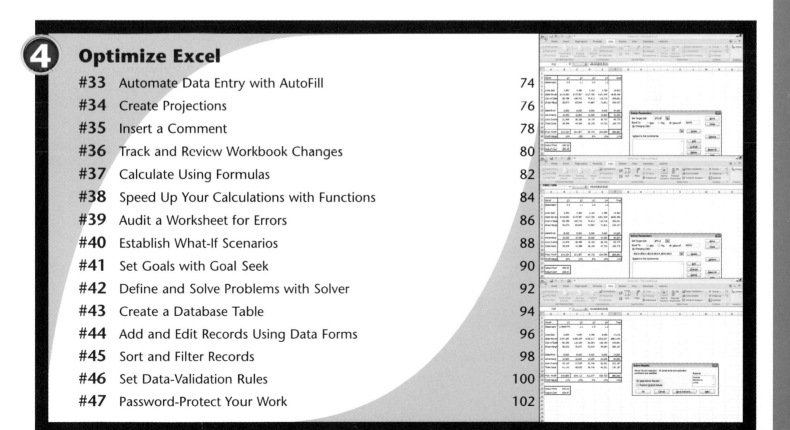

Table of Contents

Table of Contents

11 Manage Multiple Priorities with Outlook

Maximize the Power of Office 2007

The various applications in Microsoft Office 2007 — in particular, Word, Excel, PowerPoint, Access, and Outlook — share a common look and feel. Indeed, you can find many of the same features in each program, such as the new Ribbon feature, the Quick Access toolbar, various program window controls, and the new Office menu.

This common look and feel is helpful when you perform certain tasks within Office applications. For example, creating a new document in Word is similar to creating a new document in Excel.

The same goes for more complicated tasks, such as encrypting documents, tracking changes to a document, adding a digital signature, marking a document as final, and so on. This commonality makes mastering Office 2007 a snap.

This chapter focuses on tasks that transcend applications. That is, these tasks can be performed in more than one Office program. Although some of these tasks do apply to Access and Outlook, most relate only to Word, Excel, and PowerPoint.

Top 100

Make a document
BACKWARD COMPATIBLE

By default, documents you create with Office 2007 are saved with an *x* at the end of the file extension — for example, .docx, .xlsx, and so on. Documents with this type of file extension can be opened and read only by others who also use Office 2007.

If you frequently share documents with others who use earlier versions of the software suite, you can save the documents you create in Office 2007 in *Compatibility Mode* — a format that is compatible

with earlier versions of Office (or, in other words, a format that is *backward compatible*). Documents saved in Compatibility Mode can be opened and read by people who use earlier versions of the software. Documents in compatibility mode do not include the *x* at the end of the file extension.

Be aware that saving a document in Compatibility Mode means that those functions of Office 2007 that are not supported by earlier versions of Office are disabled.

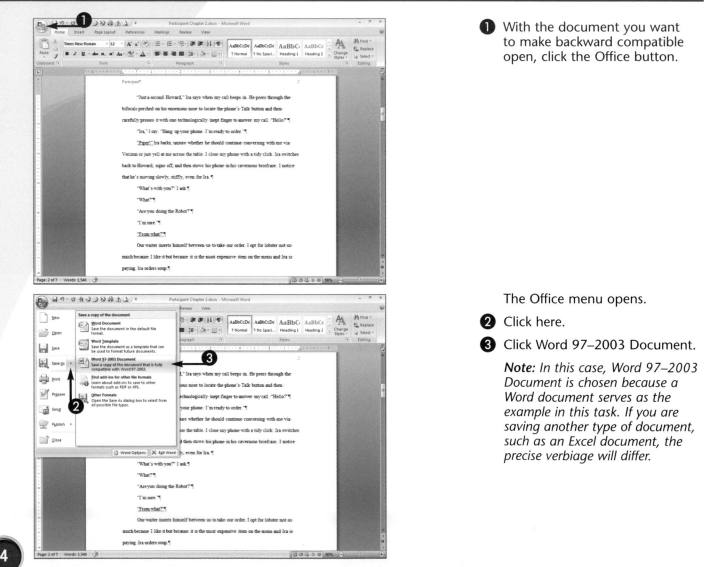

① With the document you want to make backward compatible open, click the Office button.

The Office menu opens.

② Click here.

③ Click Word 97–2003 Document.

Note: In this case, Word 97–2003 Document is chosen because a Word document serves as the example in this task. If you are saving another type of document, such as an Excel document, the precise verbiage will differ.

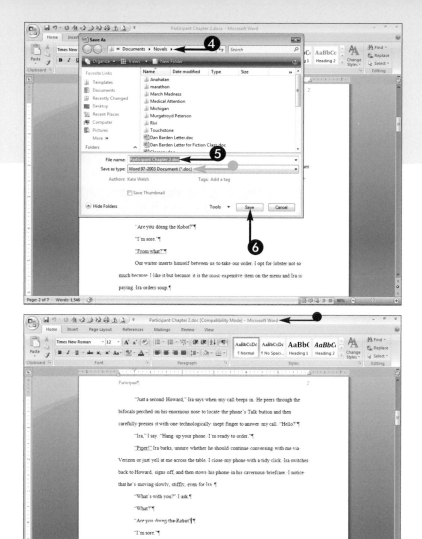

The Save As dialog box opens.

④ Locate and select the folder in which you want to save the backward-compatible document.

⑤ Type a name for the document.

● Notice that the file type listed in the Save as type field is Word 97–2003 Document.

⑥ Click Save.

● The document is saved in Compatibility Mode, as denoted in the application window's title bar.

TIP

Did You Know?

You can set up the various programs in Office to automatically save documents in Compatibility Mode. To do so, click the Office button and then click the *Program Name* Options button at the bottom of the menu. In the window that appears, click Save, click the Save files in this format drop-down arrow, select the desired format, and click OK.

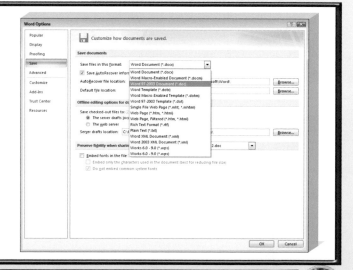

Save Office documents as
WEB PAGES

If you have access to a Web server, you can share your Office documents by saving them as Web pages. In this way, you can share your Office files with others who do not use Office.

When you save an Office document as a Web page, Office converts the document to a hypertext markup language (HTML) file. This file contains all the necessary coding to be displayed by a Web browser such as Internet Explorer 7.

Of course, simply saving an Office file as an HTML document is not enough to share it with others online. You will also need to upload the HTML file to a Web server. That requires using a Web host. You might have access to Web-hosting services through your Internet service provider; contact your provider to find out. If not, you can sign up with a Web-hosting service to place your HTML pages online. For specific instructions on uploading your Office documents to the Internet, consult with your provider.

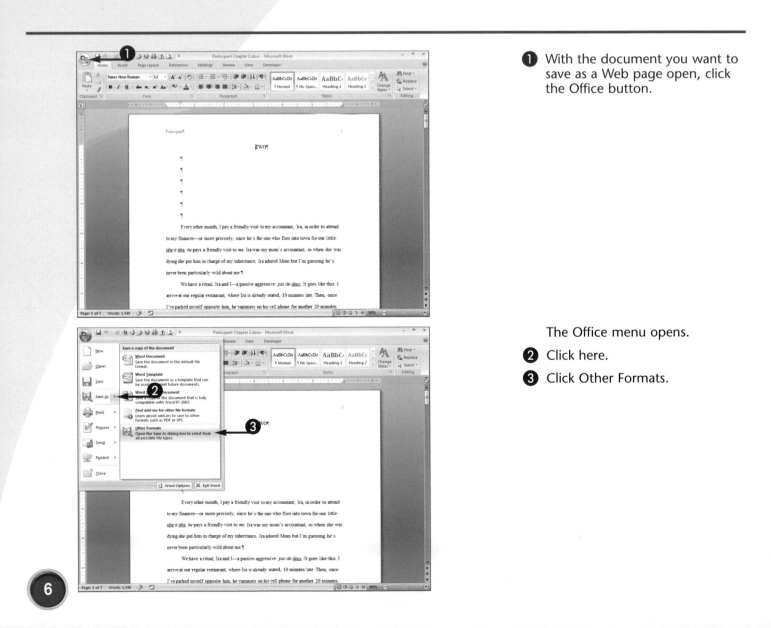

① With the document you want to save as a Web page open, click the Office button.

The Office menu opens.

② Click here.

③ Click Other Formats.

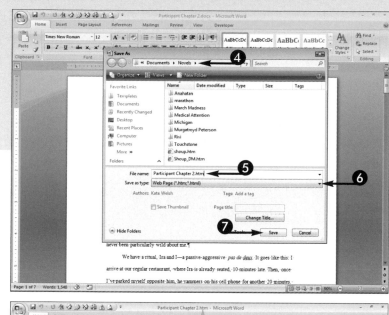

The Save As dialog box opens.

4 Locate and select the folder in which you want to save the Web page.

5 Type a name for the Web page.

6 Click here and select Web Page (*.htm, *.html) from the list that appears.

7 Click Save.

DIFFICULTY LEVEL

● The document is saved as a Web page.

TIPS

Try This!

You can change the title of the page — that is, the name of the page as it appears in the Web browser's title bar when the page is displayed. To do so, click Change Title in the Save As dialog box. Then, in the Set Page Title dialog box that appears, type the desired title and click OK.

Did You Know?

If you have access to a document management server, you can publish your Office document to that server. To do so, click the Office button, click Publish, and click Document Management Server. In the dialog box that appears, locate and select the folder on the document management server in which you want to save the document and click Save.

Automate Office tasks with MACROS

If you frequently use an Office program to complete the same task — for example, to format the cells in a spreadsheet a certain way, or to insert a table in a Word document that contains a certain number of rows and columns (as shown here) — you can expedite the process by recording a macro. When you record a macro, you essentially record a series of actions. Then, you can run the macro you recorded to automatically perform the recorded actions.

One way to access the controls for recording a macro is from the Developer tab on the Ribbon. This tab is

not displayed by default, however. To display the Developer tab, click the Office button, click *Program Name* Options, click Popular, and click the Show Developer Tab in the Ribbon check box to select it.

Note that recording a macro in Access differs somewhat from recording macros in other Office programs, such as Word, Excel, and PowerPoint. For information on creating macros in Access, see Chapter 8.

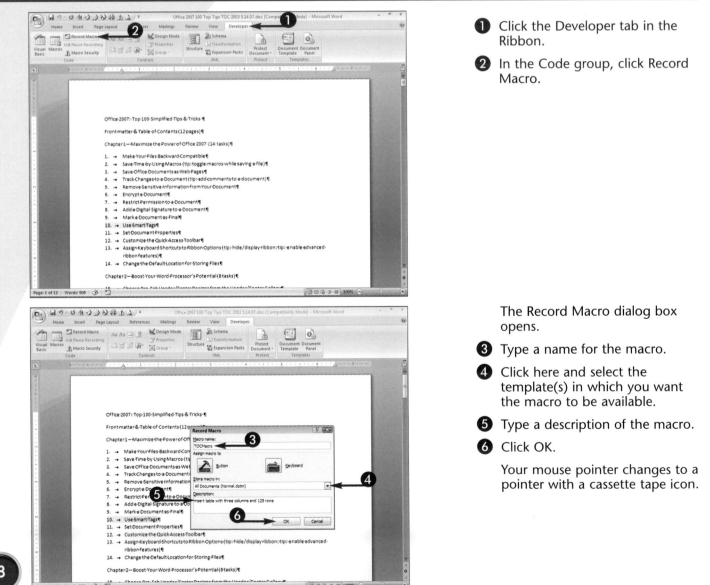

① Click the Developer tab in the Ribbon.

② In the Code group, click Record Macro.

The Record Macro dialog box opens.

③ Type a name for the macro.

④ Click here and select the template(s) in which you want the macro to be available.

⑤ Type a description of the macro.

⑥ Click OK.

Your mouse pointer changes to a pointer with a cassette tape icon.

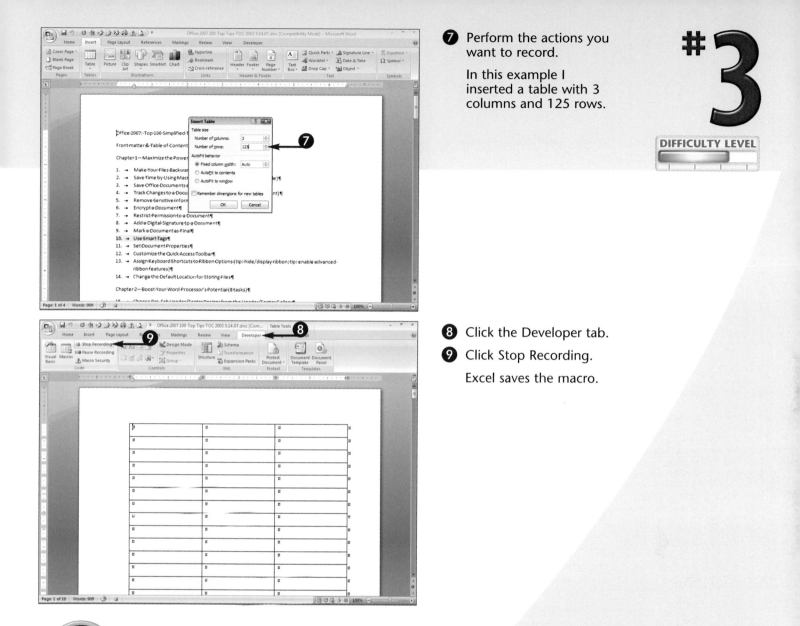

⑦ Perform the actions you want to record.

In this example I inserted a table with 3 columns and 125 rows.

#3

⑧ Click the Developer tab.

⑨ Click Stop Recording.

Excel saves the macro.

TIPS

Apply It!

To run a macro you have recorded, click the Developer tab and click Macros in the Code group. In the Macros dialog box that appears, click the macro you want to run, and then click Run.

Attention!

Because macros can be created for malicious purposes, they are often disabled by default. To enable the use of macros in a particular document, click the Office button, click *Program Name* Options, click Trust Center, click Trust Center Settings, and then click Macro Settings. Finally, click Disable all macros with notification. That way, when Office encounters a document that contains macros, it will display a security dialog box that enables you to specify whether the macros should be allowed.

Set DOCUMENT PROPERTIES

Office automatically embeds certain document properties, or *metadata*, such as the size of the document, the date it was created, and so on, in the document file. In addition to these default properties, you can supply other document properties, which you can then use to organize and identify your documents, as well as search for documents at a later date. For example, you can enter an author name, a title, a subject, keywords, a category, status information, and comments. You can also add custom properties, such as the client name, department, date completed, and even typist.

You can view certain document properties that are recorded automatically in the Open or Save As dialog box. To do so, simply click the document you want to view in either dialog box, click the down arrow next to Views, and then choose Details. To view properties of a document that you yourself add, open the document, click the Office button, click Prepare, and click Properties.

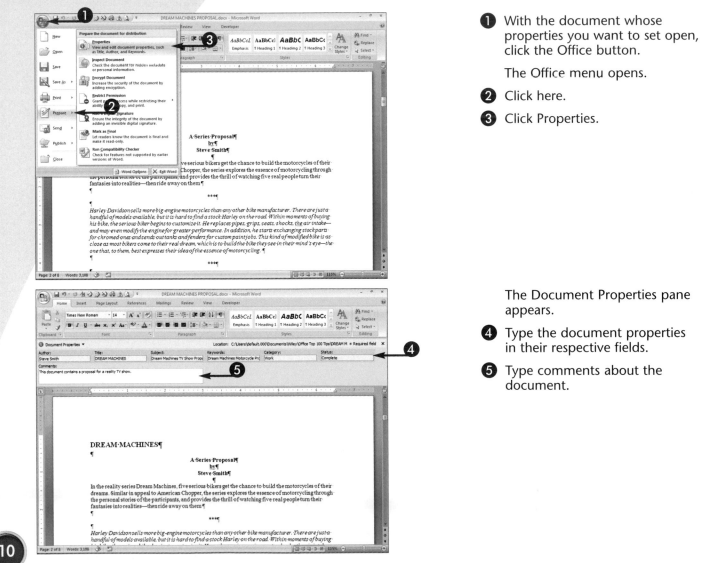

❶ With the document whose properties you want to set open, click the Office button.

The Office menu opens.

❷ Click here.

❸ Click Properties.

The Document Properties pane appears.

❹ Type the document properties in their respective fields.

❺ Type comments about the document.

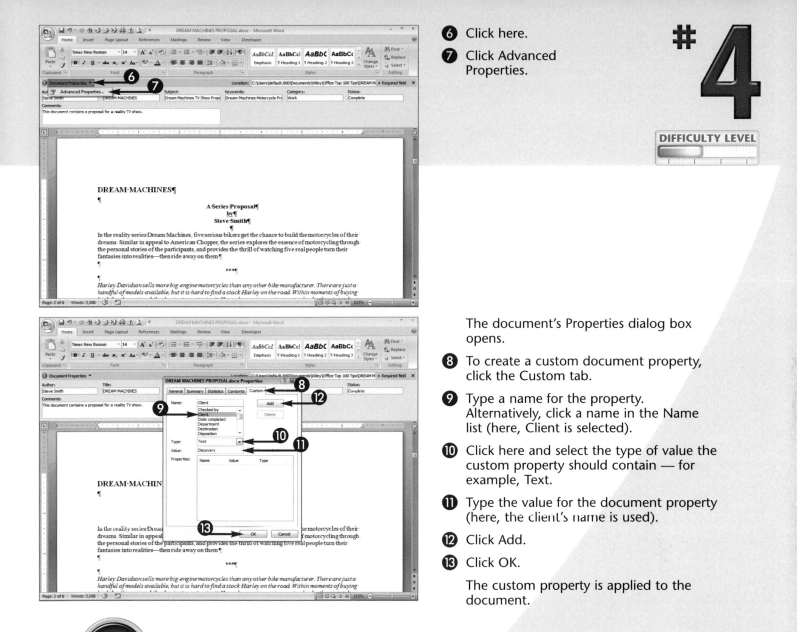

6 Click here.

7 Click Advanced Properties.

The document's Properties dialog box opens.

8 To create a custom document property, click the Custom tab.

9 Type a name for the property. Alternatively, click a name in the Name list (here, Client is selected).

10 Click here and select the type of value the custom property should contain — for example, Text.

11 Type the value for the document property (here, the client's name is used).

12 Click Add.

13 Click OK.

The custom property is applied to the document.

TIPS

Did You Know?

In addition to enabling you to set custom properties, the Properties dialog box also enables you to see a summary of the properties set, as well as statistics about the document, such as the page count, word count, and even whether the document has been printed.

Cross-Platform!

Windows Vista users can search using document properties with the operating system's built-in search function. If you use Windows XP, however, you must first download the Windows Desktop Search tool from the Microsoft Web site.

More Options!

To close the Document Properties pane, click the Close button in the pane's upper-right corner. You can click the Cancel button to close the Properties dialog box without saving any changes.

REMOVE SENSITIVE INFORMATION
from your document

If you plan to share an Office document with others, whether via e-mail or by some other method, you might want to first ensure that the document is void of personal, company, or other private information that may be stored in the document's metadata or in the document itself.

This information might include comments, tracked changes, or annotations; information about the document's author, status, category, keywords, and so on; hidden information (such as text, rows, columns, worksheets, or what have you) or content marked "invisible"; server properties; custom XML data; and more. (Note that if you remove hidden data from a document, you might not be able to restore it.) To locate and remove this data, you can use the 2007 Office Document Inspector.

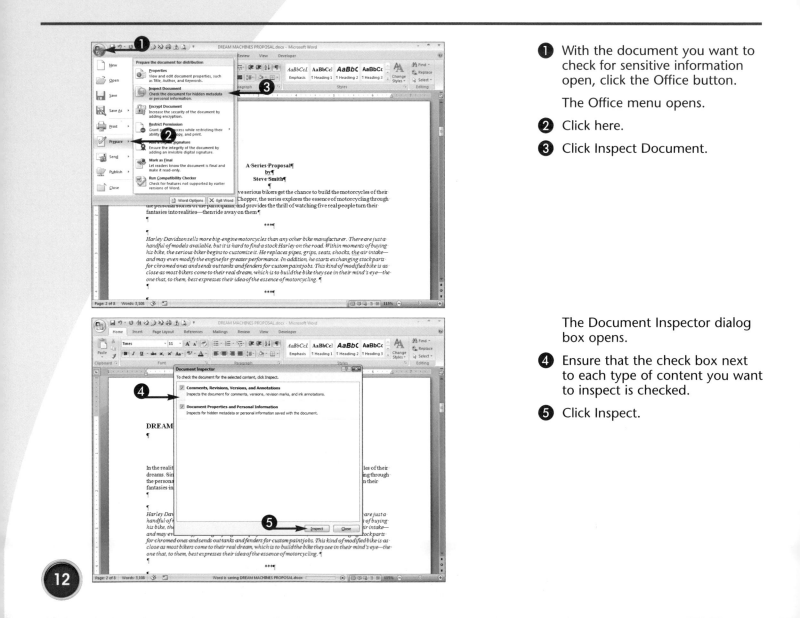

1 With the document you want to check for sensitive information open, click the Office button.

The Office menu opens.

2 Click here.

3 Click Inspect Document.

The Document Inspector dialog box opens.

4 Ensure that the check box next to each type of content you want to inspect is checked.

5 Click Inspect.

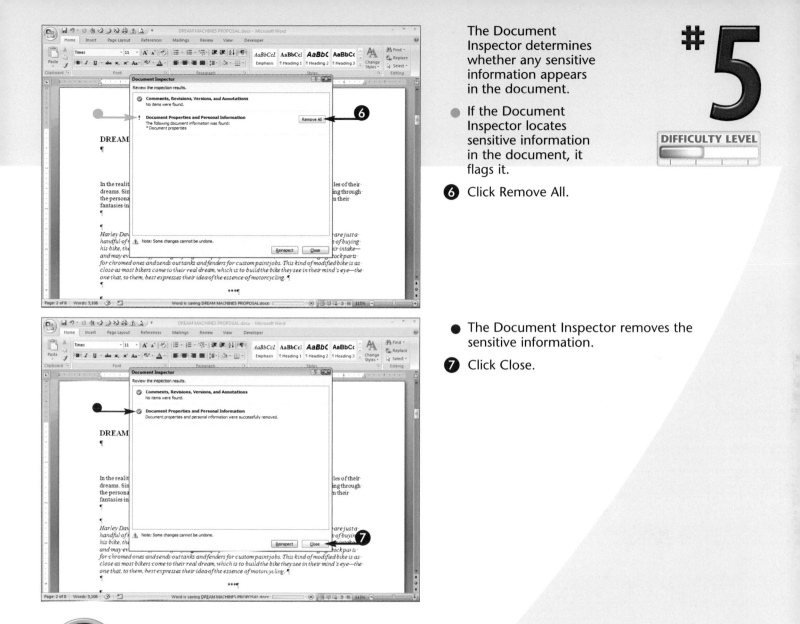

The Document Inspector determines whether any sensitive information appears in the document.

● If the Document Inspector locates sensitive information in the document, it flags it.

6 Click Remove All.

● The Document Inspector removes the sensitive information.

7 Click Close.

TIPS

Caution!
If you are not sure whether you want to remove the information flagged by Document Inspector, cancel the inspection and use the appropriate Office tools to view the information. For example, if document properties are flagged, then view the document properties to see whether you want to eliminate them from the document.

Caution!
You cannot undo the effects of removing information with Document Inspector. You can, however, restore the removed information by closing the document without saving the changes made by the inspection process.

Did You Know?
Be aware that the particulars of using Document Inspector vary slightly depending on whether you are using it in Word 2007, Excel 2007, or PowerPoint 2007.

ENCRYPT
a document

If you are working on a document that contains sensitive information, you might want to encrypt it. That way, for someone to open the document and view its contents, he or she will need to enter a password, which you set. When you encrypt an Office document, you set a password for it; to open the document, the password is required.

Be aware that if you forget the password, you will not be able to open the document, even if you are the person who encrypted it. For this reason, it is imperative that you choose a password that you will not forget, or that you write the password down and keep it in a safe place. That said, the password should not be easy for others to guess. The strongest passwords contain at least eight characters and are composed of a mixture of uppercase and lowercase letters, numbers, and symbols. Avoid using common passwords such as pet names, birth dates, and so on.

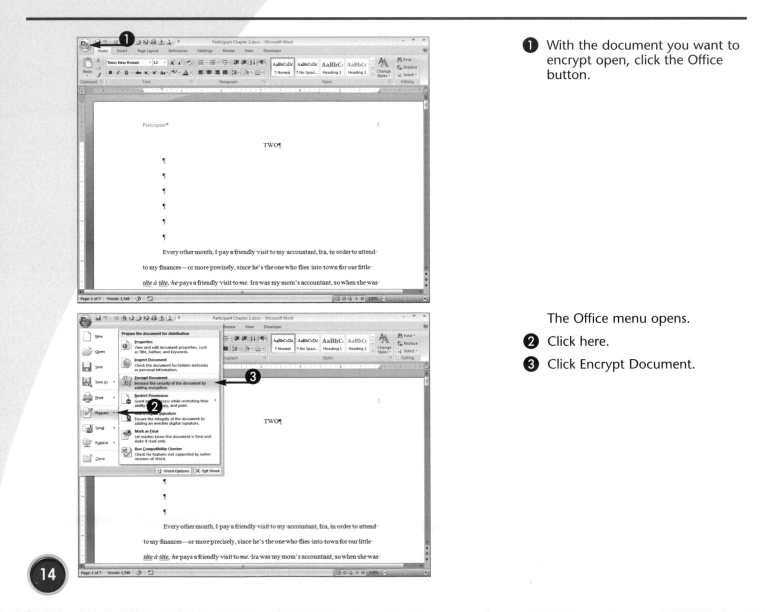

① With the document you want to encrypt open, click the Office button.

The Office menu opens.

② Click here.

③ Click Encrypt Document.

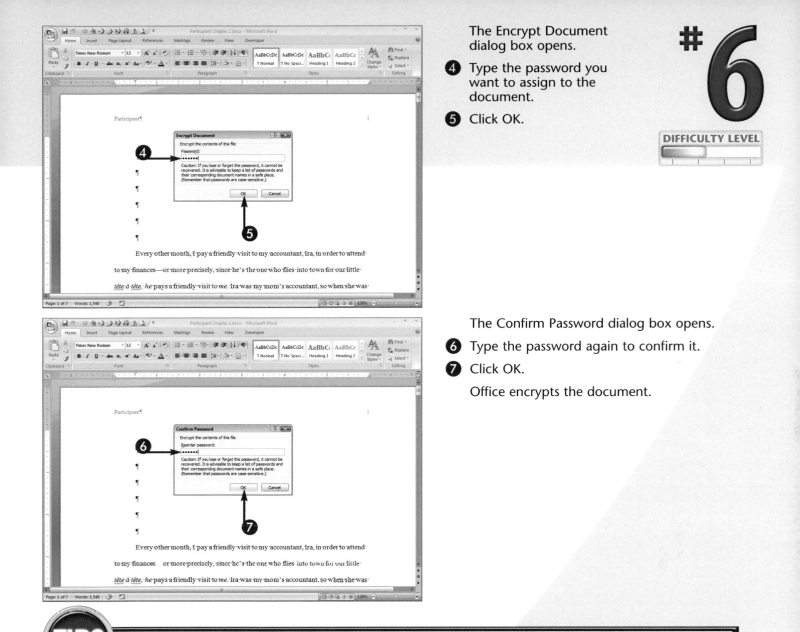

The Encrypt Document dialog box opens.

4 Type the password you want to assign to the document.

5 Click OK.

The Confirm Password dialog box opens.

6 Type the password again to confirm it.

7 Click OK.

Office encrypts the document.

TIPS

Apply It!

Open an encrypted document just as you would any other document — for example, by double-clicking it. When you do, Office displays the Password dialog box; type the password and click OK.

Remove It!

To unencrypt a document, open it, click the Office button, and click Save As. In the dialog box that opens, click the Tools drop-down arrow and choose General Options; then delete the password in the Password to open field.

DIGITALLY SIGN
a document

To authenticate an Office document, you can add a digital signature to it. First, however, you must create a digital ID and have a current *digital certificate*, which is a means of proving identity. A digital certificate is issued by a *certificate authority*, which is a trusted third-party entity. (If you do not have a digital ID, you are prompted to create one as you complete this task.)

A digital signature contains a *message digest*, which contains a reduced version of the document's

contents, and a *private key*, which is used to encrypt the message digest on the signer's computer. When you sign a document, the encrypted version of the message digest is appended to the document; the digest is then decrypted by the recipient using the *public key*, included in the digital certificate associated with the signature. In this way, the recipient can confirm the origin of the document and that the contents of the document did not change during transit.

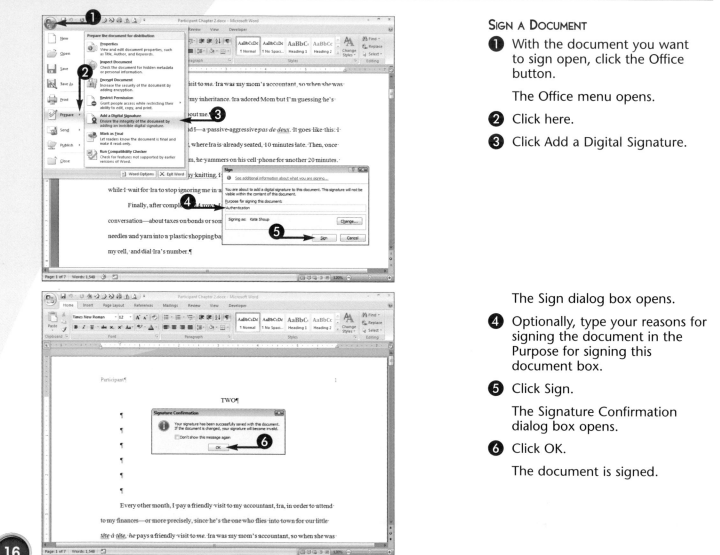

SIGN A DOCUMENT

❶ With the document you want to sign open, click the Office button.

The Office menu opens.

❷ Click here.

❸ Click Add a Digital Signature.

The Sign dialog box opens.

❹ Optionally, type your reasons for signing the document in the Purpose for signing this document box.

❺ Click Sign.

The Signature Confirmation dialog box opens.

❻ Click OK.

The document is signed.

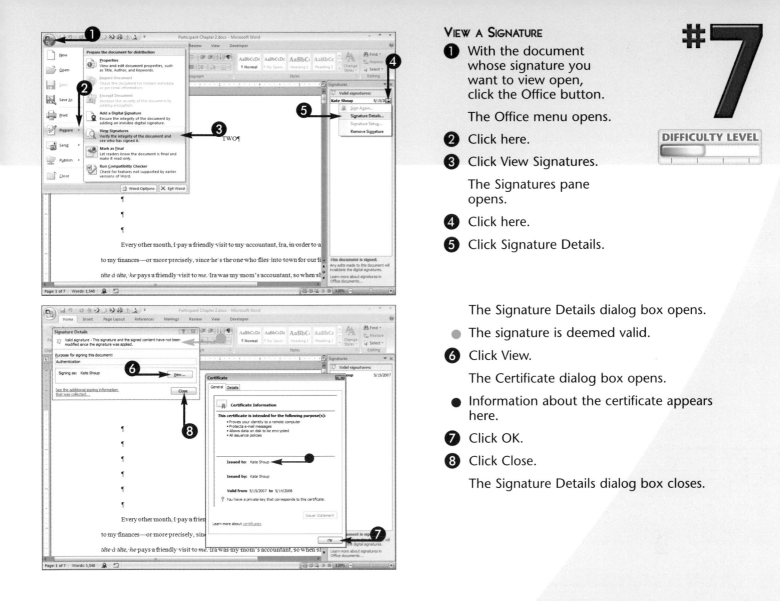

VIEW A SIGNATURE

1 With the document whose signature you want to view open, click the Office button.

The Office menu opens.

2 Click here.

3 Click View Signatures.

The Signatures pane opens.

4 Click here.

5 Click Signature Details.

The Signature Details dialog box opens.

● The signature is deemed valid.

6 Click View.

The Certificate dialog box opens.

● Information about the certificate appears here.

7 Click OK.

8 Click Close.

The Signature Details dialog box closes.

TIP

Important!

You are not required to obtain a digital certificate from a certificate authority in order to create a digital ID and sign your Office documents; instead, you can create your own. To do so, click Create your own digital ID instead of Get a digital ID from a Microsoft partner in the Get a Digital ID dialog box, which is displayed automatically if no digital ID is present on your computer. Then, in the Create a Digital ID dialog box that appears, enter the requested information — name, e-mail address, organization, and location — and click Create. Note, however, that when you share a file signed with a digital ID you created, it cannot be authenticated by users on other machines.

Get a Digital ID

In order to sign a Microsoft Office document, you need a digital ID. You have two options for getting a digital ID:

◉ **Get a digital ID from a Microsoft partner**

If you use a digital ID from a Microsoft partner, other people will be able to verify the authenticity of your signature.

○ **Create your own digital ID**

If you create your own digital ID, other people will not be able to verify the authenticity of your signature. You will be able to verify the authenticity of your signature, but only on this computer.

Learn more about digital IDs in Office...

OK   Cancel

Mark a document as FINAL

After you finish working on a document — that is, you have proofread it and accepted any revisions made with the Track Changes feature — you can mark it as final. Marking a document as final makes the file read-only, thereby preventing changes from being made to the document. The document can, however, be opened and read by others. (Note that the file is read-only when opened by users whose systems run Office 2007. If the document is saved in Compatibility Mode and opened in an earlier version of Office, the file will not open in read-only mode.)

Marking a file as final is not a security feature. That is, it does not permanently and irrevocably lock the document to prevent further edits. Anyone with access to the document can revoke the Mark as Final status. Steps for revoking Mark as Final status appear among the tips at the end of this section.

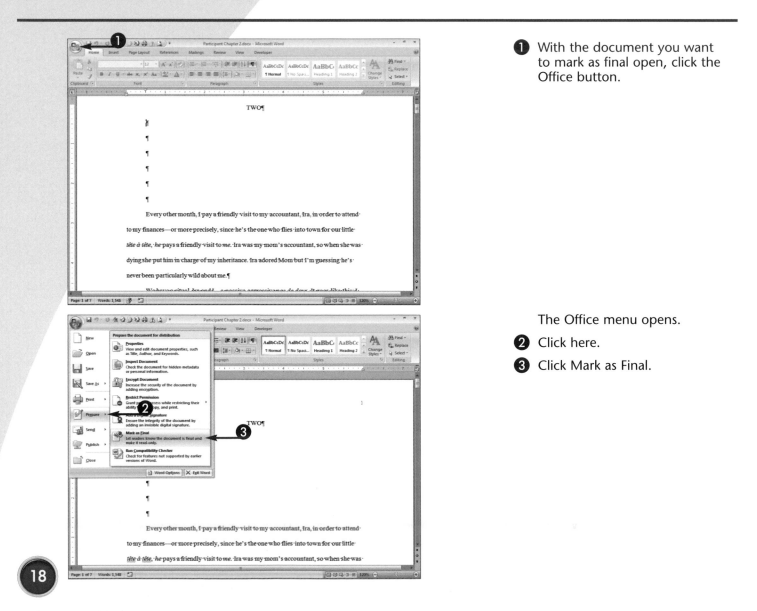

① With the document you want to mark as final open, click the Office button.

The Office menu opens.

② Click here.

③ Click Mark as Final.

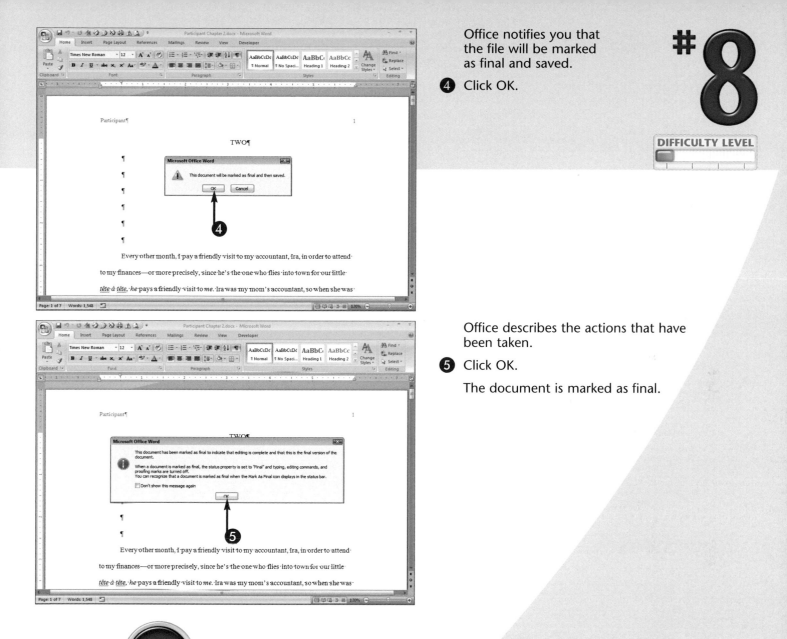

Office notifies you that the file will be marked as final and saved.

④ Click OK.

Office describes the actions that have been taken.

⑤ Click OK.

The document is marked as final.

TIPS

Did You Know?

If a document has been marked as final, it displays a special Mark as Final icon along the bottom of the screen.

Did You Know?

When a document is marked as final, the document's Status property changes to Final. That means you can search for the document using that status as a criterion.

Remove It!

You revoke the Mark as Final status the same way you apply it: by clicking the Office button, clicking Prepare, and clicking Mark as Final. Revoking Marked as Final status means the document can again be edited.

Enable
SMART TAGS

Several Office programs support the use of smart tags, which are labels that indicate that the document contains data of a particular type, and enable you to perform certain tasks using that data.

For example, if Office detects a name in your document, it can display a *smart tag indicator*, a purple dotted line. You can click the smart tag indicator to open the contact record in Outlook that is associated with that name, add the name to your Outlook contacts, schedule a meeting with the person, or insert the person's address. (The precise

options available to you when you click the smart tag indicator depend on what type of data is detected.)

To use smart tags, you must first enable them. In addition to using the smart tags that are available within Office, you can obtain additional smart tags from Microsoft as well as from third-party companies.

Note that you can embed smart tags in Excel and PowerPoint documents; that way, others who open the document on their own computers can view the smart tags.

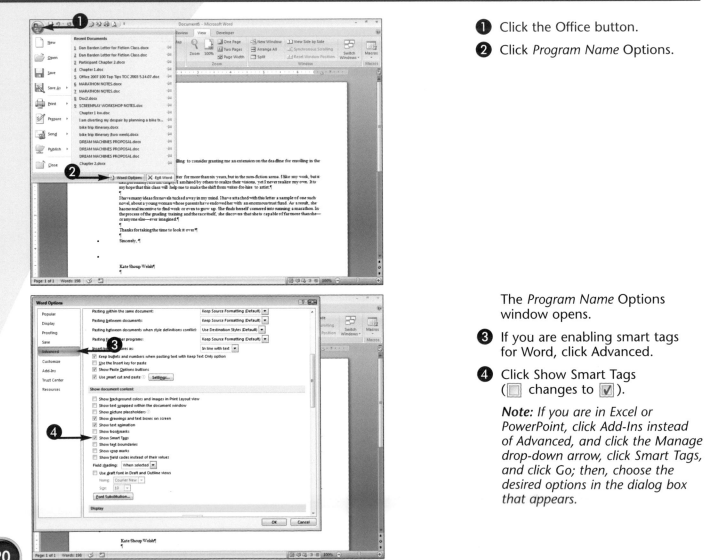

❶ Click the Office button.

❷ Click *Program Name* Options.

The *Program Name* Options window opens.

❸ If you are enabling smart tags for Word, click Advanced.

❹ Click Show Smart Tags (☐ changes to ☑).

Note: If you are in Excel or PowerPoint, click Add-Ins instead of Advanced, and click the Manage drop-down arrow, click Smart Tags, and click Go; then, choose the desired options in the dialog box that appears.

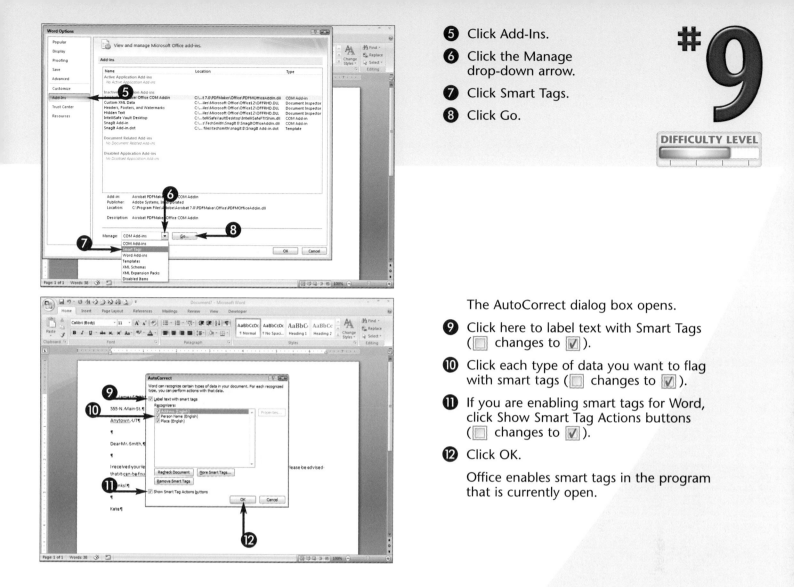

⑤ Click Add-Ins.

⑥ Click the Manage drop-down arrow.

⑦ Click Smart Tags.

⑧ Click Go.

The AutoCorrect dialog box opens.

⑨ Click here to label text with Smart Tags (☐ changes to ☑).

⑩ Click each type of data you want to flag with smart tags (☐ changes to ☑).

⑪ If you are enabling smart tags for Word, click Show Smart Tag Actions buttons (☐ changes to ☑).

⑫ Click OK.

Office enables smart tags in the program that is currently open.

TIPS

Check It Out!

To obtain additional smart tags, open the AutoCorrect dialog box and click More Smart Tags. Office launches a special page on Microsoft Office Online that enables you to access links to additional smart tags created by Microsoft as well as by third-party software vendors. You can also find links to tools for building your own smart tags.

More Options!

Similar to smart tags are AutoCorrect and Paste Options tools. AutoCorrect works by displaying an AutoCorrect button anytime an Office program corrects text that you enter; click the button to undo or adjust the correction. Paste Options displays a Paste button when you paste data into a document; click it to specify how you want the content pasted in.

Customize the
QUICK ACCESS TOOLBAR

The Quick Access toolbar provides easy access to often-used commands such as Save and Undo. You can customize the Quick Access toolbar to change which commands are available.

Office enables you to add commands to the Quick Access toolbar three different ways. One is to select the desired command from the Customize Quick Access Toolbar menu. Another is to use the *Program Name* Options dialog box. Finally, you can simply

right-click the command you want to add in the Ribbon and click Add to Quick Access Toolbar.

In addition to adding commands to the Quick Access toolbar, you can also move it from its default spot above the Ribbon to a spot below the Ribbon. To do so, click the arrow in the Quick Access toolbar and click Show Below the Ribbon from the menu that appears.

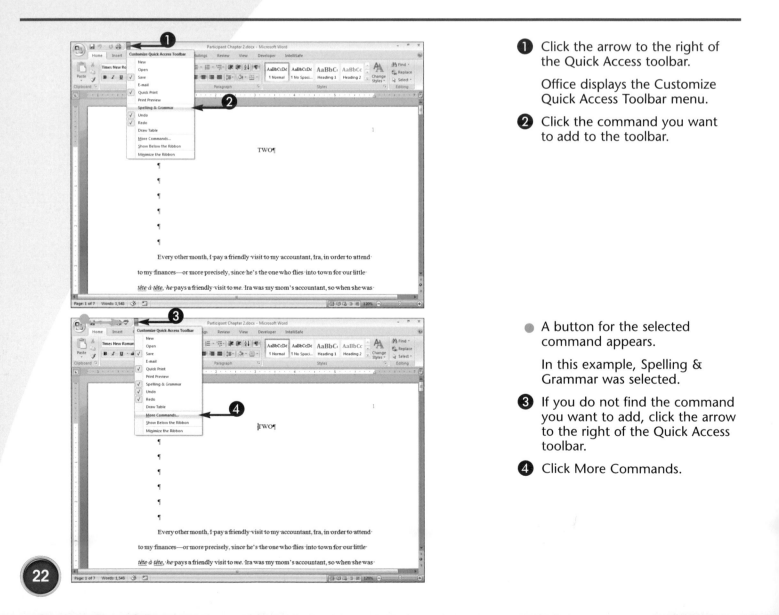

1 Click the arrow to the right of the Quick Access toolbar.

Office displays the Customize Quick Access Toolbar menu.

2 Click the command you want to add to the toolbar.

● A button for the selected command appears.

In this example, Spelling & Grammar was selected.

3 If you do not find the command you want to add, click the arrow to the right of the Quick Access toolbar.

4 Click More Commands.

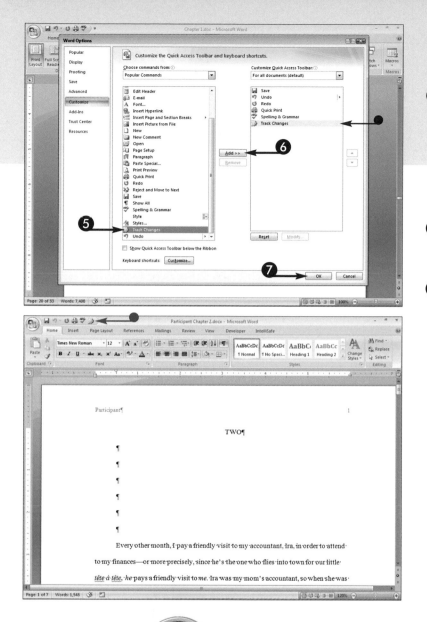

The *Program Name* Options window opens with Quick Access toolbar options displayed.

5 In the window's left pane, click the command you want to add.

Note: *If the command you want to add is not displayed, click the Choose commands from drop-down arrow and select All Commands.*

6 Click Add.

● The command is added to window's right pane.

7 Click OK.

● A button for the selected command appears.

In this example, Track Changes was selected.

TIPS

Did You Know?

You can add groups of commands in the Ribbon to the Quick Access toolbar. To do so, right-click the group name in the Ribbon and click Add to Quick Access Toolbar. The group is stored under a single button; click the arrow next to the button to reveal the available commands in the group.

Did You Know?

To apply the change to the Quick Access toolbar to the current document only, click the Customize Quick Access Toolbar drop-down arrow in the *Program Name* Options window and choose For *Document Name*.

Customize the
RIBBON

In lieu of using the traditional menu system and toolbars, Office 2007 features what Microsoft calls the *Ribbon*. The Ribbon is designed to enable you to find the command necessary to complete a task more quickly and more intuitively than the menus of old.

To this end, the Ribbon groups related commands together, placing them under clickable tabs. Each tab pertains to a certain type of task, such as formatting text, inserting items into a document, laying out a

page, reviewing a document, and so on. The tabs displayed depend on which Office program is open, and what type of task is being performed.

If you feel the Ribbon consumes too much space in your Office windows, you can minimize it, displaying it in full only when it is needed.

If you prefer, you can access the commands displayed in the Ribbon using your keyboard.

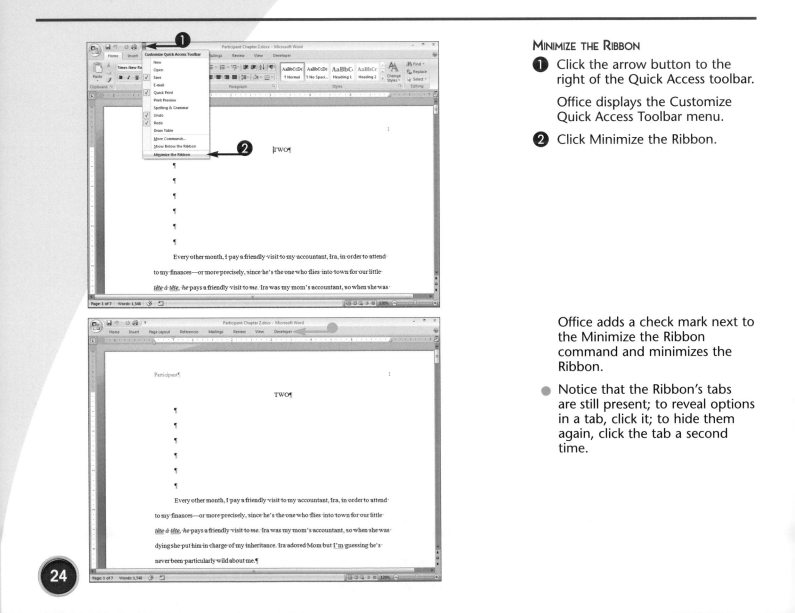

MINIMIZE THE RIBBON

① Click the arrow button to the right of the Quick Access toolbar.

Office displays the Customize Quick Access Toolbar menu.

② Click Minimize the Ribbon.

Office adds a check mark next to the Minimize the Ribbon command and minimizes the Ribbon.

● Notice that the Ribbon's tabs are still present; to reveal options in a tab, click it; to hide them again, click the tab a second time.

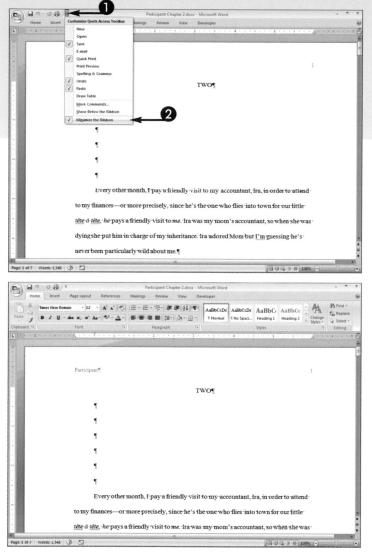

ReDisplay the Ribbon

1 Click the arrow to the right of the Quick Access toolbar.

Office displays the Customize Quick Access Toolbar menu.

2 Click Minimize the Ribbon.

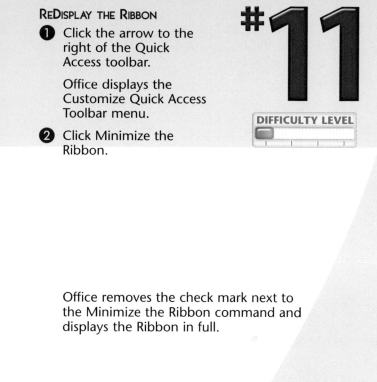

DIFFICULTY LEVEL

Office removes the check mark next to the Minimize the Ribbon command and displays the Ribbon in full.

TIPS

Try This!
To quickly minimize the Ribbon, double-click any of its tabs. To redisplay it, double-click a tab a second time.

More Options!
Just as the menus in older versions of Microsoft Office supported the use of keyboard shortcuts to execute various commands, so, too, does the Ribbon. To see what keyboard shortcuts apply, press and release the Alt key on your keyboard; Office shows *key tips*, which denote the key used in conjunction with the Alt key in the keyboard shortcut. (Note that pressing the key indicated by the key tip may reveal more key tips. For example, you might press Alt+N to switch to the Insert tab; when you do, Office displays key tips for the various commands located on that tab.)

Change the
SAVE SETTINGS

By default, Office saves your documents in your Documents folder (or, if you are using a version of Windows that precedes Windows Vista, the My Documents folder). You may find, however, that another folder is more suitable. For example, if you only create PowerPoint presentations for a particular client, you might configure Office to save PowerPoint files you create in the folder you have created for that client by default.

In addition to changing where Office stores your Word, Excel, PowerPoint, and other Office files by default, you can also specify what file extension

should be used. For example, suppose your Word files should be backward compatible by default. In that case, you can opt to save all files you create using Office 2007 in Compatibility Mode (that is, in Word 97–2003 format).

Assuming you want Office to auto-save your documents (recommended), you can also indicate how frequently the auto-save operation should occur. Auto-saving too frequently can slow your computer; auto-saving too infrequently can cause you to lose more data in the event of a system crash.

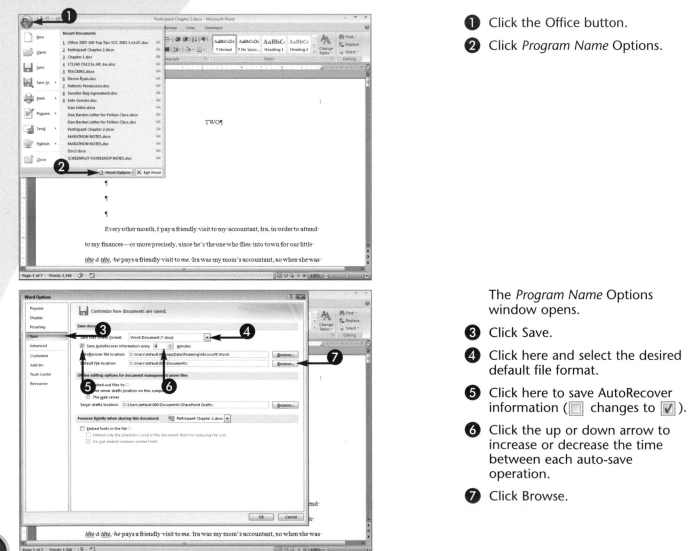

① Click the Office button.

② Click *Program Name* Options.

The *Program Name* Options window opens.

③ Click Save.

④ Click here and select the desired default file format.

⑤ Click here to save AutoRecover information (☐ changes to ☑).

⑥ Click the up or down arrow to increase or decrease the time between each auto-save operation.

⑦ Click Browse.

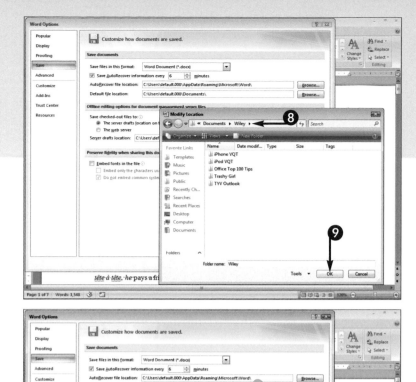

The Modify Location dialog box opens.

8 Open the folder in which you want to save documents created by this Office program by default.

9 Click OK.

● The folder you chose appears in the Default file location field.

10 Click OK.

The *Program Name* Options window closes, and your changes are applied.

TIPS

More Options!

To ensure that others who view your Word or PowerPoint document see it with the correct fonts, select the Embed fonts in the file check box in the *Program Name* Options window's Save screen. To reduce the size of your file, opt to embed font information for those characters used in the document only, and to *not* embed common system fonts. (This option is available for Word only.)

Try This!

If you want to change the author name that is associated with your documents, open the *Program Name* Options window and, in the Popular screen, type the desired name in the User Name field. Optionally, if using Word or PowerPoint, you can also change the author initials.

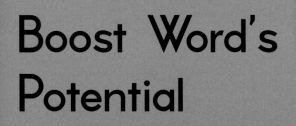

Chapter 2

Boost Word's Potential

If you have a project that involves text of any kind — be it correspondence, a report, or what have you — you can harness the power of Word 2007 to quickly and easily generate a professional-looking document.

Word 2007 features a host of tools designed to improve your efficiency no matter what type of document you need to create, from prefabricated header and footer styles to building blocks for creating your own styles. The program's Research tools provide quick access to reference materials such as thesauri,

dictionaries, and encyclopedias. You can even use Word to translate the text in your document into a different language.

In addition to enabling you to generate your own documents, Word 2007 also eases the process of sharing your documents with others. For example, the program's Track Changes feature enables you to easily pinpoint where edits have been made and by whom. And of course, by providing features to expedite blogging, Word enables you to share your writing with the world.

Top 100

Add a HEADER/FOOTER BUILDING BLOCK to the gallery

Word offers a gallery of several predefined header and footer designs, called *building blocks*. Alternatively, you can create your own header/footer building blocks — for example, one that contains your name and contact information in the color and font of your choice — and add that design to the gallery. That way, anytime you need to insert that particular header or footer, rather than reconstructing it, you can simply click it in the gallery.

In addition to creating header/footer building blocks, you can also create building blocks with other custom

Office elements, such as cover pages, pull quotes, and so on. Building blocks might also contain specific text or a graphic that you want to reuse.

If, when attempting to create or apply a building block, you find that the required commands are grayed out, it is likely because the necessary add-ins have been disabled. To enable them, click the Office button, choose Word Options, click Add-Ins, click Disabled Items in the Manage list, and then click Go. Next, click Building Blocks.dotx and click Enable. To implement the change, restart Word.

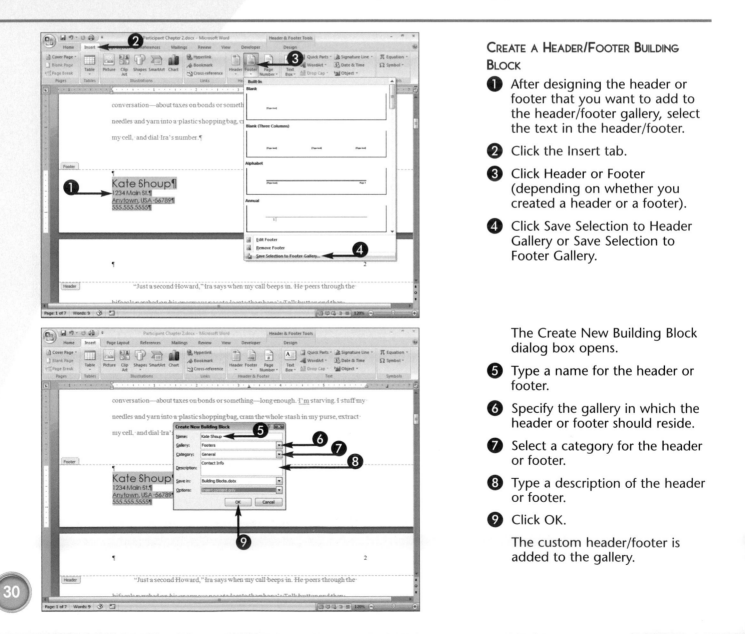

CREATE A HEADER/FOOTER BUILDING BLOCK

1. After designing the header or footer that you want to add to the header/footer gallery, select the text in the header/footer.

2. Click the Insert tab.

3. Click Header or Footer (depending on whether you created a header or a footer).

4. Click Save Selection to Header Gallery or Save Selection to Footer Gallery.

The Create New Building Block dialog box opens.

5. Type a name for the header or footer.

6. Specify the gallery in which the header or footer should reside.

7. Select a category for the header or footer.

8. Type a description of the header or footer.

9. Click OK.

The custom header/footer is added to the gallery.

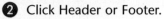

APPLY A HEADER/FOOTER BUILDING BLOCK

① With the document into which you want to insert the header or footer open, click the Insert tab.

② Click Header or Footer.

③ Click the header or footer you want to add. (You might need to scroll down in the gallery to locate it.)

#13

DIFFICULTY LEVEL

● The header or footer is inserted in the document.

TIP

More Options!

If your document contains section breaks, you can apply different headers and footers to each section. Click in the section for which you want to create a unique header or footer, click Header or Footer in the Insert tab, and click Edit Header or Edit Footer. The Design tab appears in the Ribbon; click Link to Previous to deselect it. Then create the new header/footer or insert a header/footer building block from the gallery. (Repeat for each section in your document.) Designing separate headers and footers for even and odd pages is similar; just select the Different Odd & Even Pages check box in the Design tab instead of clicking Link to Previous and add the different headers/footers as normal.

Chapter 2: Boost Word's Potential

SHARE BUILDING BLOCKS
with others

Although Word offers several predefined Office elements, such as headers and footers, cover pages, pull quotes, and so on, you can also create your own and add them to Word's gallery of choices. These elements, called *building blocks*, might contain specific text or a graphic you want to reuse — for example, your company logo or your name and contact information in the color and font of your choice.

You can share the building blocks you create by embedding them in a Word template, which you can

then distribute to others. Anytime someone applies the template you distribute to a document, the building blocks you embedded will become available in that document.

To attach a template to a document, open the document, click the Office button, and click Word Options. In the window that appears, click Add-ins, click the Manage drop-down arrow, click Templates, and click Go. Finally, click Attach in the Templates and Add-ins dialog box, locate and select the template you want to attach, and click OK.

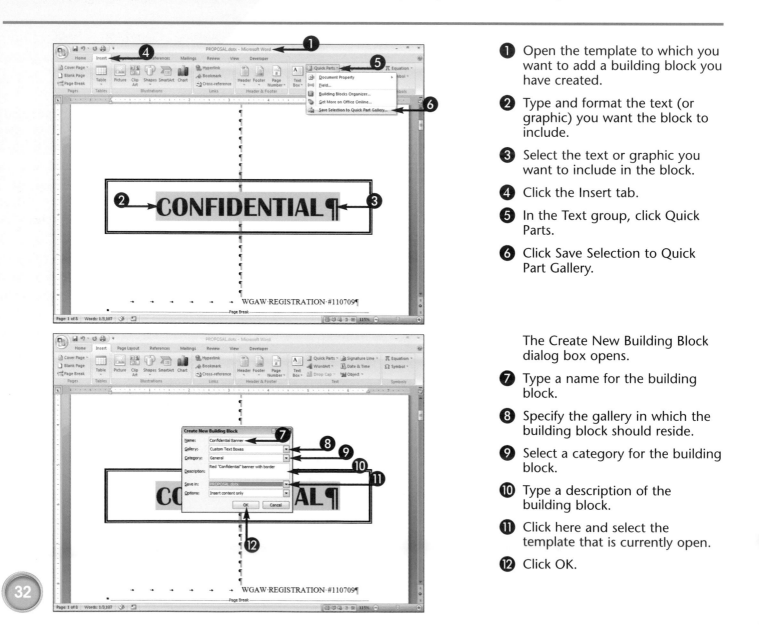

① Open the template to which you want to add a building block you have created.

② Type and format the text (or graphic) you want the block to include.

③ Select the text or graphic you want to include in the block.

④ Click the Insert tab.

⑤ In the Text group, click Quick Parts.

⑥ Click Save Selection to Quick Part Gallery.

The Create New Building Block dialog box opens.

⑦ Type a name for the building block.

⑧ Specify the gallery in which the building block should reside.

⑨ Select a category for the building block.

⑩ Type a description of the building block.

⑪ Click here and select the template that is currently open.

⑫ Click OK.

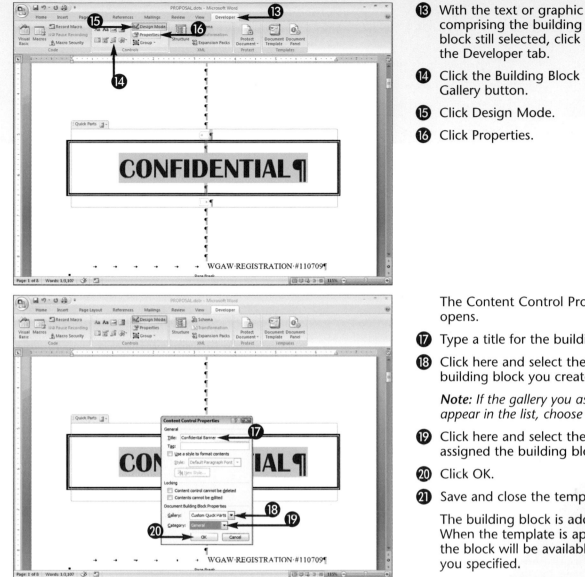

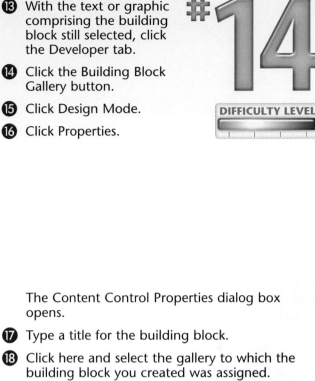

⑬ With the text or graphic comprising the building block still selected, click the Developer tab.

⑭ Click the Building Block Gallery button.

⑮ Click Design Mode.

⑯ Click Properties.

The Content Control Properties dialog box opens.

⑰ Type a title for the building block.

⑱ Click here and select the gallery to which the building block you created was assigned.

Note: If the gallery you assigned does not appear in the list, choose Custom Quick Parts.

⑲ Click here and select the category you assigned the building block.

⑳ Click OK.

㉑ Save and close the template.

The building block is added to the template. When the template is applied to a document, the block will be available from the gallery you specified.

TIPS

Apply It!

To insert a building block that has been saved in a template into a document, attach the template to the document, click in the document in the spot where you want the building block to appear, click the Insert tab, click Quick Parts in the Insert group, and click Building Blocks Organizer. Finally, locate and click the block you want to insert and click Insert.

Important!

To include any paragraph formatting you have applied in the building block, ensure that the paragraph mark at the end of the paragraph is also selected. If no paragraph marks are visible, click the Home tab and, in the Paragraph group, click Show/Hide.

Work with the
DOCUMENT MAP

If your document contains text that has been formatted with a Heading style, you can use a special pane in Word 2007 called the Document Map pane to navigate that document.

If your document contains multiple levels of headings, you can opt to display them in the Document Map pane. Alternatively, you can display top-level headings only. If you decide to display top-level headings, you can choose to expand the outline to view subheadings beneath a top-level

heading by clicking the plus sign to the left of the heading.

The Document Map pane acts like an interactive outline. Each item in the Document Map pane represents a heading in your document; you can click a heading in the pane to move to that heading in your document. Especially if your document is very long, being able to quickly jump from spot to spot can be a real timesaver!

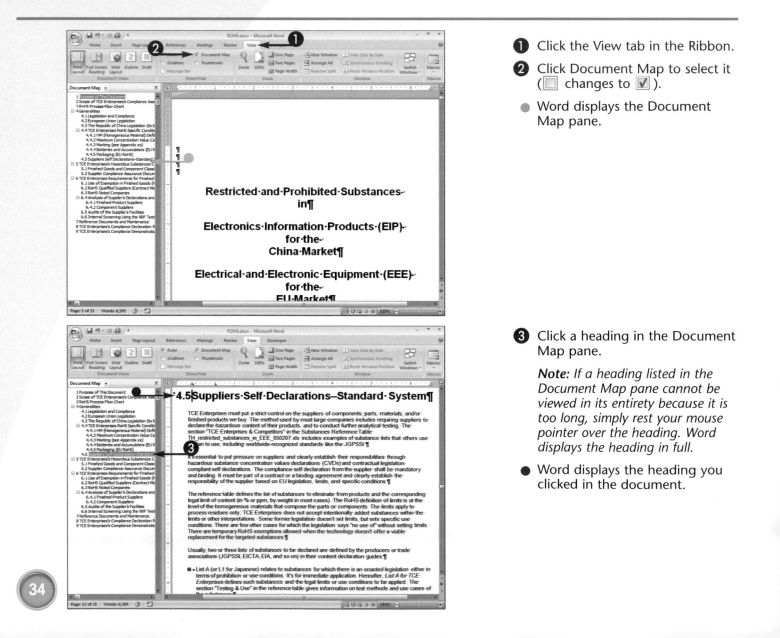

1 Click the View tab in the Ribbon.

2 Click Document Map to select it (☐ changes to ☑).

● Word displays the Document Map pane.

3 Click a heading in the Document Map pane.

Note: If a heading listed in the Document Map pane cannot be viewed in its entirety because it is too long, simply rest your mouse pointer over the heading. Word displays the heading in full.

● Word displays the heading you clicked in the document.

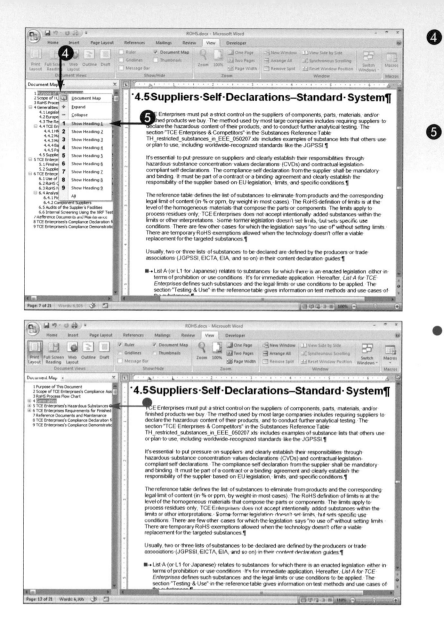

4 To change which headings are displayed — for example, to show top-level headings only — right-click any heading in the Document Map pane.

5 Choose the level of heading you want to view.

DIFFICULTY LEVEL

● The Document Map pane displays headings of the level you chose and higher.

TIPS

Did You Know?
To change the width of the Document Map pane, place your mouse pointer over the right edge of the pane. The pointer changes to a two-sided arrow; click and drag to the right or left to make the column wider or more narrow, respectively.

Remove It!
Close the Document Map pane by clicking its Close button. Alternatively, change to a different view; when you do, the Document Map pane disappears automatically.

Scan document content with
THUMBNAILS

Sometimes, especially when you are working with a very long document, being able to quickly scan through the document to locate a particular page can be very helpful. To enable this, Word 2007 includes the Thumbnails pane. You can use this pane to navigate your open document by sight rather than by, say, heading, as you do with the Document Map pane.

The Thumbnails pane displays a small image (that is, a *thumbnail*) of each page in your document. To

make locating the page you need even easier, the Thumbnails pane displays the number of each page below its thumbnail image. The page currently displayed in the main portion of the Word window is highlighted in orange in the Thumbnails pane.

You can switch back and forth between the Thumbnails pane and Document Map pane by clicking the drop-down arrow at the top of the pane and choosing Document Map or Thumbnails, respectively.

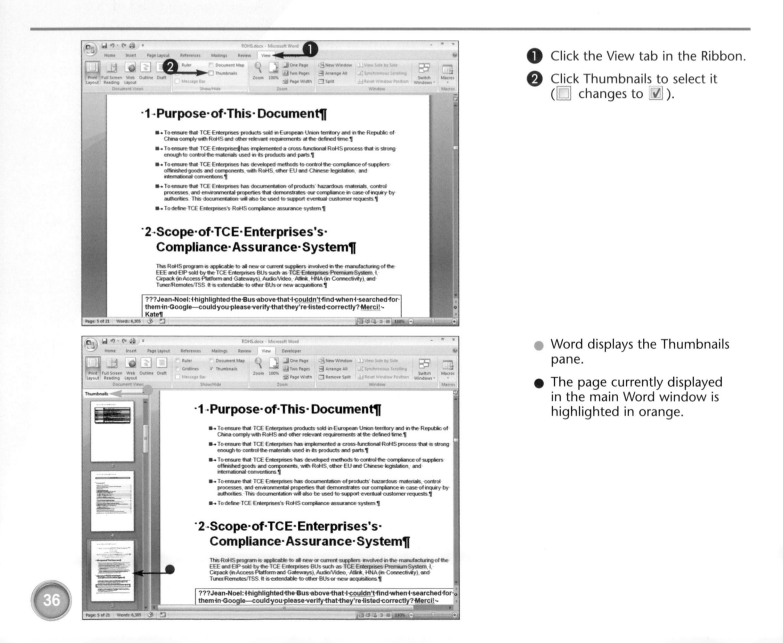

① Click the View tab in the Ribbon.

② Click Thumbnails to select it (☐ changes to ☑).

● Word displays the Thumbnails pane.

● The page currently displayed in the main Word window is highlighted in orange.

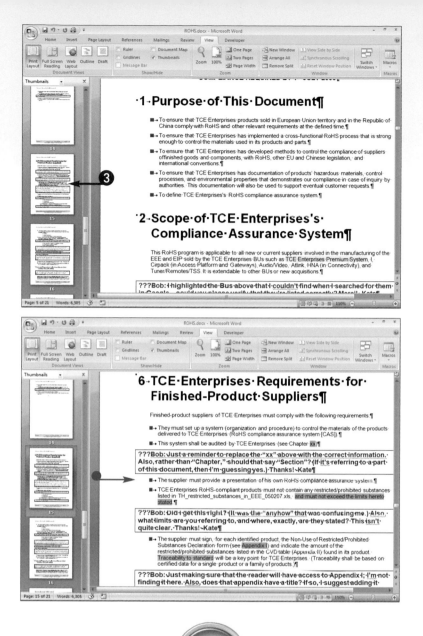

3 Click an image in the Thumbnails pane to switch to a different page.

Note: *Use the scroll bar to the right of the pane to move up and down through the thumbnail images.*

#16

DIFFICULTY LEVEL

● Word displays the page you clicked in the document.

TIPS

Did You Know?

To change the width of the Thumbnails pane, place your mouse pointer over the right edge of the pane. The pointer changes to a two-sided arrow; click and drag to the right or left to make the column wider or more narrow, respectively.

Remove It!

Close the Thumbnails pane by clicking its Close button. Alternatively, change to a different view; when you do, the Thumbnails pane will disappear automatically.

TRACK CHANGES
in a document

If you work in an environment in which you share your Word documents with others, you can use the program's Track Changes feature to help you keep track of changes made to the file by you and by others.

When Track Changes is enabled, Word tracks edits such as formatting changes and text additions and deletions. Additions appear inline in the text; deletions appear either inline in the text or in balloons in the right margin, depending on the document view. For example, in Word, using Draft view displays deletions inline; using Print Layout view, however, displays deletions in balloons in the right margin. If multiple people review the document, each person's changes will appear in a different color to help you keep track of who made which edits.

When you review a document that has been edited with Track Changes on, Word flags each change in the document, which you can then accept or reject.

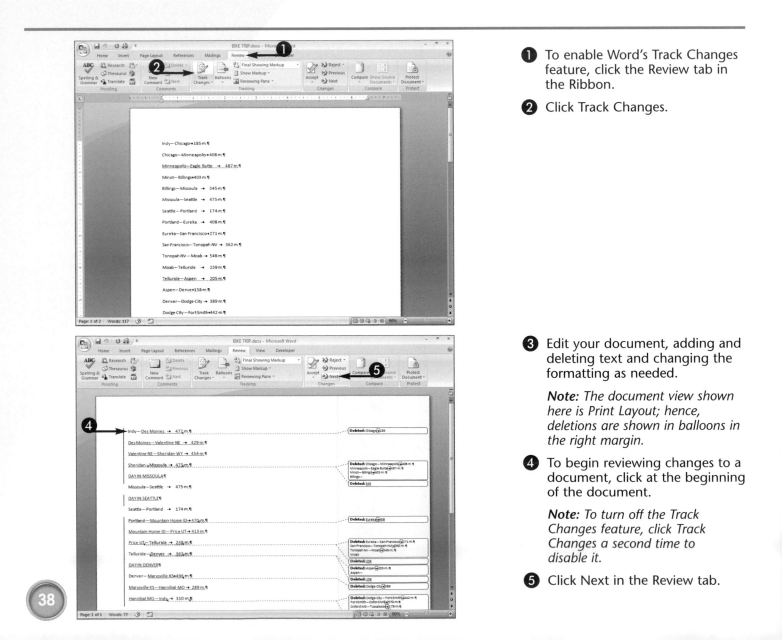

1. To enable Word's Track Changes feature, click the Review tab in the Ribbon.

2. Click Track Changes.

3. Edit your document, adding and deleting text and changing the formatting as needed.

    Note: The document view shown here is Print Layout; hence, deletions are shown in balloons in the right margin.

4. To begin reviewing changes to a document, click at the beginning of the document.

    Note: To turn off the Track Changes feature, click Track Changes a second time to disable it.

5. Click Next in the Review tab.

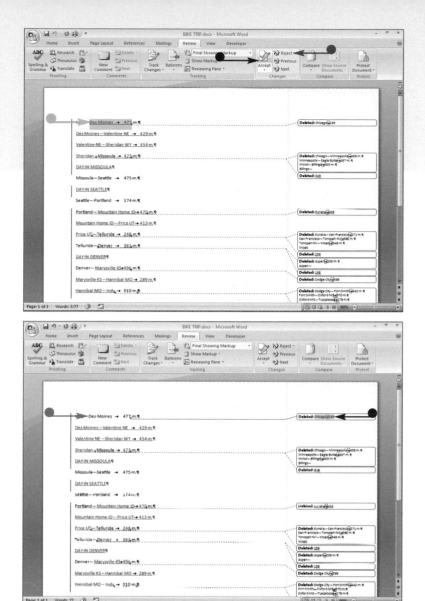

● Word highlights the first change in the document.

● To accept the change, click Accept in the Review tab.

● To reject the change, click Reject in the Review tab.

Note: To accept all changes in the document, click the down arrow under Accept and click Accept All Changes in Document.

● Depending on which button you clicked, Word accepts (as shown here) or rejects the change.

● Word automatically highlights the next change in the document, which you can choose to accept or reject.

TIP

Did You Know?

By default, insertions appear as underlined text, and deletions appear either in balloons or as strikethrough text, depending on the view. To change these and other settings, click the down arrow beside Track Changes and choose Change Tracking Options. The Track Changes Options dialog box opens; change the settings as desired.

COMPARE DOCUMENTS

If you or someone else makes changes to a document without first enabling the Track Changes feature, but you want to determine exactly what edits were made, you can compare the edited document with the original.

When you compare an original document with an updated version, the result is a third file that flags the discrepancies between the two documents. (The two source documents — that is, the original and revised versions — remain unchanged.) These discrepancies look exactly like edits made with Track Changes enabled; that is, formatting changes and

text additions and deletions become visible. Additions appear inline in the text; deletions appear either inline in the text or in balloons in the right margin, depending on the document view. For example, in Word, using Draft view displays deletions inline; using Print view, however, displays deletions in balloons in the right margin.

You review a file generated by comparing documents the same way you review a file that has been edited with Track Changes enabled. Word flags each change in the document, which you can then accept or reject.

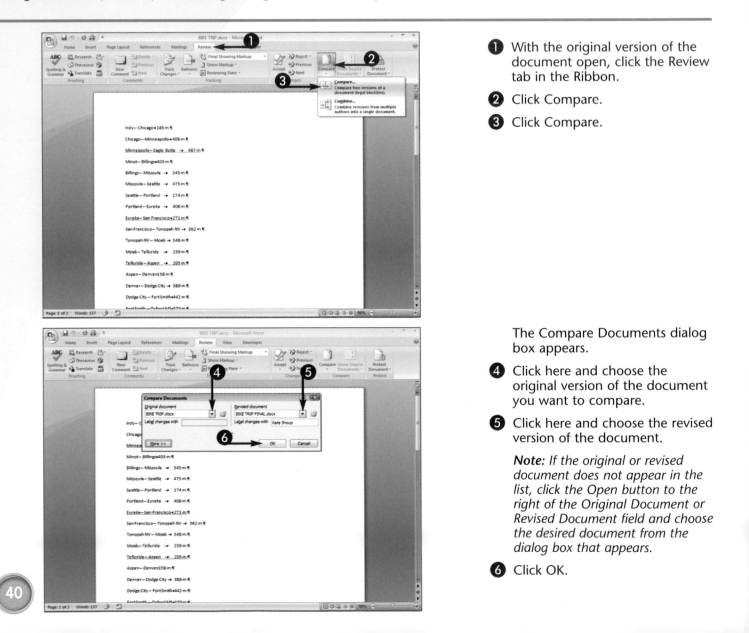

❶ With the original version of the document open, click the Review tab in the Ribbon.

❷ Click Compare.

❸ Click Compare.

The Compare Documents dialog box appears.

❹ Click here and choose the original version of the document you want to compare.

❺ Click here and choose the revised version of the document.

Note: If the original or revised document does not appear in the list, click the Open button to the right of the Original Document or Revised Document field and choose the desired document from the dialog box that appears.

❻ Click OK.

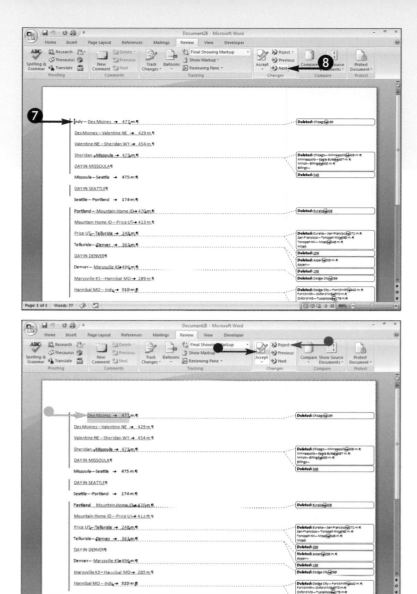

Word compares the document, flagging discrepancies such as text additions and deletions as well as formatting changes.

Note: *The document view shown here is Print Layout; hence, deletions are shown in balloons in the right margin.*

DIFFICULTY LEVEL

7 To begin reviewing the discrepancies, click at the beginning of the document.

8 Click Next on the Review tab.

● Word highlights the first discrepancy in the document.

● To accept the change, click Accept in the Review tab (as shown here).

● To reject the change, click Reject in the Review tab.

Note: *To accept all changes in the document, click the down arrow under Accept and click Accept All Changes in Document.*

Depending on which button you clicked, Word accepts or rejects the change, and automatically highlights the next one in the document, which you can choose to accept or reject.

 **TIPS**

Did You Know?

To combine multiple revised files into a single document, click Compare on the Review tab and choose Combine. Select the original version of the document from the Original Document list, and select any of the reviewed versions from the Revised Document list. Click More and, under Show Changes In, click Original Document, and then click OK. Repeat for each revised version of the document.

More Options!

Another way to collaborate with others on a document is to use Word's Comments feature. To add a comment, select the text on which you want to comment, click New Comment in the Comments group of the Review tab, and type your comment in the balloon or field that appears.

TRANSLATE TEXT

In today's global economy, being able to communicate with others who speak different languages is imperative. Fortunately, Word contains translation tools, including bilingual dictionaries and machine-translation functions, that enable you to quickly and easily translate words or phrases that you write in your native tongue into one of several other languages (and vice versa).

Word can translate text to and from many languages, including Arabic, Chinese, Dutch, English, French, German, Greek, Italian, Japanese, Korean, Portuguese, Russian, Spanish, and Swedish. (Note, however, that your ability to translate text to and from all these languages may be limited by your computer's operating system.)

If you need to translate more than the occasional word or phrase and instead need to translate an entire document, you can use Word to access fee-based online translation services.

Note that while translating text in this manner can convey the basics of the content, the full meaning and tone of the text may be lost. If it is imperative that the specifics of what the text contains be conveyed, human translation is recommended.

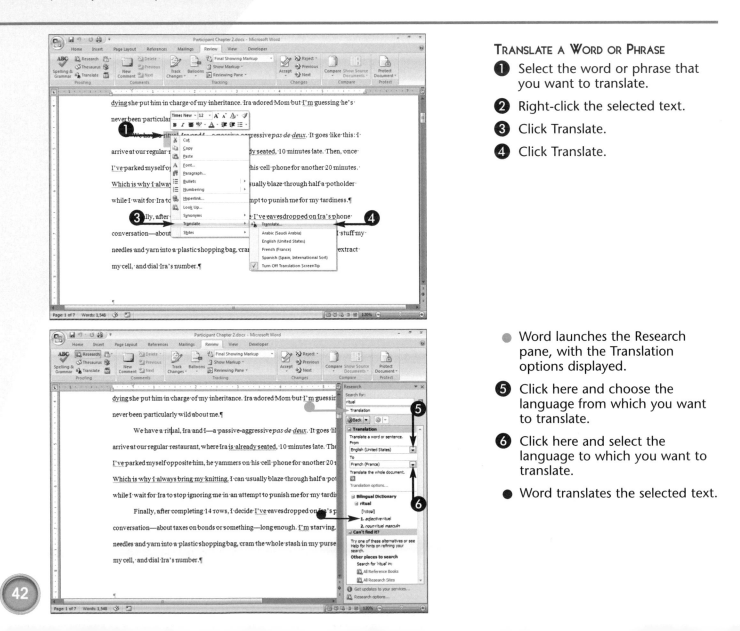

TRANSLATE A WORD OR PHRASE

❶ Select the word or phrase that you want to translate.

❷ Right-click the selected text.

❸ Click Translate.

❹ Click Translate.

● Word launches the Research pane, with the Translation options displayed.

❺ Click here and choose the language from which you want to translate.

❻ Click here and select the language to which you want to translate.

● Word translates the selected text.

TRANSLATE A DOCUMENT

1 With the document you want to translate open in Word, click the Review tab.

2 Click Translate.

● Word launches the Research pane, with the Translation options displayed.

3 Click here and select the language from which you want to translate.

4 Click here and select the language to which you want to translate.

5 Click here under Translate the whole document.

● Word notifies you that it will send your document to a Web-based translation service.

6 Click Yes.

Word displays the translated text in your Web browser.

Note: You might find that only a portion of your document has been translated. In order for the rest of the document to be translated, you may need to pay a fee.

TIPS

Did You Know?

If you only need to translate the occasional word, enable Word's Translation ScreenTip feature. To do so, right-click in the body of a document, click Translate, and click the language into which you need to translate; then, simply hover your mouse pointer over the word in question. Word displays a translation for the word. To disable this feature, again right-click in the document and click Translate, but this time click Turn Off Translation ScreenTip.

Important!

If you are using Word's Translate function for the first time, you may be prompted to install the necessary bilingual dictionaries. Click OK.

Remove It!

To close the Research pane, click the Close button in the pane's upper-right corner.

Use Word's
THESAURUS AND DICTIONARY

If you are having trouble finding just the right word or phrase, you can use Word's thesaurus tool to find words with similar meanings (that is, synonyms) as well as words with the opposite meaning (that is, antonyms). Word even enables you to access thesauri in different languages. For example, if you are writing a document in French, you can use Word's French thesaurus just as you would use the English version when composing in English. In addition, Word includes a dictionary tool, which you can use to look up words of whose meanings you are not quite certain.

You access these tools from within Word's Research pane, from which you also access the program's translation tools and other reference-based features such as an encyclopedia, as well as research sites including HighBeam Research, the MSN Money Stock Quotes site, and the Thomson Gale Company Profiles site.

Another way to use the thesaurus and dictionary tools is to right-click the word for which you want to see synonyms or a definition. Word displays a context menu from which you can choose the desired option.

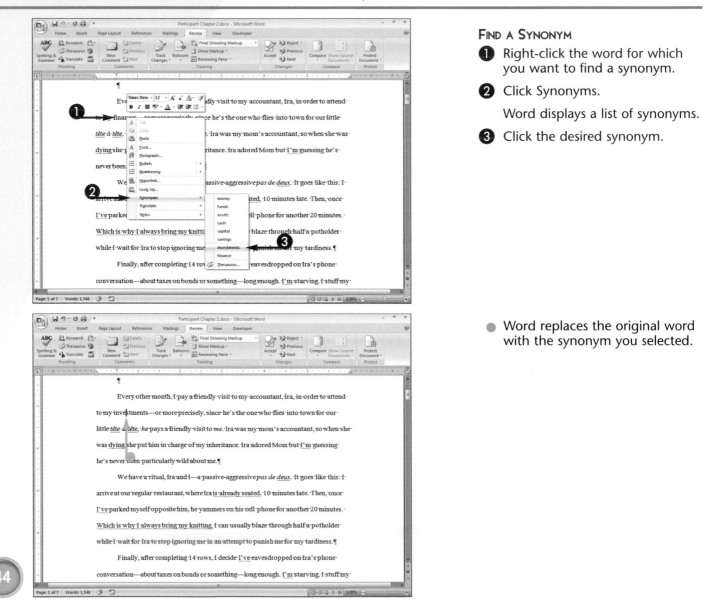

FIND A SYNONYM

1 Right-click the word for which you want to find a synonym.

2 Click Synonyms.

Word displays a list of synonyms.

3 Click the desired synonym.

● Word replaces the original word with the synonym you selected.

LOOK UP A WORD

1 Right-click the word you want to look up.

2 Click Look Up.

DIFFICULTY LEVEL

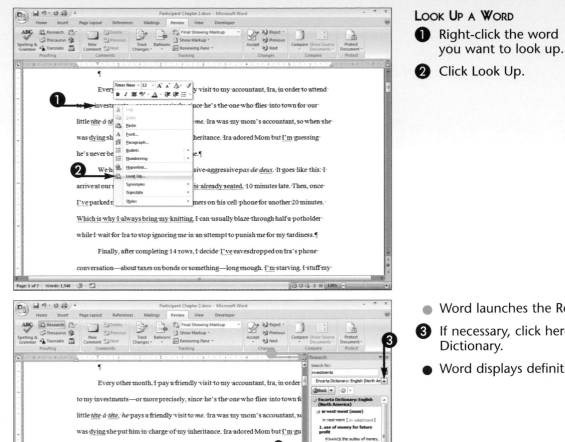

● Word launches the Research pane.

3 If necessary, click here and select Encarta Dictionary.

● Word displays definitions of the word.

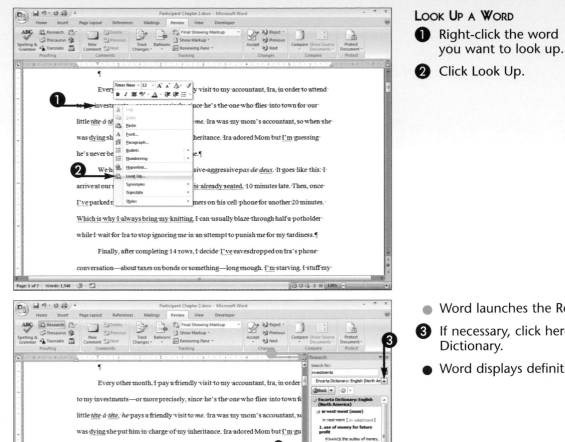

TIPS

Try This!

Another way to open Word's Research pane is to click the Research button in the Ribbon's Review tab.

More Options!

Word's Research pane offers easy access to MSN Encarta, a free Web-based encyclopedia. To use it, open the Research pane. Then either type the topic you want to research in the pane's Search For field or Alt+click a word in your document that you want to research. Next, click the drop-down arrow near the top of the pane and choose Encarta Encyclopedia from the menu that appears. The pane displays a list of links to articles that relate to the word you typed or clicked; click one to launch your Web browser and access the MSN Encarta page with the related article displayed.

Create a
BLOG POST

A portmanteau of *Web log*, a *blog* is a sort of online journal. A blog might provide commentary on a topic as broad as global warming or as specific as the day-to-day activities of a single individual. Blogs can include text, images, links to other Web pages and blogs, and more.

Recent years have seen an explosion in the number of blogs on the Internet, with some estimates pegging the current number at more than 71,000,000. To accommodate this growing legion of bloggers, Microsoft has developed tools for composing and publishing blogs to sites such as MSN Spaces and Blogger from within Word.

Composing blog posts within Word offers several advantages. First, you can use many of Word's formatting features, as well as its spelling- and grammar-checking capabilities on your blog entries. Second, you need not be connected to the Internet until you are ready to publish your piece.

To publish posts written in Word to your blog, you must first establish an account with a blogging site such as Blogger, and then register that account with Word.

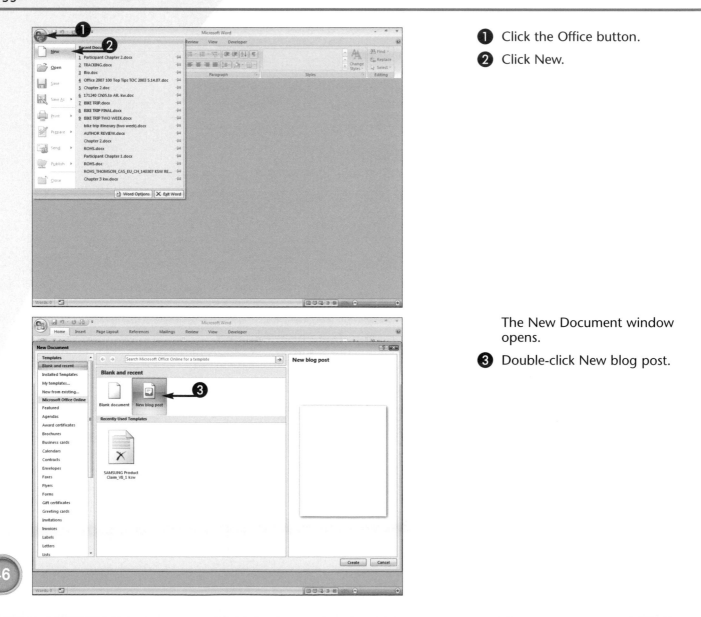

❶ Click the Office button.

❷ Click New.

The New Document window opens.

❸ Double-click New blog post.

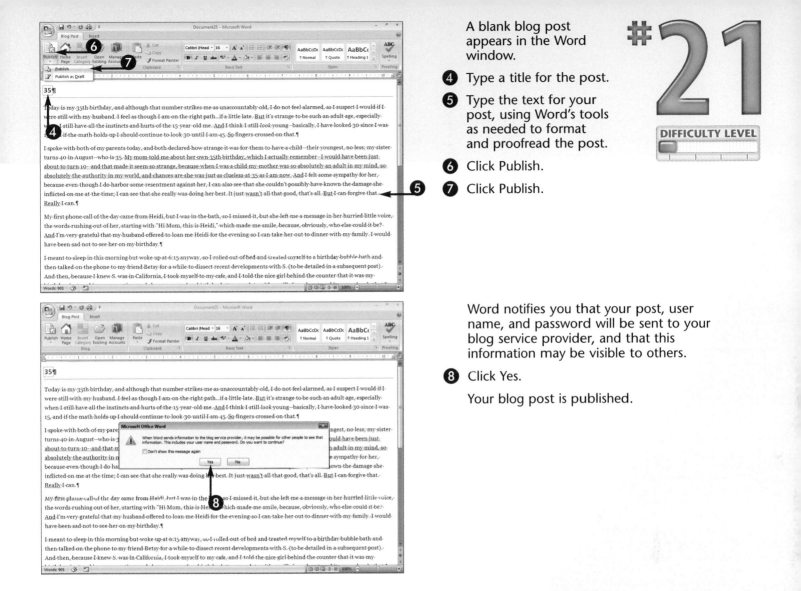

A blank blog post appears in the Word window.

④ Type a title for the post.

⑤ Type the text for your post, using Word's tools as needed to format and proofread the post.

⑥ Click Publish.

⑦ Click Publish.

Word notifies you that your post, user name, and password will be sent to your blog service provider, and that this information may be visible to others.

⑧ Click Yes.

Your blog post is published.

TIPS

Important!

If you are using Word to create a new blog post for the first time, Word will prompt you to register your blog account. When it does, click Register, click the Blog drop-down arrow, and choose your blog service provider. Click Next, enter the user name and password for your blog account, select the Remember Password check box if you want Word to log you on automatically, and click OK.

Important!

Some blog providers automate the process of uploading photos to your blog; others require that you establish a separate account with a picture provider — that is, a site that is devoted solely to storing photos. To determine whether you need a picture provider account, check with your blog provider.

Jazz Up Your Work with Word

The thrust behind the design of this new version of Word is to enable users to spend less time formatting their documents and more time writing. To that end, this version of Word includes several tools to expedite formatting your document. For example, Word's Drop Cap feature enables you to draw your reader's attention to your text by enlarging the first letter of a paragraph.

Other Word tools help you save time by generating special elements for your documents. One such special element is a bibliography, which lists the books, Web sites, and other sources used in the course of researching and writing your document. You simply add citations to the document that include the relevant information, and Word does the rest. Another special element you can generate automatically in Word is a table of

contents that contains all the headings in your document.

To ensure that your document meets the strict standards of academic and professional environments, you can use Word to insert footnotes and endnotes. Word numbers these footnotes, automatically updating them as you add, delete, and move text in your document. This saves you the time and trouble of tracking these items yourself.

Finally, to help you make your documents look more professional, Word includes tools for creating a cover page, including several built-in designs from which you can choose; adding Excel charts to your documents; embedding a watermark on pages in your document; and more.

Create a
BIBLIOGRAPHY

If you are writing an academic paper, you will almost certainly be required to include a bibliography. Word enables you to automatically generate a bibliography and format its entries using the style guide of your choice. Style-guide options include American Psychological Association (APA), Modern Language Association (MLA), and *The Chicago Manual of Style*. To specify which style guide you want to use, click the References tab, click Citations & Bibliography, click the Style drop-down arrow, and choose a style guide from the list that appears.

For Word to determine which entries should appear in the bibliography, you must cite sources in your document as you work. Word then collects the information from these citations to generate the bibliography. When you add a source to a document, Word saves it for use in subsequent documents, meaning that instead of reentering the information, you can search for the existing source.

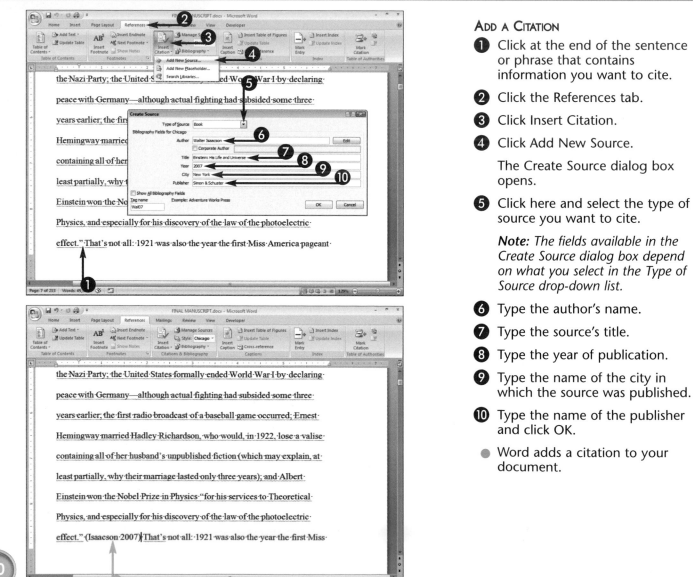

ADD A CITATION

1. Click at the end of the sentence or phrase that contains information you want to cite.

2. Click the References tab.

3. Click Insert Citation.

4. Click Add New Source.

   The Create Source dialog box opens.

5. Click here and select the type of source you want to cite.

   Note: The fields available in the Create Source dialog box depend on what you select in the Type of Source drop-down list.

6. Type the author's name.

7. Type the source's title.

8. Type the year of publication.

9. Type the name of the city in which the source was published.

10. Type the name of the publisher and click OK.

● Word adds a citation to your document.

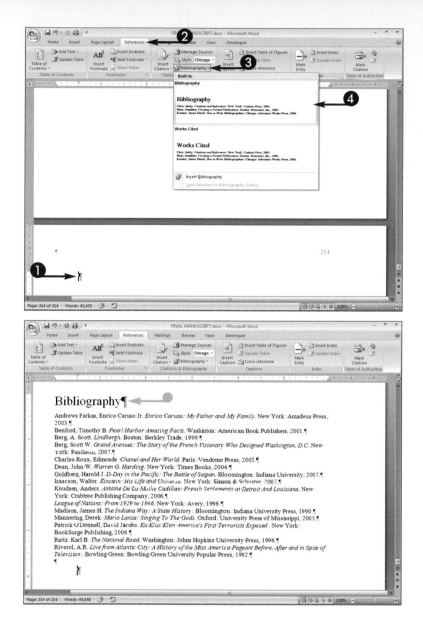

GENERATE THE BIBLIOGRAPHY

1 Click the spot in the document where you want the bibliography to appear (typically at the end).

2 Click the References tab.

3 Click Bibliography.

4 Click one of the gallery options to insert a predesigned bibliography into your document.

● Word inserts the bibliography.

DIFFICULTY LEVEL

#22

TIPS

Did You Know?

To reuse a source from another document, click Manage Sources in the Citations & Bibliography group. Then, under Master List in the Manage Sources dialog box, click the citation you want to add to your current document, click Copy, and click Close.

More Options!

If you know you want to add a citation to your document, but you don't have all the necessary information, you can create a placeholder. Click Insert Citation in the Citations & Bibliography group, choose Add New Placeholder, and type a name for the placeholder in the dialog box that appears. Later, add citation information by clicking Manage Sources in the Citations & Bibliography group, clicking the placeholder under Current List, clicking Edit, and entering the necessary information.

Insert
FOOTNOTES AND ENDNOTES

You can use Word to insert footnotes and endnotes in your document. A *footnote* is an explanatory note, usually in a smaller font, inserted at the bottom of a page to cite the source of or further explain information that appears on that page. The information to which the footnote pertains is flagged, usually with a superscript numeral, but sometimes with a symbol, such as a dagger symbol. *Endnotes* are like footnotes, but appear at the end of a section or document rather than at the bottom of a page.

When you insert footnotes or endnotes in a document, Word automatically numbers them. As you add, delete, and move text in your document, any associated footnotes or endnotes are likewise added, deleted, or moved, as well as renumbered.

To delete a footnote or endnote, but leave the text in the document to which it refers intact, select the superscript numeral or symbol flagging the footnote or endnote and press the Delete key on your keyboard. Word deletes the flag as well as the note.

① Click in your document where you want to add the numeral or symbol indicating a footnote or endnote.

② Click the References tab.

③ Click Insert Footnote (as shown here) or Insert Endnote.

● A superscript numeral or symbol appears at the cursor location.

④ Type the information you want to include in the footnote.

⑤ Click the diagonal arrow in the Footnotes group on the Ribbon.

The Footnote and Endnote dialog box appears.

6 Click here and select where on the page the footnote should appear.

7 Click here and select the desired number format.

8 Click here and select the number, letter, or symbol that should appear first.

9 Click here and specify whether the numbering should be continuous, restart at the beginning of each section, or restart at the beginning of each page.

10 Click Convert.

The Convert Notes dialog box opens.

11 To convert the footnotes in your document to endnotes, click Convert all footnotes to endnotes (◎ changes to ●).

12 Click OK.

13 Click Insert.

23

DIFFICULTY LEVEL

TIPS

Customize It!

If a footnote or endnote runs to a second page, you can add standard text, called a *continuation notice*, to it to indicate that it continues on the next page. To do so, first switch to Draft view. Then, in the References tab, click Show Notes in the Footnotes group. If prompted, specify whether you want to create a continuation notice for the footnotes or the endnotes in the document, click the Footnotes or Endnotes drop-down arrow and click Footnote Continuation Notice or Endnote Continuation Notice, and type the text you want to use in the notice.

Important!

You must be in Print Layout view to add a footnote or endnote.

Generate a
TABLE OF CONTENTS

If your document requires a table of contents (TOC), you can use Word to generate one automatically. By default, a TOC generated in Word contains text that is formatted in one of Word's predefined heading styles. Word generates the TOC by searching for these styles, copying text that has been formatted with them, and pasting it into the TOC.

If you used custom styles in your document to create headings rather than Word's built-in styles, you can still generate a TOC; you simply indicate what style Word should search for in your document when determining what the TOC should contain.

Regardless of whether you use Word's predefined heading styles to generate the TOC or you create a TOC that cites text formatted with custom styles, you can choose from Word's gallery of TOC styles to establish its look and feel.

If you edit your document, you can update your TOC to reflect the changes. Click Update Table in the References tab's Table of Contents group and specify whether you want to update page numbers only or the entire table.

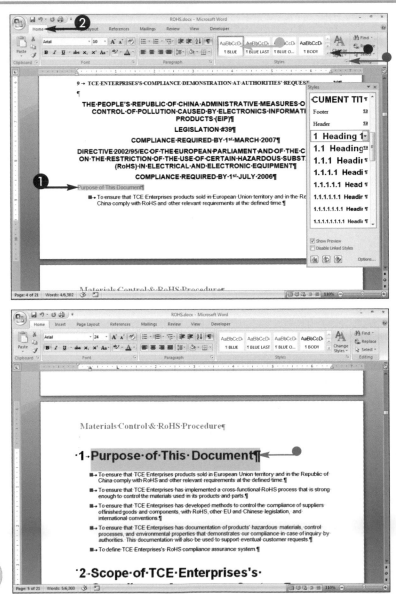

STYLE TEXT AS HEADINGS

1 Select text in your document that you want to style as a heading.

2 Click the Home tab.

● Click the style you want to select it.

● If the style you want to apply does not appear in the Styles group, click the More button and choose the desired style from the Quick Style gallery.

● If the style you want to apply does not appear in the Quick Style gallery, click here and select the desired style from the Styles task pane.

● Word applies the style you chose to the selected text.

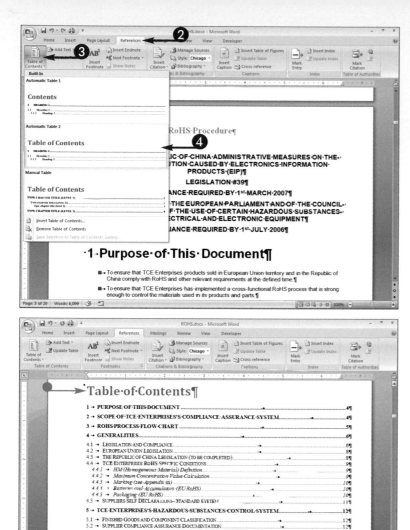

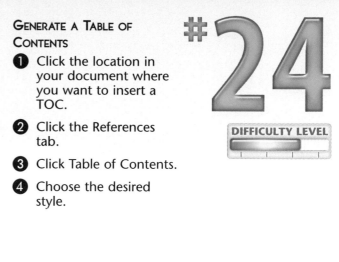

1 Click the location in your document where you want to insert a TOC.

2 Click the References tab.

3 Click Table of Contents.

4 Choose the desired style.

#24

DIFFICULTY LEVEL

● Word generates the TOC.

Note: To delete a TOC, click Table of Contents in the References tab's Table of Contents group and click Remove Table of Contents.

TIP

Customize It!

If you need to generate a TOC using custom styles rather than Word's predefined header styles, click Table of Contents on the References tab and choose Insert Table of Contents. The Table of Contents dialog box opens; click Options. In the Table of Contents Options dialog box, under Available Styles, locate the top-level heading style you applied to your document; then type the number **1** in the corresponding field to indicate that it should appear in the TOC as a level-1 heading. Repeat for additional heading styles, typing **2**, **3**, **4**, and so on to indicate their levels. Click OK to close the Table of Contents Options dialog box, and click OK again to close the Table of Contents dialog box.

Insert a
COVER PAGE

To add a professional touch to your documents, you can add a cover page. For example, you might include a special cover page for an annual report that is sent to investors.

Word enables you to insert predefined cover pages from its Cover Pages gallery. Alternatively, you can create your own cover page and save it to the gallery for future use.

Regardless of whether the cover page you add to your document is a predefined cover page supplied

by Word or a custom cover page you converted to a building block, the process of adding the cover page to your document is essentially the same.

Once a cover page is added to your document, you simply select the placeholder text and type over it with text of your own. You can also change the look and feel of the cover page just as you would any other page in Word — by using the program's various formatting tools.

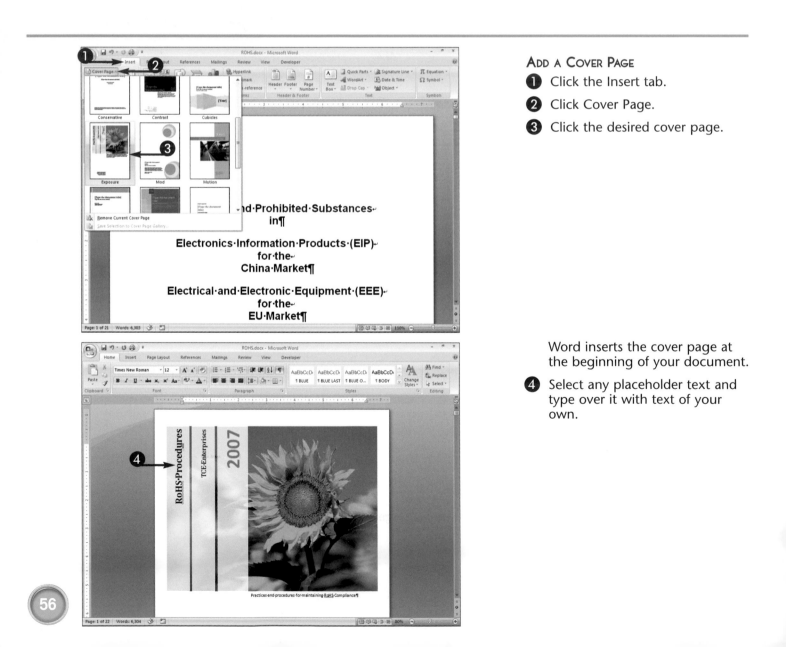

ADD A COVER PAGE

① Click the Insert tab.

② Click Cover Page.

③ Click the desired cover page.

Word inserts the cover page at the beginning of your document.

④ Select any placeholder text and type over it with text of your own.

56

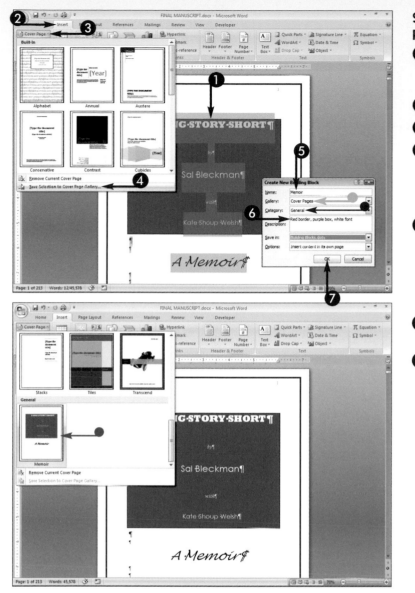

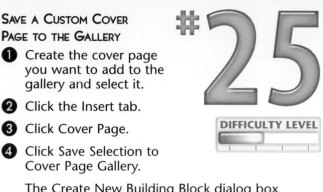

25

SAVE A CUSTOM COVER PAGE TO THE GALLERY

DIFFICULTY LEVEL

❶ Create the cover page you want to add to the gallery and select it.

❷ Click the Insert tab.

❸ Click Cover Page.

❹ Click Save Selection to Cover Page Gallery.

The Create New Building Block dialog box opens.

❺ Type a name for the cover page.

● The new cover page is saved in the Cover Pages gallery by default.

● The new cover page is assigned the General category by default.

❻ Optionally, type a description for the cover page.

❼ Click OK.

● Word adds the custom cover page to the Cover Pages gallery.

TIPS

Customize It!

If your document contains page numbers, you probably want to omit them from the cover page. Depending on whether the cover page you added was a predefined one or one you created, you may need to do this by hand. Click anywhere in the document, click the Page Layout tab, click the diagonal arrow in the bottom-right corner of the Page Setup group, and click the Layout tab in the dialog box that appears. Finally, click the Different First Page check box to select it and then click OK.

Remove It!

If you add a cover page to your document but later decide you want to remove it, click the Insert tab, click Cover Page, and click Remove the Current Cover Page.

Generate an
INDEX

If your document requires an index, you can use Word to build one. Before Word can build an index, however, you must mark any words or phrases in your document that should appear in your index. When you do, Word adds a special XE (short for *index entry*) field to the document that includes the marked word or phrase, as well as any cross-reference information you care to add.

When you create an index, Word searches for the marked words and phrases, sorts them alphabetically, adds the appropriate page-number references, locates and removes duplicate entries that cite the same page number, and then generates the index.

When you mark index entries, you have a few options. One is to mark a single word or phrase. Another is to create entries for text that spans a range of pages. When you do the latter, you first select the text to which you want the entry to refer, and then create a bookmark for that text. When generating the index, Word refers to the bookmark information to determine the correct page range.

MARK A WORD OR PHRASE FOR AN INDEX

1 Select text you want to mark.

2 Click the References tab.

3 Click Mark Entry.

The Mark Index Entry dialog box opens.

4 If the selected text does not appear as it should in the index, delete it and type the desired text. (If the entry is a person's name, type his or her last name first.)

5 Click Current Page.

6 Click Mark to create an entry for the word or phrase on this page only, or click Mark All to create entries for all occurrences in the document.

● Word adds an XE field to your document.

Note: If you can't see the XE field, click the Show/Hide button on the Ribbon's Home tab.

7 Click Close.

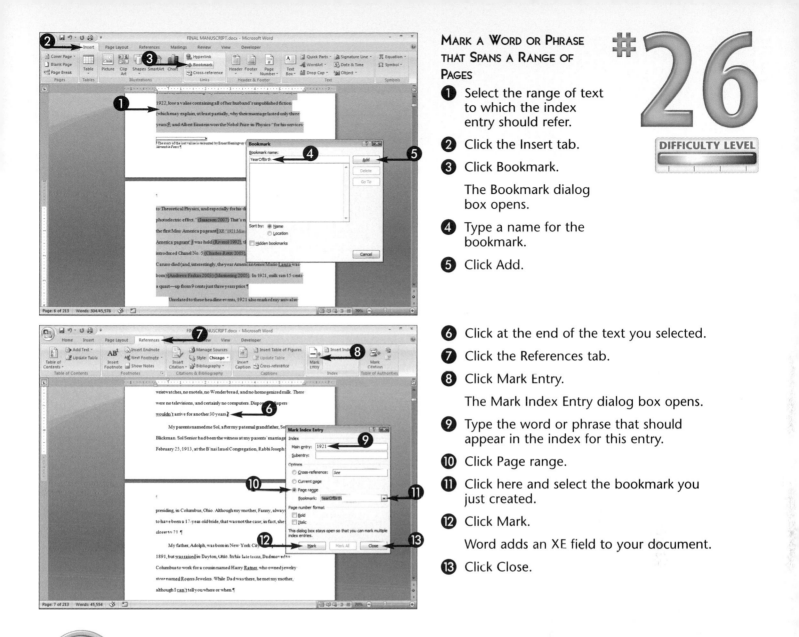

MARK A WORD OR PHRASE THAT SPANS A RANGE OF PAGES

⬛26

DIFFICULTY LEVEL

1 Select the range of text to which the index entry should refer.

2 Click the Insert tab.

3 Click Bookmark.

The Bookmark dialog box opens.

4 Type a name for the bookmark.

5 Click Add.

6 Click at the end of the text you selected.

7 Click the References tab.

8 Click Mark Entry.

The Mark Index Entry dialog box opens.

9 Type the word or phrase that should appear in the index for this entry.

10 Click Page range.

11 Click here and select the bookmark you just created.

12 Click Mark.

Word adds an XE field to your document.

13 Click Close.

TIPS

More Options!

If the text you selected should appear as a subentry rather than a main entry, type the entry under which the selected text should appear in the Main Entry field, and then type the selected text in the Subentry field. If the text should appear as a subentry *and* a main entry, add two XE fields — one for the main entry and one for the subentry. To include a third-level entry, type the subentry under which the third-level entry should appear, add a colon, and then type the third-level entry.

Put It Together!

To create index entries that refer to other entries, click Cross-reference in the Mark Index Entry dialog box and type the word or phrase to which this entry should refer.

Generate an
INDEX

After you have marked all the words and phrases in your document that you want to appear as index entries, you can create the index by either selecting one of Word's built-in index designs or creating a custom design.

If you make a change to your document — for example, adding more index entries, editing existing entries, or changing the text such that the page numbers in the existing index are no longer correct — you can update the index to reflect the change.

Note that to edit an existing index entry, you must find the XE field for the entry and change the text inside the field's quotation marks as needed. To change the contents of an XE field that appears multiple times in your document, click the Replace button in the Home tab, type the XE string you need to change in the Find What field (for example, XE "Winston Churchill"), type the replacement text in the Replace With field (for example, XE "Churchill, Winston"), and click Replace All.

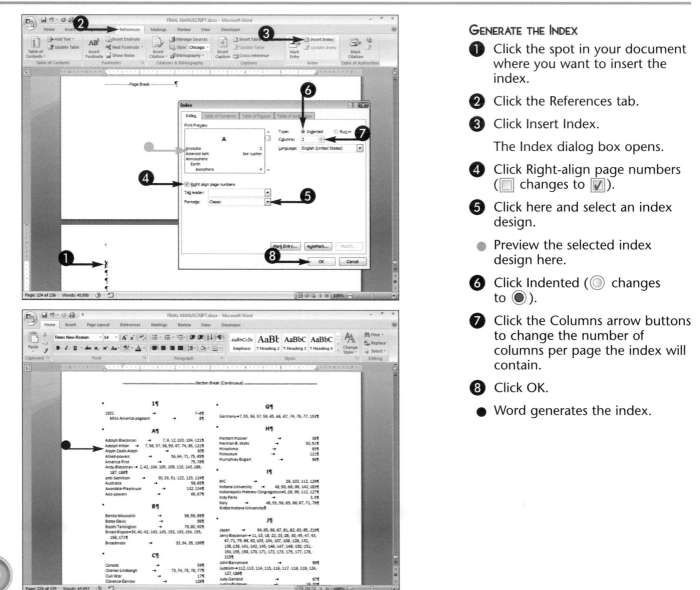

GENERATE THE INDEX

1 Click the spot in your document where you want to insert the index.

2 Click the References tab.

3 Click Insert Index.

The Index dialog box opens.

4 Click Right-align page numbers (☐ changes to ☑).

5 Click here and select an index design.

● Preview the selected index design here.

6 Click Indented (◎ changes to ◉).

7 Click the Columns arrow buttons to change the number of columns per page the index will contain.

8 Click OK.

● Word generates the index.

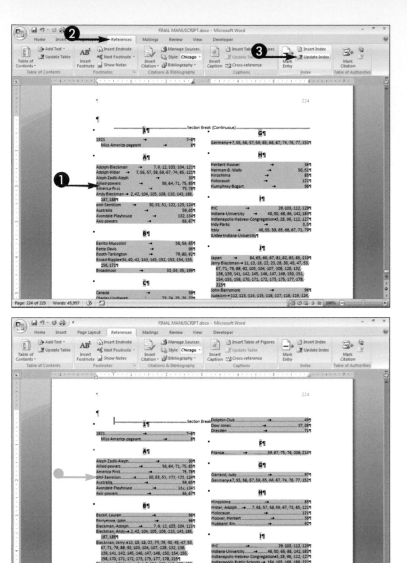

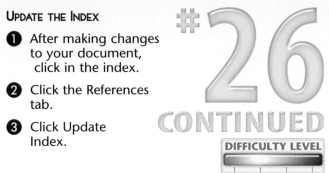
UPDATE THE INDEX

① After making changes to your document, click in the index.

② Click the References tab.

③ Click Update Index.

● Word updates the index to reflect changes to the document that have occurred since the original index was generated.

TIPS

Customize It!

If you want your index to use a custom layout, click the Formats drop-down arrow in the Index dialog box, choose From Template, and click Modify. The Style dialog box opens; click the index style you want to change, and again click Modify. Finally, select the desired options in the Formatting section. To add this custom index style to the template so that all documents you create with the template can use the style, click All Documents Based on the Template.

Remove It!

You delete an index entry by selecting the entire XE field, including the braces ({}) that surround it, and pressing the Delete key on your keyboard. Be sure to update the index after deleting any entries!

Add a
CROSS-REFERENCE

DIFFICULTY LEVEL

Suppose you want to insert text in one part of your document that refers the reader to a different part of the document for more information. To do so, you can insert a cross-reference. Cross-references can refer readers to text that is styled as a heading, to footnotes, to bookmarks, to captions, and to numbered paragraphs.

Before inserting a cross-reference, you will probably want to type some introductory text, such as "For more information, refer to." Then add the cross-reference after the text to complete the thought.

If the item to which a cross-reference refers is moved or changed, you can update the cross-reference to reflect the edit. To do so, select the cross-reference you want to update, right-click the selection, and click Update Field. To update all cross-references in the document, select the entire document rather than a single cross-reference.

Note that you can create cross-references only to items in the document that already exist. That is, you cannot create a cross-reference for a document element you have not yet created.

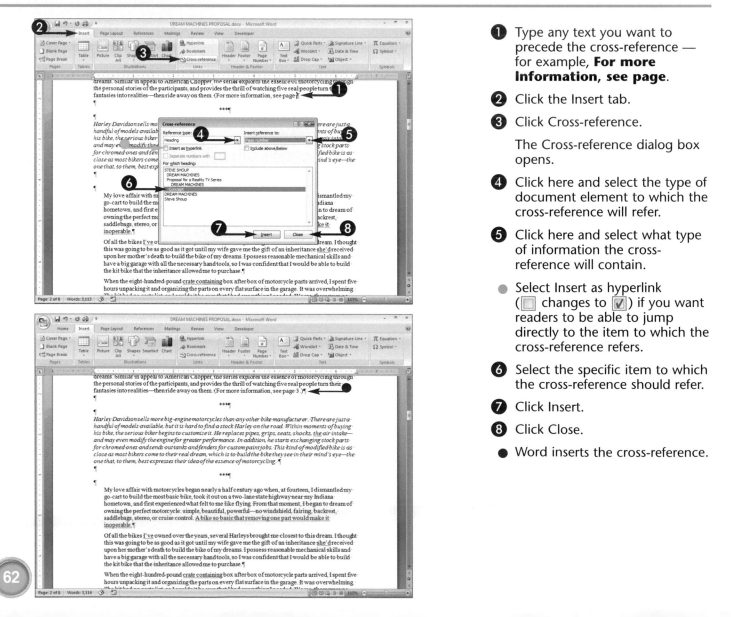

① Type any text you want to precede the cross-reference — for example, **For more Information, see page**.

② Click the Insert tab.

③ Click Cross-reference.

The Cross-reference dialog box opens.

④ Click here and select the type of document element to which the cross-reference will refer.

⑤ Click here and select what type of information the cross-reference will contain.

● Select Insert as hyperlink (☐ changes to ☑) if you want readers to be able to jump directly to the item to which the cross-reference refers.

⑥ Select the specific item to which the cross-reference should refer.

⑦ Click Insert.

⑧ Click Close.

● Word inserts the cross-reference.

Emphasize text with
DROP CAPS

DIFFICULTY LEVEL

A great way to direct your readers' attention to your text is to use Word's Drop Cap feature. This feature enlarges the first letter of a paragraph such that the top of the letter lines up with the top of the other letters in the first line, but the bottom of the letter lines up with the bottom of the letters in the fourth or fifth line. You have probably seen drop caps used at the beginning of chapters in some novels, at the beginning of magazine articles, in the newspaper, and in other publications.

When using Word to create drop caps, you have two options. One is to place the drop cap inline with the other text in the paragraph; the other is to set the drop cap in the margin.

In addition to specifying where the drop cap should appear, you can also choose a different font for the drop cap, how many lines the drop cap should span, and how far the drop cap should be from the other text in the paragraph.

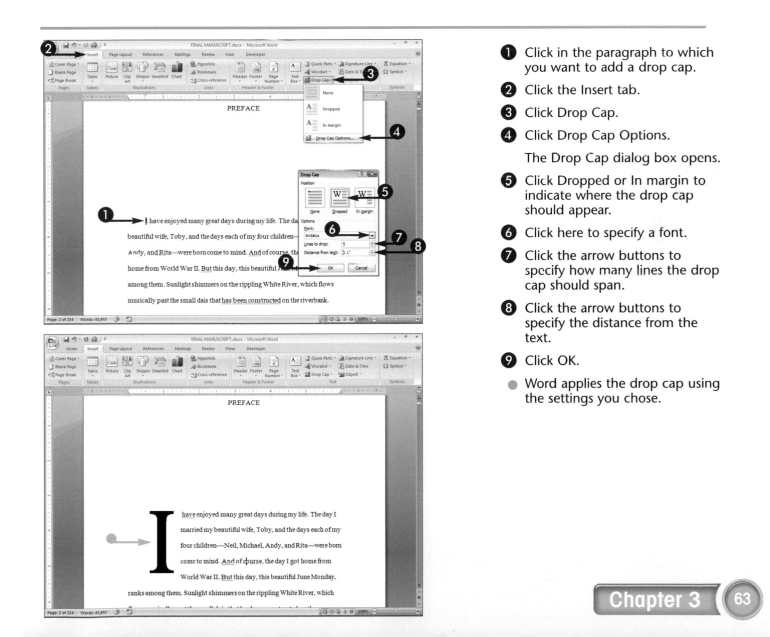

① Click in the paragraph to which you want to add a drop cap.

② Click the Insert tab.

③ Click Drop Cap.

④ Click Drop Cap Options.

The Drop Cap dialog box opens.

⑤ Click Dropped or In margin to indicate where the drop cap should appear.

⑥ Click here to specify a font.

⑦ Click the arrow buttons to specify how many lines the drop cap should span.

⑧ Click the arrow buttons to specify the distance from the text.

⑨ Click OK.

● Word applies the drop cap using the settings you chose.

Summarize information
WITH A CHART

If, in addition to having Microsoft Word 2007 installed on your computer, you also have Microsoft Excel 2007, you can create Excel charts from within Word. The chart you create will be embedded in Word, and stored in an Excel worksheet that is incorporated into the Word file.

Supported chart types include (but are not limited to) column charts, line charts, pie charts, and bar charts. Column charts work well for data arranged in both columns and rows to show changes in data over time or to compare two data sets. Line charts also work

for data arranged in both columns and rows, and are ideal for illustrating trends. Pie charts work well for data arranged in one column or row to illustrate proportional data values. Finally, bar charts, also for data arranged in a single column or row, are used to compare items in a data set.

When creating a chart, regardless of type, you can select from several predefined styles. You can then modify the chart as desired, saving it as a template for later use.

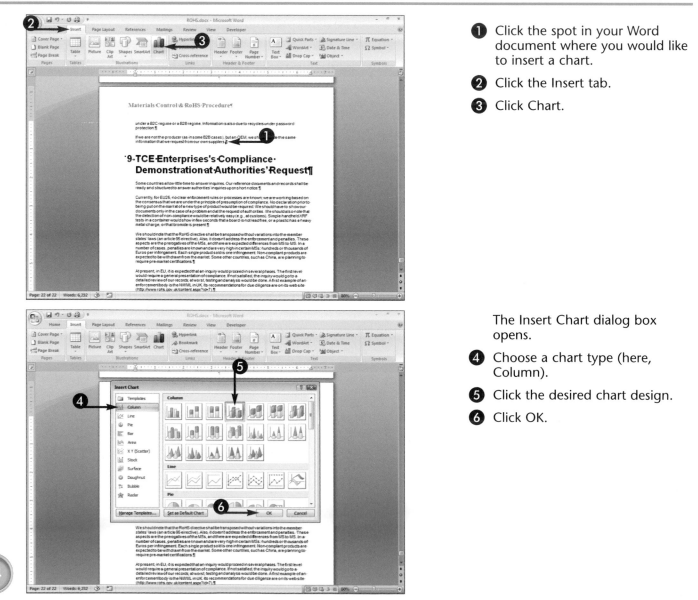

① Click the spot in your Word document where you would like to insert a chart.

② Click the Insert tab.

③ Click Chart.

The Insert Chart dialog box opens.

④ Choose a chart type (here, Column).

⑤ Click the desired chart design.

⑥ Click OK.

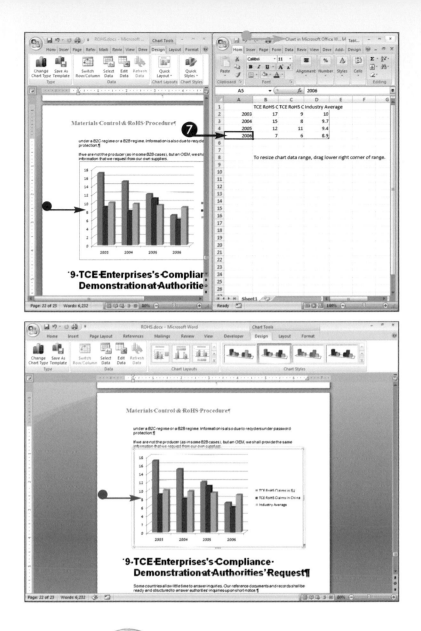

- Word launches Excel in a split window, displaying a worksheet with sample data.

- Word inserts a placeholder chart in your document.

7 Replace the sample data with your own data by clicking a cell and typing the correct data.

Note: When you are finished replacing the sample data, click the Office button in Excel, click Save As, select a file location for the Excel worksheet, type a name for the worksheet, and click Save. Then close Excel.

- The chart in the Word document is updated to reflect your changes.

TIPS

Customize It!

You can modify a chart to better suit your needs — for example, adding a title, moving the legend, changing the color or formatting, or what have you. To explore your options, click the Design, Layout, and Format tabs in the Ribbon.

Did You Know?

If you modify a chart's design, you can save the changed chart as a chart template for reuse. To do so, click the chart and, in the Design tab's Type group, click Save As Template. The Save Chart Template dialog box opens with the contents of the Charts folder displayed. Type a name for the chart and click Save. You can apply the template by selecting it in the Insert Chart dialog box's Templates folder.

Add a
WATERMARK

Traditionally speaking, a *watermark* is a faint design impressed in paper that is visible when the sheet is held to the light. To re-create the effect, you can apply a digital watermark to your Word documents.

You might apply a watermark that contains your company's logo, or perhaps the word *Draft*, *Confidential*, or *Final* to indicate the status of a document. Watermarks applied in Word are visible in Print Layout view and Full Screen view, as well as on printouts of the document.

Word offers a gallery of several predesigned text watermarks, including ones that say "Confidential" and "Do Not Copy." In addition to using these prebuilt designs, you can create and insert your own watermark. The watermark you create can contain text of your choosing, formatted using the font and color you specify. Alternatively, you can choose a picture to use as a watermark. To ensure the picture or text does not compete with the document contents, you can opt to wash it out — that is, make it appear more transparent.

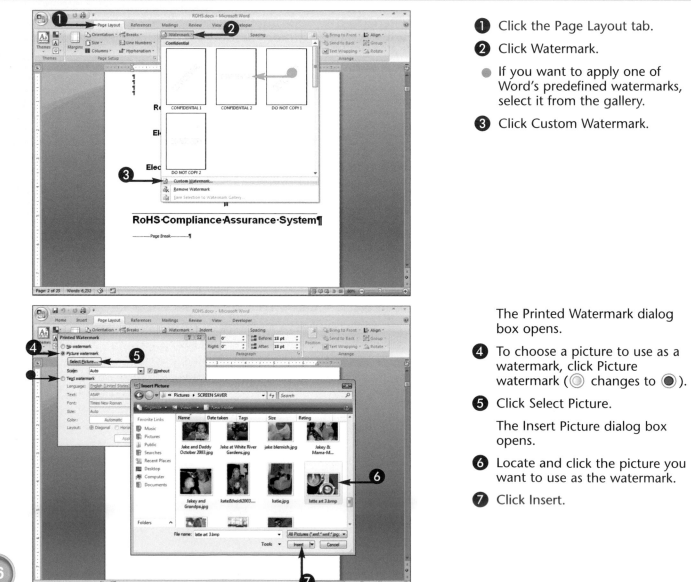

❶ Click the Page Layout tab.

❷ Click Watermark.

● If you want to apply one of Word's predefined watermarks, select it from the gallery.

❸ Click Custom Watermark.

The Printed Watermark dialog box opens.

❹ To choose a picture to use as a watermark, click Picture watermark (◯ changes to ◉).

❺ Click Select Picture.

The Insert Picture dialog box opens.

❻ Locate and click the picture you want to use as the watermark.

❼ Click Insert.

8 Click here and select how large the image should appear on the page.

9 To make the image appear more transparent, click the Washout check box (☐ changes to ☑).

● To preview how the watermark will look if applied to your document, click Apply.

10 Click OK.

#30

DIFFICULTY LEVEL

● Word applies the watermark.

Customize It!

In addition to creating custom picture watermarks, you can also create custom text watermarks. To do so, do the following:

1 Click the Text watermark radio button in the Printed Watermark dialog box.

2 Type the text you want the watermark to contain.

3 Choose a font, font size, and font color.

4 Click the Semitransparent check box to wash out the text.

5 Specify whether the text should appear diagonally or horizontally.

6 Click OK.

Remove It!

If, after adding a watermark, you change your mind, you can remove it. To do so, click Watermark in the Page Layout tab's Page Background group and choose Remove Watermark.

WRAP TEXT
around a graphic

When you insert a graphic — for example, clip art, Word Art, your own photos, charts, drawing objects, and so on — into a Word document, you can specify how the text before and after the graphic will appear.

For example, you can choose Word's Top and Bottom text-wrapping setting to place the graphic such that it interrupts the flow of text, leaving white space on the sides of the graphic. If space is at a premium, however, you might opt to use the Square, Tight, or Through text-wrapping setting to wrap the text around the graphic, eliminating the extra space.

Other options include Behind Text, in which case the text runs atop the graphic, and In Front of Text, in which case the graphic obscures the text.

In most cases, graphics you add to a document are square or rectangular in shape. For this reason, Word typically wraps text in a square around your graphic, regardless of the graphic's actual shape. You can, however, opt to wrap the text in such a way that it mirrors the shape of the image.

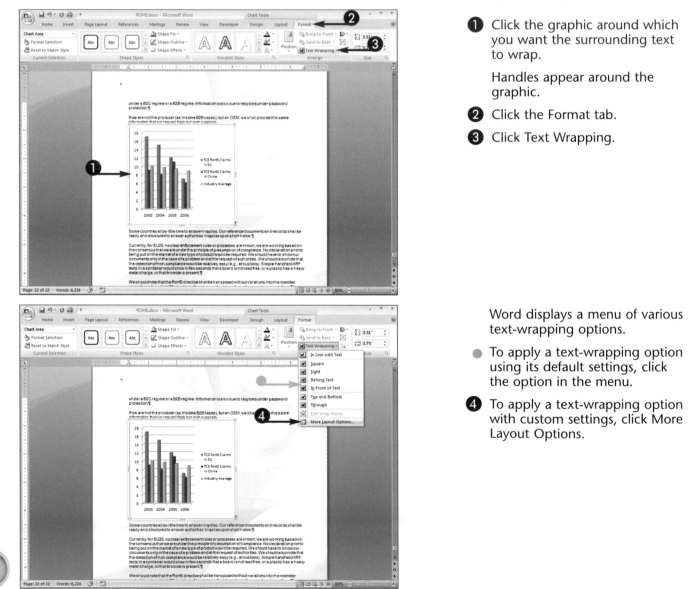

❶ Click the graphic around which you want the surrounding text to wrap.

Handles appear around the graphic.

❷ Click the Format tab.

❸ Click Text Wrapping.

Word displays a menu of various text-wrapping options.

● To apply a text-wrapping option using its default settings, click the option in the menu.

❹ To apply a text-wrapping option with custom settings, click More Layout Options.

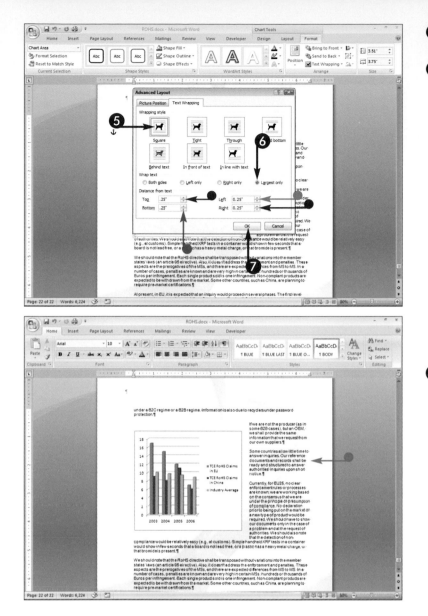

5 Click the wrapping style you want to apply.

6 Specify the area on the document relative to the graphic where the wrapped text should appear.

● Set the distance between the text above the graphic and the top of the graphic here.

● Set the distance between the text below the graphic and the bottom of the graphic here.

● Set the distance between the text to the left of the graphic and the left side of the graphic here.

● Set the distance between the text to the right of the graphic and the right side of the graphic here.

7 Click OK.

● Word wraps the text around the graphic using the settings you chose.

TIPS

Important!

The steps for inserting a graphic in your document vary depending on the type of graphic — photograph, clip art, shape, SmartArt (predesigned drawing components, useful for creating organizational charts, flow charts, and so on), or chart. Explore your options in the Insert tab's Illustrations group.

Did You Know?

In addition to wrapping text around a graphic, you can also wrap it around a table. To do so, click the table. Then, in the Ribbon's Layout tab, click Properties in the Table group. Next, under Text Wrapping, click Around. For more options — for example, settings that enable you to set the table's vertical and horizontal positions, the distance between the table and surrounding text, and so on — click Positioning in the Text Wrapping group.

ADD LINE NUMBERS
to your document

Suppose you are working on a document that is particularly dense, and that will be reviewed by others in hard copy form — for example, a lease agreement or contract, or something similar. To make it easier for others to reference portions of the document that require additional attention, you can add line numbers to the document.

The line numbers you add can be configured to restart at the top of each page or section in the document or to appear continuously throughout the document. You can also change the numbering increment — for example, entering an increment of two to include even numbers only.

Note that line numbers are visible onscreen only in Print Preview view. To switch to Print Preview view, click the View tab and click Print Preview.

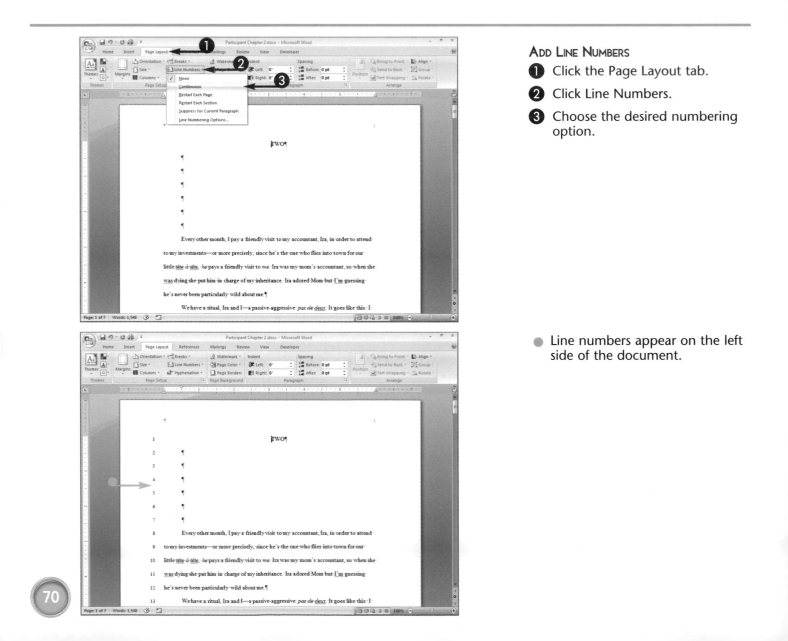

ADD LINE NUMBERS

1 Click the Page Layout tab.

2 Click Line Numbers.

3 Choose the desired numbering option.

● Line numbers appear on the left side of the document.

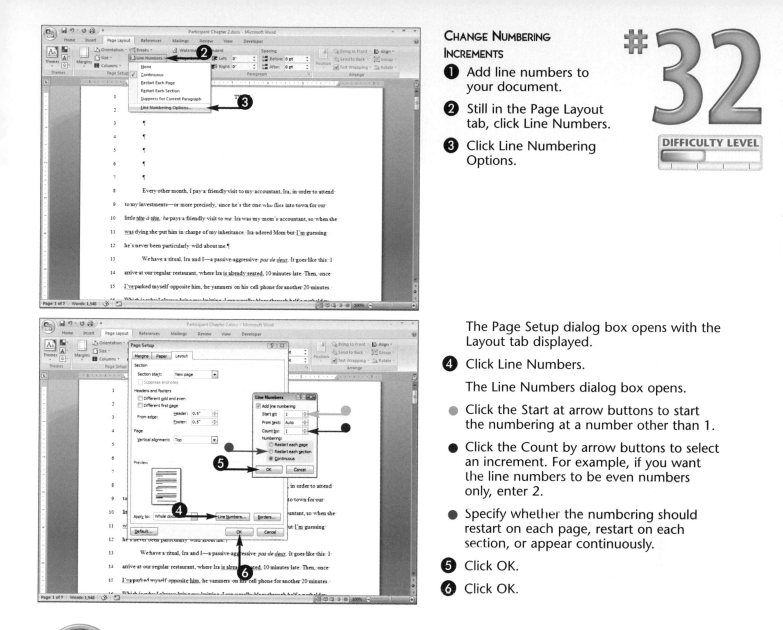

CHANGE NUMBERING INCREMENTS

1 Add line numbers to your document.

2 Still in the Page Layout tab, click Line Numbers.

3 Click Line Numbering Options.

32

DIFFICULTY LEVEL

The Page Setup dialog box opens with the Layout tab displayed.

4 Click Line Numbers.

The Line Numbers dialog box opens.

● Click the Start at arrow buttons to start the numbering at a number other than 1.

● Click the Count by arrow buttons to select an increment. For example, if you want the line numbers to be even numbers only, enter 2.

● Specify whether the numbering should restart on each page, restart on each section, or appear continuously.

5 Click OK.

6 Click OK.

TIPS

Remove It!

To remove line numbers, click the Page Layout tab, click Line Numbers, and choose None.

Did You Know?

In addition to inserting line numbers in your document, you can also insert page numbers. Page numbers can appear in the document's header or footer area, or in the document's margins. To add page numbers, click the Insert tab and, in the Header & Footer group, click Page Number. Select where on the page you want the numbers to appear, as well as how you want the numbers to look. To change the page on which the numbering starts and other numbering options, click the Insert tab, click Page Number in the Header & Footer group, and click Format Page Numbers.

Chapter 3: Jazz Up Your Work with Word   71

Optimize Excel

You can use Excel to perform a wide variety of number-crunching tasks on data, from the simplest calculation to the most complex formula. You can also use Excel to track and manage large quantities of data such as inventories, price lists, and more. You can even use Excel as a database, entering and sorting records.

Data you enter into Excel is stored in a workbook. Each workbook contains individual worksheets, which hold your data. By default, Excel workbooks have three worksheets, each identified by a tab at the bottom of the screen, but you can add or remove worksheets as needed.

A worksheet is a grid, formed by columns and rows. Columns are labeled with letters, while rows are numbered.

Every intersection of a column and row creates a cell. Cells are the receptacles for your Excel data. Every cell in an Excel worksheet has a unique name, also called an address or cell reference, which consists of the column letter and row number, with the column listed first. For example, cell A1 is the first cell in the worksheet. The next cell to the right is B1.

A group of related cells in a worksheet is called a range. Excel identifies a range by the anchor points in the upper-left and lower-right corners of the range, separated by a colon. For example, the range A1:B3 includes cells A1, A2, A3, B1, B2, and B3. Ranges are particularly useful when you begin creating formulas that reference groups of cells.

Top 100

AUTOMATE DATA ENTRY
with AutoFill

Often, the data that needs to be entered into an Excel worksheet is part of a series or pattern. In that case, you can use Excel's AutoFill feature to automate data entry.

For example, you might type the word Monday in your spreadsheet, and then use AutoFill to automatically enter the remaining days of the week. Alternatively, you might type January, and then use AutoFill to enter the remaining months of the year.

In addition to automating data entry using predefined data lists such as the ones described in

the preceding paragraph, you can create your own custom data lists for use with Excel's AutoFill feature. For example, you might create a custom list that includes the names of coworkers who work on your team, or a list of products you regularly stock.

Along with enabling you to enter predefined or custom text series, AutoFill allows you to automatically populate cells with a numerical series or pattern.

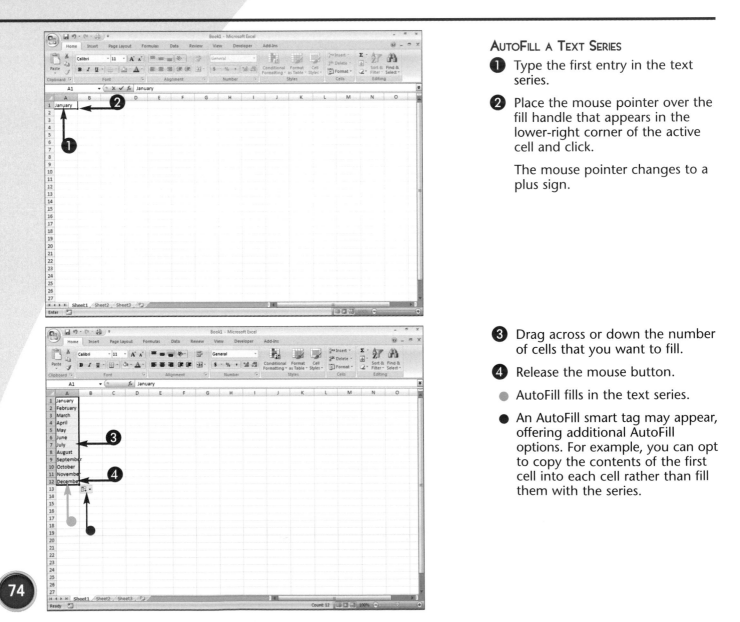

AUTOFILL A TEXT SERIES

1. Type the first entry in the text series.

2. Place the mouse pointer over the fill handle that appears in the lower-right corner of the active cell and click.

   The mouse pointer changes to a plus sign.

3. Drag across or down the number of cells that you want to fill.

4. Release the mouse button.

   ● AutoFill fills in the text series.

   ● An AutoFill smart tag may appear, offering additional AutoFill options. For example, you can opt to copy the contents of the first cell into each cell rather than fill them with the series.

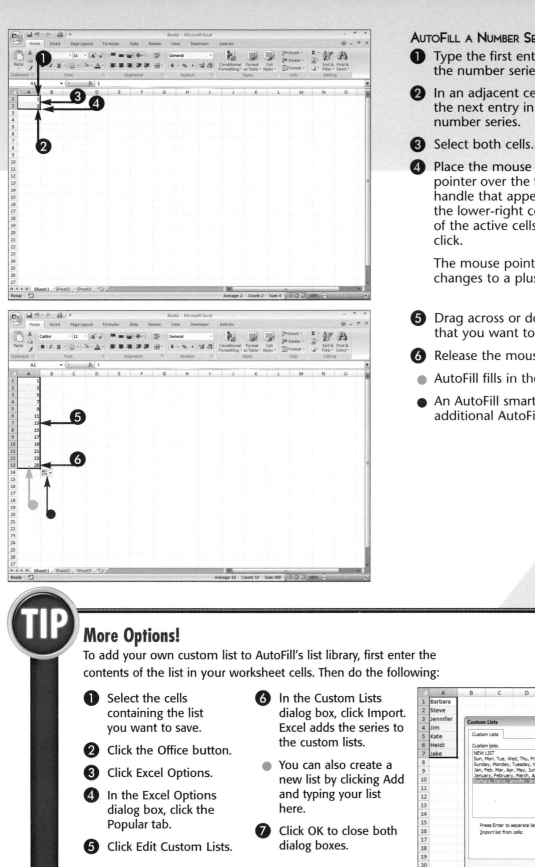

AUTOFILL A NUMBER SERIES

1 Type the first entry in the number series.

2 In an adjacent cell, type the next entry in the number series.

3 Select both cells.

4 Place the mouse pointer over the fill handle that appears in the lower-right corner of the active cells and click.

The mouse pointer changes to a plus sign.

5 Drag across or down the number of cells that you want to fill.

6 Release the mouse button.

● AutoFill fills in the number series.

● An AutoFill smart tag may appear, offering additional AutoFill options.

33

DIFFICULTY LEVEL

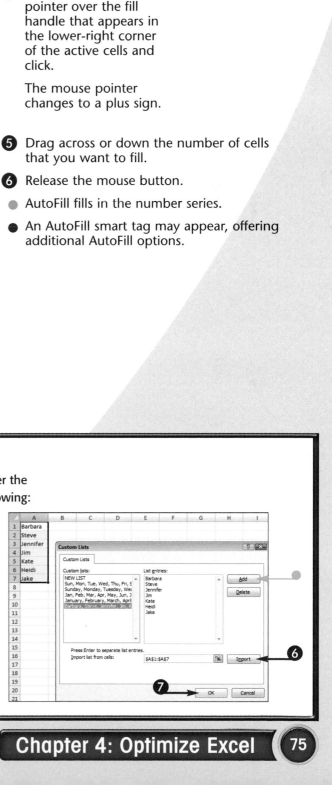

(TIP) **More Options!**

To add your own custom list to AutoFill's list library, first enter the contents of the list in your worksheet cells. Then do the following:

1 Select the cells containing the list you want to save.

2 Click the Office button.

3 Click Excel Options.

4 In the Excel Options dialog box, click the Popular tab.

5 Click Edit Custom Lists.

6 In the Custom Lists dialog box, click Import. Excel adds the series to the custom lists.

● You can also create a new list by clicking Add and typing your list here.

7 Click OK to close both dialog boxes.

Create
PROJECTIONS

You can use Excel to create projections in a manner that is similar to using the program's AutoFill feature.

Excel offers a few options for creating projections. One is to determine a linear trend — that is, to add a step value (the difference between the first and next values in the series) to each subsequent value. Another is to assess a growth trend, in which the starting value is multiplied by the step value rather than added to the value in order to obtain the next value in the series, with the resulting product and each subsequent product again being multiplied by the step value.

The easiest way to create a projection is to use Excel's automatic trending functionality. With it, you can simply right-click and drag to generate a projection. You can also create projections manually, entering a start value, a stop value, and the increment by which the trend should change. If your data is in chart form, you can still generate projections, and can even include a line in your chart to indicate the trend.

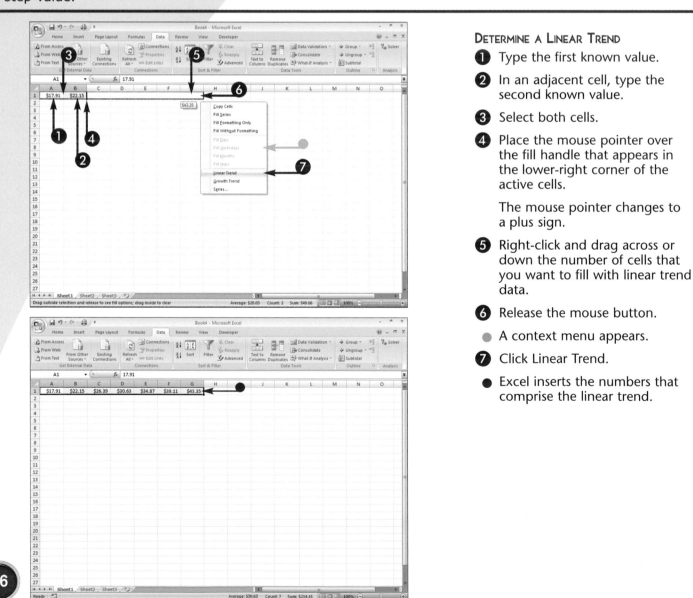

DETERMINE A LINEAR TREND

1 Type the first known value.

2 In an adjacent cell, type the second known value.

3 Select both cells.

4 Place the mouse pointer over the fill handle that appears in the lower-right corner of the active cells.

   The mouse pointer changes to a plus sign.

5 Right-click and drag across or down the number of cells that you want to fill with linear trend data.

6 Release the mouse button.

● A context menu appears.

7 Click Linear Trend.

● Excel inserts the numbers that comprise the linear trend.

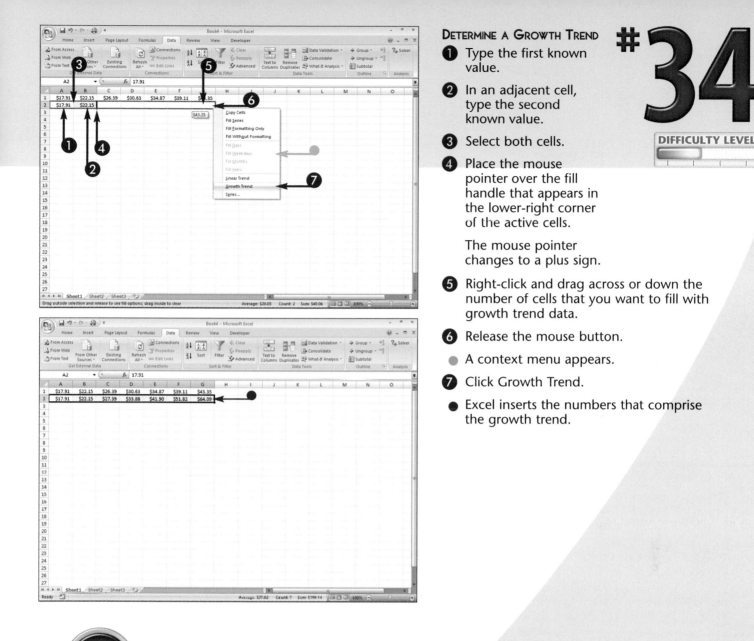

DETERMINE A GROWTH TREND

1 Type the first known value.

2 In an adjacent cell, type the second known value.

3 Select both cells.

4 Place the mouse pointer over the fill handle that appears in the lower-right corner of the active cells.

The mouse pointer changes to a plus sign.

5 Right-click and drag across or down the number of cells that you want to fill with growth trend data.

6 Release the mouse button.

● A context menu appears.

7 Click Growth Trend.

● Excel inserts the numbers that comprise the growth trend.

TIPS

More Options!

Instead of automatically projecting linear and growth trends, you can project them manually. To do so, enter the first value in the series in a cell, and then select the cell. Next, click the Home tab and, in the Editing group, click Fill and select Series. Specify whether the series should cover columns or rows, enter the value by which the series should be increased, select Linear or Growth, select the value at which you want the series to stop, and click OK.

Did You Know?

You can use chart data to create projections, adding a trend line to your chart to represent the projection. For more information about creating charts in Excel and adding trendlines to those charts, see Chapter 5.

INSERT
a comment

You can add comments to your worksheet to make a note to yourself about a particular cell's contents, or as a note for other users to see. For example, if you share your workbooks with other users, you might add comments to leave feedback about the data. By using comments, you avoid having to actually type directly in the worksheet.

Excel displays comments in a balloon. Also included in the balloon is the name of the person who entered the comment. (Note that the name that appears

matches the name entered in the Personalize section of the Excel Options dialog box's Popular tab. To open this dialog box, click the Office button in the upper-left corner of the Excel window and choose Excel Options.)

You can edit the comment text that appears in these comment balloons. To edit a comment, click the cell that contains the comment and, in the Review tab on the Ribbon, click Edit Comment. Then type over the comment text as needed.

ADD A COMMENT

1 Click the cell to which you want to add a comment.

2 Click the Review tab.

3 Click New Comment.

You can also right-click the cell and click New Comment.

● A comment balloon appears.

4 Type your comment text.

5 Click anywhere outside the comment balloon to deselect the comment.

78

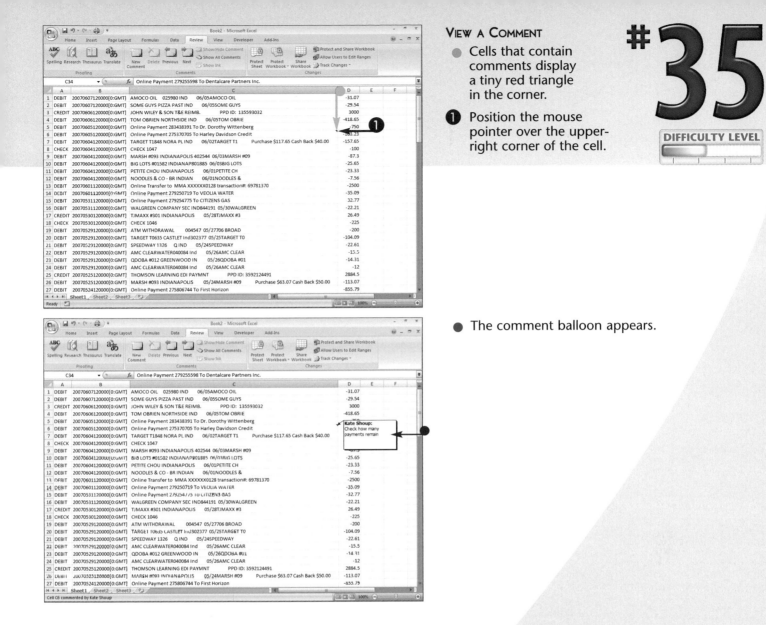

VIEW A COMMENT

● Cells that contain comments display a tiny red triangle in the corner.

① Position the mouse pointer over the upper-right corner of the cell.

#35

DIFFICULTY LEVEL

● The comment balloon appears.

TIPS

Delete It!

To remove a comment, right-click the cell containing the comment and select Delete Comment in the shortcut menu that appears. Excel immediately removes the comment from the cell.

Did You Know?

You can print the comments in your worksheet, either as they appear in the worksheet or all together at the end of the worksheet. To do so, click the Review tab in the Ribbon and click Show/Hide Comment in the Comments group. Then click the Page Layout tab and click the diagonal arrow in the bottom-right corner of the Page Setup group. Click the Sheet tab in the dialog box that appears, click the Comments drop-down arrow, select As Displayed on Sheet or At End of Sheet, and click Print.

TRACK AND REVIEW
workbook changes

If you work in an environment in which you share your Excel workbooks with others, you can use the program's Track Changes feature to help you keep track of what changes are made to a workbook, and by whom. In particular, you can see edits such as formatting changes and data additions or deletions.

The Track Changes feature uses a different color for each person's edits, making it easy to see who changed what in the workbook.

After the workbook has been edited, you can step through each edit made, accepting or rejecting it as

needed. When the review is complete, you can turn the tracking feature off by clicking the Review tab on the Ribbon, clicking Track Changes, clicking Highlight Changes, and deselecting the Track changes while editing check box in the Highlight Changes dialog box.

Be aware that Excel's Track Changes feature does not keep track of changes to worksheet names, inserted or deleted worksheets, or hidden rows or columns.

TURN ON TRACKING

1. Click the Review tab on the Ribbon.

2. Click the Track Changes drop-down arrow.

3. Click Highlight Changes.

   - The Highlight Changes dialog box appears.

4. Click Track changes while editing (☐ changes to ☑).

   This option automatically creates a shared workbook file if you have not already activated the shared workbook feature.

   - You can choose when, by whom, or where you track changes.

   - Leave this option checked to view changes to the file.

5. Click OK.

   Note: If prompted to save the workbook, locate the folder in which the workbook should be saved, type a name for the workbook, and click Save.

6. Edit the workbook.

   - Excel indicates changes in the worksheet with a small blue triangle in the upper-left corner of each edited cell.

7. To view details about a change, such as its author, move the mouse over an edited cell.

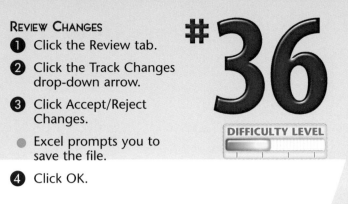

REVIEW CHANGES

❶ Click the Review tab.

❷ Click the Track Changes drop-down arrow.

❸ Click Accept/Reject Changes.

● Excel prompts you to save the file.

❹ Click OK.

 # 36

DIFFICULTY LEVEL

The Select Changes to Accept or Reject dialog box appears.

❺ Click options for which changes you want to view (☐ changes to ☑).

❻ Click OK.

The Accept or Reject Changes dialog box appears.

❼ Specify an action for each edit.

You can click Accept to add the change to the final worksheet.

To reject the change, click Reject.

● You can click one of these options to accept or reject all of the changes at the same time.

❽ When you have finished reviewing the edits, click Close.

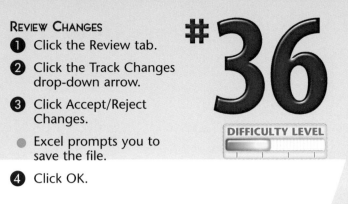

TIPS

Did You Know?

To view all changes to the workbook at the same time, click Track Changes on the Ribbon and click Highlight Changes. Then, in the Highlight Changes dialog box, select List changes on a new sheet to open a special History sheet in the workbook, which breaks down the details of each edit, including the date, time, and author. When you save the workbook, Excel deletes the History sheet.

Did You Know?

To remove a user from a shared workbook, click the Review tab on the Ribbon and click the Share Workbook button. In the Share Workbook dialog box that appears, click the name of the user you want to remove and click Remove User.

Chapter 4: Optimize Excel 81

CALCULATE
using formulas

You can use formulas to perform calculations on your Excel data. For example, you might add the contents of a column of monthly sales totals to determine the cumulative sales total.

In Excel, all formulas begin with an equal sign (=), such as =2+2. This tells Excel that any subsequent data is a formula rather than a regular cell entry.

When building a formula in Excel, you reference data in specific cells. For example, you can add the contents of two cells together, or multiply the contents of one cell by a value. You reference a value

in a cell by entering the *cell reference*, which is composed of the cell's column letter and row number. For example, cell D5 identifies the fifth cell down in column D. So, for example, if you want to add the contents of D5 and D6 together, your formula looks like this: =D5+D6.

You can even reference cells in other worksheets in your Excel formulas by specifying the worksheet name, followed by an exclamation mark, and then the cell address, like so: Sheet2!D12.

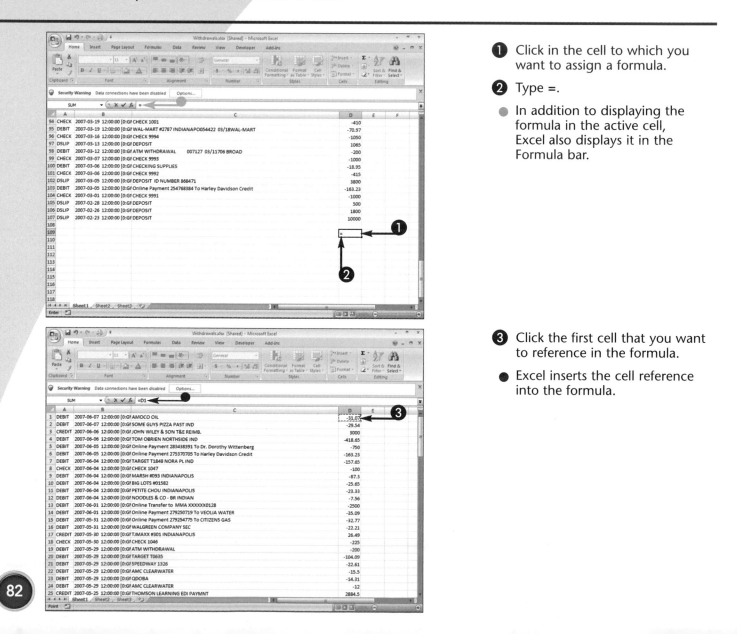

❶ Click in the cell to which you want to assign a formula.

❷ Type =.

● In addition to displaying the formula in the active cell, Excel also displays it in the Formula bar.

❸ Click the first cell that you want to reference in the formula.

● Excel inserts the cell reference into the formula.

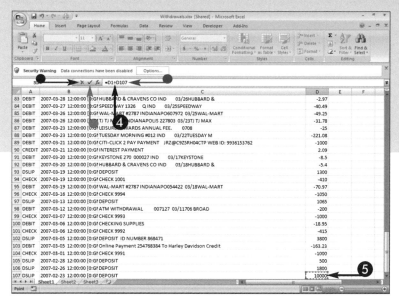

④ Type an operator for the formula.

⑤ Click the next cell that you want to reference in the formula.

● Excel inserts the cell reference into the formula.

⑥ Press Enter.

● You can also click the Enter button to accept the formula.

● Alternatively, cancel the formula by clicking the Cancel button.

Note: To edit a formula, click in the cell containing the formula and make the necessary changes in the Formula bar. Alternatively, double-click the cell and make your edits within the cell. When finished, press Enter or click the Enter button on the Formula bar.

● The formula results appear in the cell.

To view the formula in the Formula bar, simply click the cell.

● The Formula bar displays any formula assigned to the active cell.

Note: If you change any of the values in the cells referenced in the formula, the formula results automatically update to reflect the change.

TIP

Did You Know?

Commonly used operators in Excel formulas include the following:

Operator	Function	Operator	Function
+	Addition	>	Greater Than
−	Subtraction/negation	<	Less Than
*	Multiplication	>=	Greater Than or Equal To
/	Division	<=	Less Than or Equal To
%	Percent	<>	Does Not Equal
^	Exponent		

SPEED UP YOUR CALCULATIONS
with functions

A speedy way to perform calculations is to use any of the more than 300 built-in formulas in Excel, called *functions*. Functions are ready-made formulas that perform a series of operations on a specified range of values. Each function has a name. For example, the function that sums data is called the SUM function, while the formula for averaging values is called the AVERAGE function.

Functions typically use *arguments* to indicate which cells' contents you want the function to calculate. You can use the Function Arguments dialog box to select

the desired cells. This dialog box can also help you determine what values you need to enter to build the formula.

You can type functions directly into your worksheet cells or into the Formula bar. You can also use the options in the Function Library group on the Ribbon's Formulas tab to construct functions. If you are not sure which function to apply, click Insert Function in the Function Library group to launch the Insert Function dialog box for help in selecting and applying functions to your data.

① Click the cell to which you want to assign a function.

② Click the Formulas tab.

③ Click here to select the desired function category.

④ If necessary, click the arrow next to the desired subcategory to reveal function options.

⑤ Click the function you want to apply.

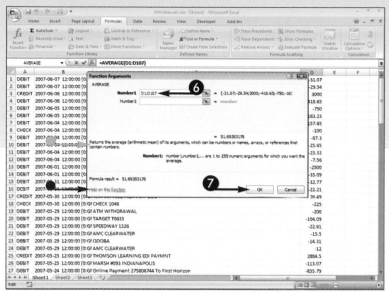

Excel displays the Function Arguments dialog box.

⑥ Specify the cells for each argument required by the function.

If you select a cell or range of cells directly in the worksheet, Excel automatically adds the references to the argument.

You can also type a range or cell address into the argument text box.

● The dialog box displays information about the function here.

● Click here to get help information about the function.

⑦ When finished constructing the arguments, click OK.

● Excel displays the function results in the cell.

● The function appears in the Formula bar.

![TIPS]

Did You Know?

One of the most popular functions available in Excel is the AUTOSUM function. AUTOSUM automatically totals the contents of cells. For example, you can quickly total columns of sales figures. AUTOSUM works by guessing which cells you want to total, although you can also specify exactly which cells to sum. To use AUTOSUM, click in the cell where you want to insert a sum total, click the Formulas tab on the Ribbon, and click AutoSum in the Function Library group.

Try This!

If the Function Arguments dialog box is covering cells you need to select, click the Collapse button at the end of the argument text box to minimize the dialog box.

AUDIT A WORKSHEET
for errors

If you see an error message, you should double-check your formula to ensure that you referenced the correct cells. One way to do so is to click the smart tag icon that is displayed by Excel alongside any errors it detects; doing so displays a menu of options, including options for correcting the error. For example, you can click Help on this error to find out more about the error message.

To help you with errors that arise when dealing with larger worksheets in Excel, you can use Excel's Formula Auditing tools to examine and correct

formula errors. In particular, the Error Checking feature looks through your worksheet for errors and helps you find solutions.

Auditing tools can trace the path of your formula components and check each cell reference that contributes to the formula. When tracing the relationships between cells, you can display tracer lines to find *precedents* (that is, cells referred to in a formula) and *dependents* (cells that contain formula results).

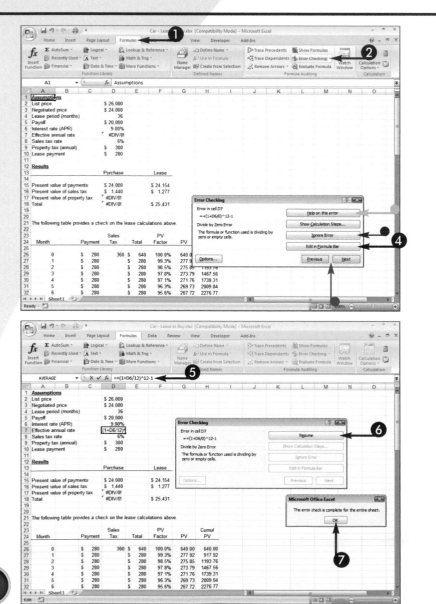

CHECK ERRORS

❶ Click the Formulas tab.

❷ Click Error Checking.

Excel displays the Error Checking dialog box and highlights the first cell containing an error.

● To find help with an error, you can click here.

● To ignore the error, click Ignore Error.

● You can click Previous and Next to scroll through all of the errors on the worksheet.

❹ To fix the error, click Edit in Formula Bar.

❺ Make edits to the cell references in the Formula bar.

❻ Click Resume.

When the error check is complete, a prompt box appears.

❼ Click OK.

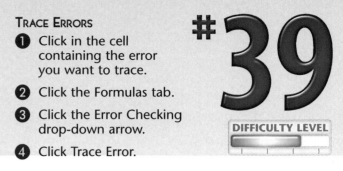

TRACE ERRORS

❶ Click in the cell containing the error you want to trace.

❷ Click the Formulas tab.

❸ Click the Error Checking drop-down arrow.

❹ Click Trace Error.

● Excel displays trace lines from the current cell to any cells referenced in the formula.

You can make changes to the cell contents or changes to the formula to correct the error.

❺ Click Remove Arrows to turn off the trace lines.

TIPS

Did You Know?

You can click Evaluate Formula in the Formulas tab's Formula Auditing group to check over a formula or function step by step. Simply click the cell containing the formula you want to evaluate and click Evaluate Formula; Excel opens the Evaluate Formula dialog box, where you can evaluate each portion of the formula to check it for correct references and values.

Try This!

To quickly ascertain the relationships among various cells in your worksheet, click a cell, click the Formulas tab on the Ribbon, and click Trace Precedents or Trace Dependents in the Formula Auditing group. Excel displays trace lines from the current cell to related cells — that is, cells with formulas that reference it or vice versa.

Establish
WHAT-IF SCENARIOS

You can perform what-if speculations on your data. For example, you might do so to examine what would happen if you increased shipping fees or product prices. To perform these what-if speculations, you use Excel's Scenario Manager tool. Scenario Manager keeps track of what-if scenarios you run on a workbook, enabling you to revisit and make changes to the scenarios as needed.

It is a good practice to save a copy of the original workbook before using Scenario Manager to perform what-if scenarios on it. That way, you ensure that

your data is not permanently replaced with the what-if data by accident. Alternatively, create a scenario that employs the original values; then, you can revert to that original scenario any time.

You can generate a report that summarizes what-if scenarios performed on a workbook. This report lists all inputs and results for each scenario.

To remove a scenario you no longer want, re-open the Scenario Manager dialog box, click the scenario you want to remove, and then click Delete.

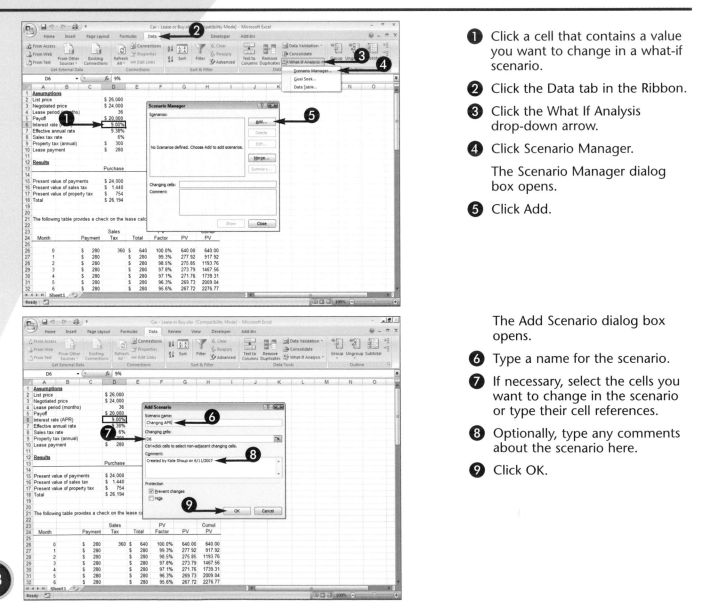

❶ Click a cell that contains a value you want to change in a what-if scenario.

❷ Click the Data tab in the Ribbon.

❸ Click the What If Analysis drop-down arrow.

❹ Click Scenario Manager.

The Scenario Manager dialog box opens.

❺ Click Add.

The Add Scenario dialog box opens.

❻ Type a name for the scenario.

❼ If necessary, select the cells you want to change in the scenario or type their cell references.

❽ Optionally, type any comments about the scenario here.

❾ Click OK.

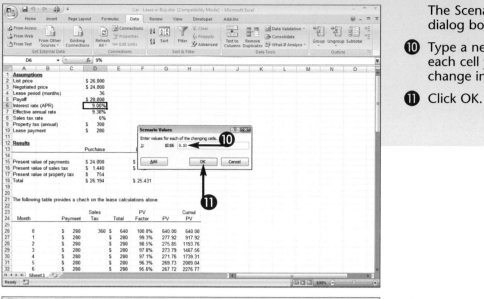

The Scenario Values dialog box appears.

🔟 Type a new value for each cell you want to change in the scenario.

⓫ Click OK.

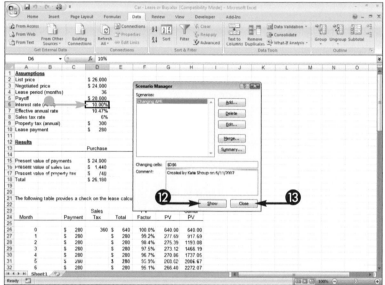

⓬ Click Show to view the scenario results in your worksheet.

● The results are displayed.

⓭ Click Close to close the Scenario Manager dialog box.

Excel closes the Scenario Manager dialog box; the last applied scenario remains in the worksheet.

TIPS

Try This!

To generate a summary report that compares the results of multiple scenarios either by listing them side by side or by arranging them in a pivot table, click the What If Analysis drop-down arrow in the Data tab's Data Tools group, click Scenario Manager, and then click Summary. In the dialog box that appears, click Scenario Summary or Scenario Pivot Table and enter the references for cells whose values are changed by the scenario. Then click OK.

Apply It!

To view the results of a scenario, open the Scenario Manager dialog box as normal (click What If Analysis in the Data tab's Data Tools group and click Scenario Manager), click the scenario you want to view, and click Show.

Set goals with
GOAL SEEK

Where Excel's Scenario Manager enables you to run "what-if" speculations by tweaking various variables in your spreadsheet, Goal Seek does just the opposite: It enables you to set the desired result and work backward to determine which variables need to be tweaked to attain it. For example, suppose you are trying to calculate how much you can afford to spend each month on a new car. By entering the maximum amount you are willing to spend, Goal Seek can help you work backward to determine the maximum loan amount based on such variables as interest rate, duration of loan, and so on.

You can use Goal Seek to solve single-variable equations of any kind. For example, although one of the most popular uses of Goal Seek is figuring out loan amounts and payments, you can also use Goal Seek to help you figure out how much you need to sell to reach a sales goal (for example, to determine how many units must be sold to attain net earnings of $50,000, as outlined here).

❶ Click the target cell — that is, the cell that will contain the "goal" value (here, cell D6).

❷ Click the Data tab on the Ribbon.

❸ Click the What-If Analysis drop-down arrow.

❹ Click Goal Seek.

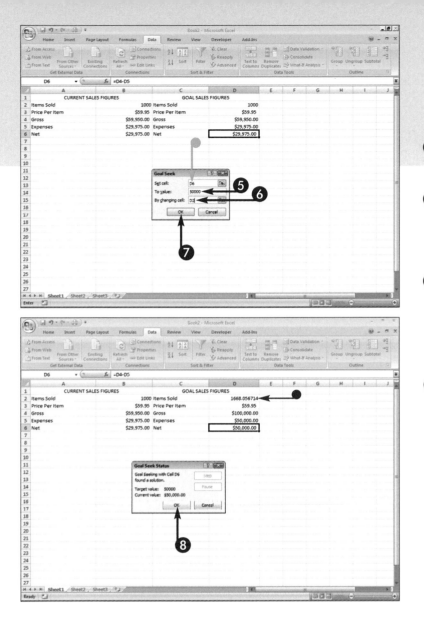

The Goal Seek dialog box opens.

● Notice that the Set cell value has already been filled in with the cell you clicked in step **1**.

5 Type your goal value (here, the desired net earnings).

6 Select or type the cell whose value you want to change to attain the goal value (here, D2, or the number of units sold).

7 Click OK.

The Goal Seek Status dialog box opens.

● Goal Seek has determined how many units must be sold to reach the goal.

8 Click OK.

The Goal Seek Status dialog box closes.

TIPS

More Options!

You use Goal Seek when you want to produce a specific value by adjusting one input cell that influences the value. If you require adjustments to more than one input cell, use Excel's Solver tool instead. Solver is an add-in you can use for complex problems that use multiple variables. For more information about Solver, see Task #42.

Try This!

If the Goal Seek dialog box is covering cells you need to select, click the button on the right side of the Set cell or By changing cell field to minimize the dialog box.

Define and solve problems with
SOLVER

Goal Seek enables you to produce a specific value by adjusting one input cell that influences the value. In contrast, Excel's Solver tool enables you to produce a value using multiple variables.

To use Solver, you define the target cell along with the cells that Solver can modify to obtain a different value in the target cell. Solver then analyzes the formulas used to establish the value in the target cell and makes changes to the cells you specify to come up with different solutions.

Solver is one of several add-in programs that come with Excel. In order to use Solver, you must first load the add-in. To do so, click the Office button in the upper-left corner of the screen and click Excel Options. Click the Add-Ins entry along the left side of the Excel Options dialog box, click the Manage drop-down arrow along the bottom of the dialog box, click Excel Add-Ins, and click Go. Finally, in the Add-Ins dialog box, click the Solver Add-in check box and click OK.

① Click the Data tab.

② Click Solver.

Note: If no Solver button appears on the Data tab, try unloading and reloading the Solver add-in. (To unload the add-in, uncheck the Solver Add-in check box in the Add-Ins dialog box mentioned in the introduction to this task and click OK.)

The Solver Parameters dialog box opens.

③ Type the reference for the target cell — that is, the cell that will contain the "goal" value (here, cell F15).

④ Click an Equal To option (◎ changes to ◉).

⑤ Type the target value.

⑥ Enter the reference for each cell that Solver should adjust to attain the desired result.

To enter multiple noncontiguous cells, separate each cell reference with a comma.

● If you are not sure which cells should be adjusted, click Guess. Solver automatically proposes adjustable cells based on the target cell.

⑦ Click Solve.

The Solver Results dialog box opens.

● Excel makes changes to the designated target cell.

⑧ Select whether you want to save the solution or restore to the original values (◎ changes to ◉).

● If you click Keep Solver Solution (◎ changes to ◉), you can save the results as a report. To do so, click a report type.

● To save the changes as a scenario, click here.

⑨ Click OK.

Excel closes the Solver Results dialog box.

TIPS

More Options!
You can set constraints for the adjustable cells, the target cell, or any other cells related to the target cell to limit the solutions provided by Solver. To add constraints, click the Add button in the Solver Parameters dialog box and define the constraints in the Add Constraint dialog box.

Add Constraint

Cell Reference: Constraint:
$B$18   <=   45

OK   Cancel   Add   Help

Try This!
If the Solver Parameters dialog box is covering cells you need to select, click the button on the right side of the Set Target Cell or By Changing Cells field to minimize the dialog box.

Create a
DATABASE TABLE

You can use an Excel worksheet to build a database table to manage large lists of data. A database table is simply a collection of related records, such as a phone directory, address list, inventory, and so on. After creating a database table, you can perform a variety of analysis, sorting, and filtering techniques on the data in the database table.

A database table is composed of fields, which break the table into manageable pieces. For example, a database table containing an address book will likely include fields with labels such as Name, Address, and

Phone Number. You fill in these fields to create a *database record*. A database record might consist of the name, address, and phone number of a single individual.

Before you create a database table in Excel, take a bit of time to plan it out, deciding what kind of data you want the database table to store and how it should be organized. Otherwise, you may later discover that you have omitted important fields and have to reorganize your database table.

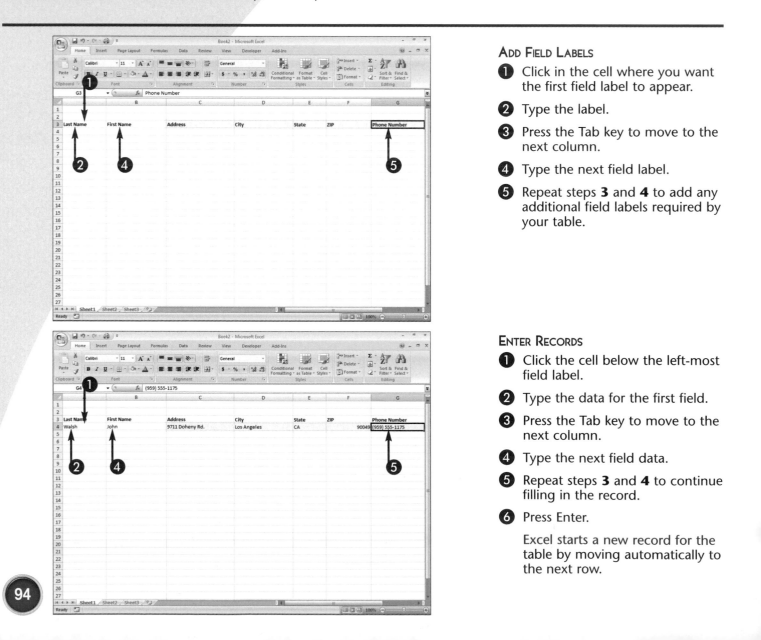

ADD FIELD LABELS

① Click in the cell where you want the first field label to appear.

② Type the label.

③ Press the Tab key to move to the next column.

④ Type the next field label.

⑤ Repeat steps **3** and **4** to add any additional field labels required by your table.

ENTER RECORDS

① Click the cell below the left-most field label.

② Type the data for the first field.

③ Press the Tab key to move to the next column.

④ Type the next field data.

⑤ Repeat steps **3** and **4** to continue filling in the record.

⑥ Press Enter.

Excel starts a new record for the table by moving automatically to the next row.

43

7 Repeat steps **2** to **6** until all the necessary records have been added.

CONVERT THE DATA TO A DATABASE TABLE

1 Select the data you want to convert into a database table.

DIFFICULTY LEVEL

2 Click the Insert tab.

3 Click Table.

The Create Table dialog box opens.

● By default, the selected range appears here. If the range is not correct, you can select the correct cell references.

● Select this option if it is necessary to include the headers in your table.

4 Click OK.

Excel turns the data into a table, fills the cells of the table with blue shading, and displays filter drop-down arrows for each field.

● The Table Tools Design tab also appears onscreen.

● To filter a list, click here and select the data you want to filter out.

TIP

Did You Know?

Entering data into a table can be tedious. To speed up the task, you can use Excel's PickList feature, which is activated as soon as you create the first record in your database table and remembers the previous field entries so you can repeat them, if necessary:

1 Right-click a cell in a new record.

2 Click Pick From Drop-down List.

A list of choices appears.

3 Click an entry to repeat it in the current cell.

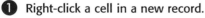

ADD AND EDIT RECORDS
using data forms

If you have converted data in a spreadsheet into a database table, you can add information to that table using a data form instead of typing it directly into the cells in the sheet. (For help converting data in Excel spreadsheets into database tables, refer to the preceding task.)

In Excel, data forms are special dialog boxes that contain all the fields in your table. For example, if your database table contains a Name field, an Address field, a City field, a State field, and a ZIP field, so too will the database table's Data Forms

dialog box. You can type the information for a database record into the dialog box rather than into the spreadsheet. (Note that you can also edit existing records from a data form dialog box.)

To access the command used to display the data form dialog box, you must first add it to the Quick Access toolbar. To do so, click the Office button, click Excel Options, and, in the dialog box that appears, click the Choose Commands From drop-down arrow, click Form in the list, click Add, and click OK.

① Click the first cell of any record in your database table.

② Click the Form button.

A data form dialog box opens.

③ Click New.

4 Type the data for the first field.

5 Press Tab.

6 Repeat steps **4** and **5** to continue filling out the fields.

● To fill out another new record, click New.

7 Click Close.

44

● Excel adds the record(s) to the database table.

TIPS

Try This!
Click the Find Prev and Find Next buttons in the data form dialog box to navigate records in a database table. Edit records by typing over the existing values in the data form dialog box's fields.

Delete It!
To delete a record, click the first cell in any record in the table and open the data form dialog box. Then click the Find Prev or Find Next button as many times as necessary to locate the record you want to delete. Finally, click the Delete button in the dialog box, and click OK to confirm the deletion. Alternatively, select the row in the table that contains the record you want to delete and then press the Delete key on your keyboard.

SORT AND FILTER
records

You can sort your database table to reorganize the information it contains. For example, you might want to sort a client table alphabetically by last name.

The easiest type of sort is a quick sort, which enables you to sort by a single criterion — for example, by last name. To perform a quick sort, simply click the drop-down arrow next to the name of the field by which you want to sort and click Sort A to Z (that is, ascending order) or Sort Z to A (that is, descending order). In the case of numbers, an ascending sort lists numbers from lowest to highest, while a

descending sort lists numbers from highest to lowest.

Another way to sort is to use the Sort dialog box. With it, you can sort by multiple fields.

Another option is to filter your records using Excel's AutoFilter tool. Unlike conducting a sort, which sorts the entire table, using AutoFilter selects certain records to display based on your criteria, while hiding the other records that do not match the criteria.

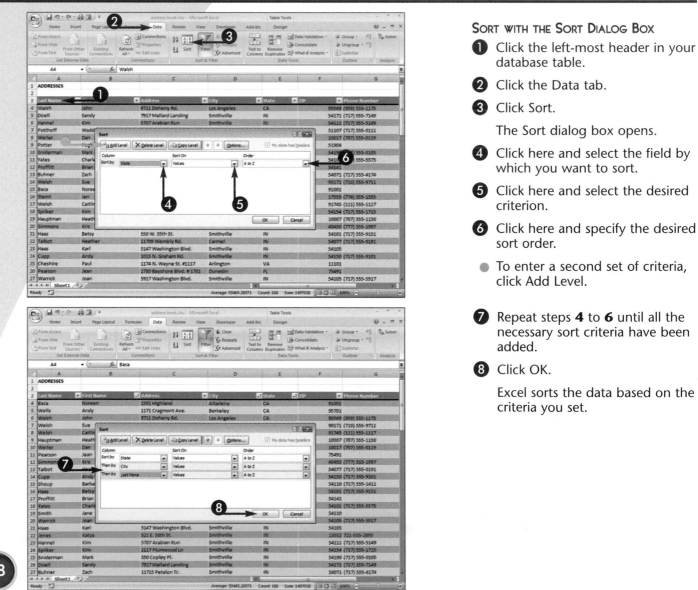

SORT WITH THE SORT DIALOG BOX

1 Click the left-most header in your database table.

2 Click the Data tab.

3 Click Sort.

The Sort dialog box opens.

4 Click here and select the field by which you want to sort.

5 Click here and select the desired criterion.

6 Click here and specify the desired sort order.

● To enter a second set of criteria, click Add Level.

7 Repeat steps **4** to **6** until all the necessary sort criteria have been added.

8 Click OK.

Excel sorts the data based on the criteria you set.

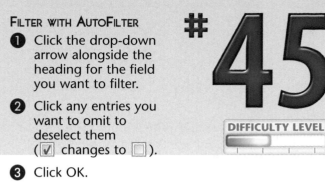

FILTER WITH AUTOFILTER

1 Click the drop-down arrow alongside the heading for the field you want to filter.

2 Click any entries you want to omit to deselect them (☑ changes to ☐).

3 Click OK.

Excel displays only those records whose entries were left checked.

TIPS

More Options!

You can activate the Advanced command on the Data tab to open the Advanced Filter dialog box. Here you can further customize the filter by selecting operators and values to apply on the filtered data.

Try This!

If you clear a filter but want to apply it again, click the Data tab and click the Reapply button in the Sort & Filter group.

Advanced Filter

Action

○ Filter the list, in-place
○ Copy to another location

List range: $A$3:$G$31
Criteria range:
Copy to:

☐ Unique records only

OK   Cancel

Set DATA-VALIDATION RULES

To ensure that the data entered into your database table is of a valid type, you can set up your database table to control exactly what kinds of data are allowed in the cells. This is handy if other people use your database table to enter records. You can make sure that they type the right kind of data in a cell by assigning a data-validation rule.

In addition to ensuring that the right types of characters are entered — for example, text or numbers — you can also set up data-validation rules

to, for example, restrict entries to a certain range of dates. You can also set up rules to limit data-entry choices by offering a drop-down list of options.

If users type the wrong data, such as text data instead of numerical data, Excel displays an error dialog box. You can configure Excel to include the text of your choosing in this dialog box — for example, instructions to the user with regard to what type of data can be entered.

① Select the range of cells to which you want to apply a data-validation rule.

② Click the Data tab.

③ Click Data Validation.

The Data Validation dialog box opens.

④ Click the Settings tab.

⑤ Click here and select the type of data you want entered into each cell in the selected range.

● Optionally, define data parameters.

You can set up Excel to display a message to users when they click a cell in the selected range, indicating what type of information should be entered into the cell.

⑥ Click the Input Message tab.

⑦ Click the Show input message when cell is selected (☐ changes to ☑).

⑧ Type a title for the input message.

⑨ Type the contents of the input message.

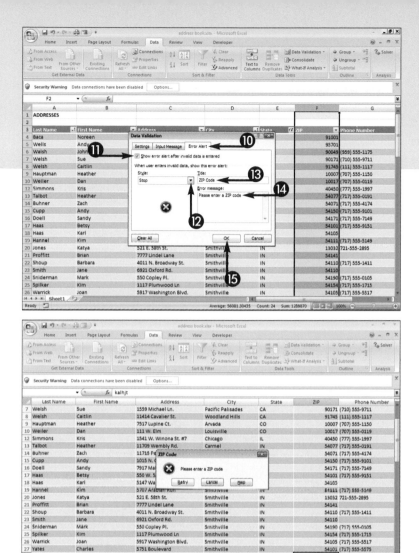

⑩ Click the Error Alert tab.

⑪ Click Show error alert after invalid data is entered (☐ changes to ☑).

⑫ Click here and select the type of icon that should appear in the Error Alert dialog box.

⑬ Type the text that you want to appear in the Error Alert dialog box's title bar.

⑭ Type the message that should be conveyed by the Error Alert dialog box.

⑮ Click OK.

Excel displays the Error Alert dialog box when someone attempts to enter invalid data in a cell in the selected range.

TIPS

Try This!

To create a drop-down list of options from which users can choose when entering data into your database table, click the Allow drop-down arrow in the Data Validation dialog box's Settings tab and choose List. Then, in the Source field, type the options you want to appear in the list, placing a comma between each entry. (Note that the width of the cell to which data validation is being applied determines the width of the drop-down list. To ensure that items in the list are not truncated, consider widening the cell.)

Remove It!

To remove data validation, select the range containing the data validation rule and then reopen the Data Validation dialog box. Click Clear All; this turns off the data-validation rules.

PASSWORD-PROTECT
your work

You can assign a password to an Excel workbook to prevent users from making changes to the number and order of worksheets and to preserve the size and arrangement of windows. The best passwords contain a mix of uppercase and lowercase letters, numbers, and symbols.

Password-protecting a workbook does not affect users' ability to enter or change data into the workbook. That requires you to password-protect sheets in your workbook. Users can still view the worksheet, but the assigned password protection prevents them from making any changes to the data.

If you no longer want to password-protect a workbook or worksheet, you can easily remove the password protection. To unprotect a password-protected workbook, click the Review tab in the Ribbon and click Protect Workbook. The Unprotect Workbook dialog box appears; type the password and click OK. Unprotect a password-protected worksheet by right-clicking the sheet's tab and choosing Unprotect Sheet; in the Unprotect Sheet dialog box that opens, type the password and click OK.

PASSWORD-PROTECT A WORKBOOK

① With the workbook you want to password-protect open in Excel, click the Review tab.

② Click Protect Workbook.

③ Click Protect Structure and Windows.

The Protect Structure and Windows dialog box opens.

④ Click Windows (☐ changes to ☑).

This selection preserves the sizing and display of the windows. The structure of the workbook (the number and arrangement of worksheets) is protected by default.

⑤ To allow users to view the workbook but not make changes, type a password.

⑥ Click OK.

The Confirm Password dialog box appears.

⑦ Retype the password exactly as you typed it in step **5**.

⑧ Click OK.

Excel assigns the password to the workbook. The next time you or any other user opens the workbook, features for deleting, moving, and renaming worksheets will be unavailable.

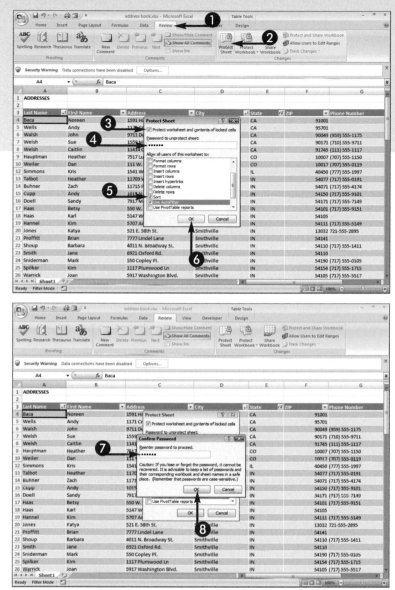

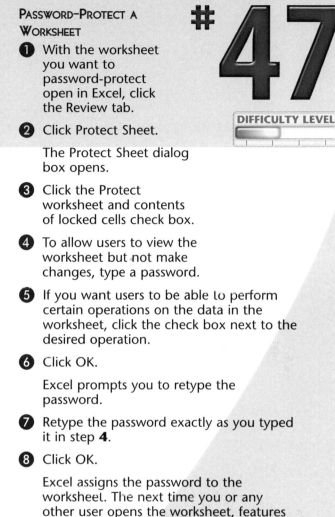

① With the worksheet you want to password-protect open in Excel, click the Review tab.

② Click Protect Sheet.

The Protect Sheet dialog box opens.

③ Click the Protect worksheet and contents of locked cells check box.

④ To allow users to view the worksheet but not make changes, type a password.

⑤ If you want users to be able to perform certain operations on the data in the worksheet, click the check box next to the desired operation.

⑥ Click OK.

Excel prompts you to retype the password.

⑦ Retype the password exactly as you typed it in step **4**.

⑧ Click OK.

Excel assigns the password to the worksheet. The next time you or any other user opens the worksheet, features for deleting, moving, and renaming worksheets will be unavailable.

TIPS

Caution!

It is critical that you remember your Excel passwords. If you lose a password, you cannot make changes to a password-protected file. Consider writing the password down and keeping it in a safe place.

More Options!

You can prevent others from even opening a workbook. To do so, click the Office button and click Save As. In the dialog box that appears, click Tools and click General Options. Then type the desired password in the Password to Open field. Optionally, you can prevent others from modifying the workbook by typing a password in the Password to Modify field. (This password should be different from the one used to open the file.) Then click OK.

Chapter 5

Unleash Your Inner Spreadsheet

Being able to crunch numbers or build database tables is of little use if the data is difficult or impossible for others to comprehend.

Fortunately, you can mitigate this by using Excel's formatting tools. For example, you can apply themes to your workbooks to create a more polished and professional look, as well as add colors, patterns, and borders to cells to make them stand out. You can even use digital images as backgrounds in your worksheets.

To draw attention to cells that meet criteria you set, you can apply conditional formatting. For example, you might set a rule to highlight cells that contain values greater than, less than, equal to, or between a range of specified values. This enables you to detect problems, patterns, and trends at a glance.

Another way to display your data is in chart form. Whether you are depicting rising or falling sales or actual costs compared to projected costs, charts can make it easy for others to understand your data. Excel supports the creation of a variety of chart types — including column charts, line charts, pie charts, and bar charts — and offers a number of predefined chart styles and colors.

To ensure that others can read the data in your worksheet's cells, you can change the alignment. You can also enable Excel's text-wrapping feature, which automatically increases a cell's row height to make room for the data it contains. Finally, Excel's various print settings enable you to generate printouts that maximize readability.

Top 100

Apply
WORKBOOK THEMES

DIFFICULTY LEVEL

You can use Excel's Themes Gallery to apply a combination of formatting settings to your spreadsheet.

To use themes to their fullest, you must apply styles to your worksheet, such as a heading style to any column headings or a title style to the worksheet title. To do so, select the cell to which you want to apply the style, click the Home tab, click the Cell Styles button in the Cells group, and choose a style.

If you want the worksheet to display the theme's background color, you must apply a background color

beforehand. Select the cells to which the color should be applied, click the Home tab, click the drop-down arrow next to the Fill Color button, and choose a color.

You can modify a theme you have applied using the Colors, Fonts, and Effects buttons in the Page Layout tab's Themes group. You can then save the modified theme for reuse. Click the Themes button on the Page Layout tab, click Save Current Theme, and save the theme with a new name in the dialog box that appears.

---

① Click the Page Layout tab.

② Click Themes.

Excel displays the Themes Gallery.

③ Choose the theme you want to apply.

Excel applies the theme.

Add emphasis with
BORDERS

You can add borders to your worksheet cells to help define the contents or more clearly separate the data from surrounding cells. You can apply a border to all four sides of a cell or range of cells or to just one, two, or three sides. Any borders you add to the sheet print out along with worksheet data.

One way to add borders is to select the cell or cells around which you want to apply a border, click the Home tab, click the drop-down arrow next to the Borders button, and click a border style in the list that appears.

Another way is to create a custom border. That way, in addition to specifying which and how many sides of the cell or cells should sport a border, you can choose a line style and color. (Color options include Theme Colors, which mesh with whatever theme is currently applied to the worksheet, as well as a wider range of standard colors.) You create a custom border using Excel's Format Cells dialog box.

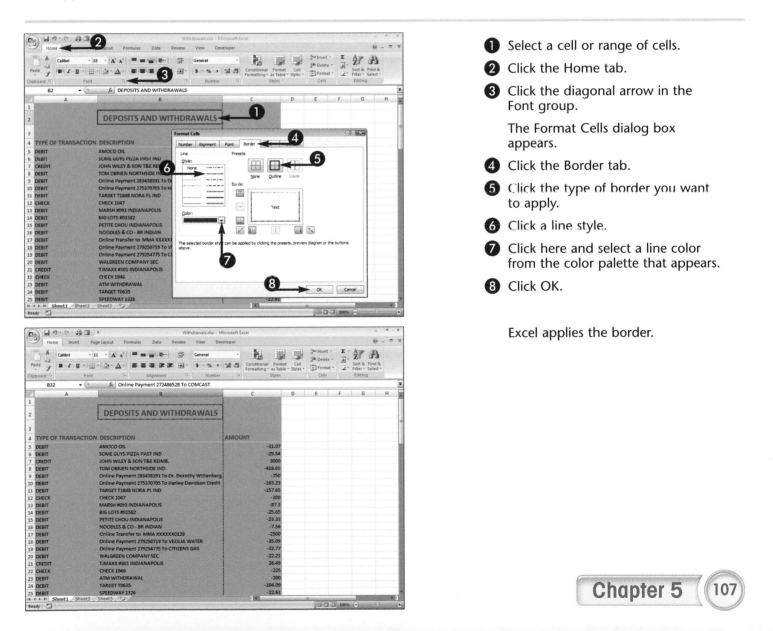

1 Select a cell or range of cells.

2 Click the Home tab.

3 Click the diagonal arrow in the Font group.

 The Format Cells dialog box appears.

4 Click the Border tab.

5 Click the type of border you want to apply.

6 Click a line style.

7 Click here and select a line color from the color palette that appears.

8 Click OK.

 Excel applies the border.

COLOR, PATTERN, OR IMAGE

You can add a background color or pattern to the cells in your worksheet to beautify it. Excel offers a variety of preset colors and patterns from which you can choose to create just the right look for your worksheet data.

One way to apply a background color is to select the cells to which you want to apply the color, click the Home tab, click the drop-down arrow next to the Fill Color button, and choose a color from the palette that appears. In addition, you can apply custom colors.

In addition to adding a color or pattern to cells to serve as a background for your worksheet, you can also add a photo or other digital image. For example, if your worksheet documents sales, you might add a picture of a product.

Regardless of whether you apply a background color, pattern, or image to your spreadsheet, make sure it does not clash with the cell data or render it illegible. If it does conflict, you might need to change the color of the worksheet data.

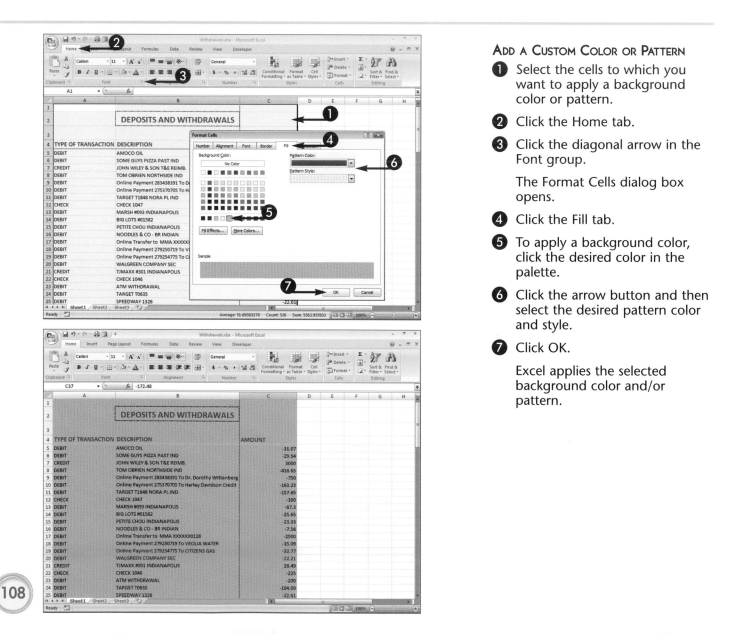

ADD A CUSTOM COLOR OR PATTERN

1. Select the cells to which you want to apply a background color or pattern.

2. Click the Home tab.

3. Click the diagonal arrow in the Font group.

   The Format Cells dialog box opens.

4. Click the Fill tab.

5. To apply a background color, click the desired color in the palette.

6. Click the arrow button and then select the desired pattern color and style.

7. Click OK.

   Excel applies the selected background color and/or pattern.

ADD A BACKGROUND IMAGE

1 With the worksheet to which you want to apply a background open in Excel, click the Page Layout tab.

2 Click Background.

The Sheet Background dialog box opens.

3 Locate and click the image you want to apply to the background.

4 Click Insert.

Excel applies the selected background image.

TIPS

Try This!

Even if you do not have a color printer, you can take advantage of the various shades of gray to add background colors to your worksheet cells. You can also experiment with the palette of solid colors to create varying degrees of background shading in grayscale tones.

Delete It!

To remove all of the formatting in a cell, including background colors or patterns, select the cell, click the Home tab, and then click Cell Styles. In the gallery of styles that appears, click Normal. This removes all the formatting that has been applied. To delete a background image, click Delete Background in the Page Layout tab.

Color-code your data with
CONDITIONAL FORMATTING

You can use Excel's conditional formatting functionality to assign certain formatting only when the value of the cell meets a specified condition. This enables you to detect problems, patterns, and trends at a glance.

Excel offers several predefined rules for conditional formatting. For example, you can set a rule to highlight cells that contain values greater than, less than, equal to, or between a range of specified values; contain specific text (as shown here) or dates; contain duplicate values; contain the top ten or bottom ten values; contain above-average or below-average values; and more.

You can format cells that meet conditions you set by changing the font or cell background. You can also apply data bars, where the length of the bar represents the value in the cell; color scales, which enable you to compare cells in a range using a gradation of color; and icon sets, which enable you to classify data into categories with each category represented by a particular icon.

If none of the predefined rules suits your needs, you can modify or create a new one.

1. Select the range to which you want to apply conditional formatting.

2. Click the Home tab.

3. Click Conditional Formatting.

A menu containing several types of predefined rules appears.

4. Click the desired rule category (here, Highlight Cells Rules).

5. Click the desired rule (here, Text that Contains).

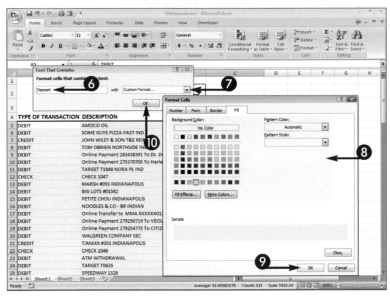

A dialog box appears, enabling you to specify the desired conditions.

6 Enter a value or text for the condition here.

7 Click here and select a format to apply.

If none of the formatting options suits your needs, select Custom Format.

The Format Cells dialog box appears.

8 Select the desired formatting options.

9 Click OK to close the Format Cells dialog box.

10 Click OK to close the dialog box in which you set your conditions.

Excel applies the conditional formatting to any cells that meet the established conditions.

DIFFICULTY LEVEL

TIPS

Try This!

To quickly locate cells to which a conditional formatting rule has been applied, click any cell in the sheet to which said formatting *has not* been applied, click the Home tab, click Find & Select, and click Conditional Formatting. To find only those cells with the same conditional formatting, click a cell to which said formatting *has* been applied, click Find & Select, choose Go To Special, click Conditional Formats, and click Same under Data Validation.

Remove It!

To remove conditional formatting from a worksheet, click the Home tab, click Conditional Formatting, and click Clear Rules from Entire Sheet. To remove conditional formatting from certain cells only, select the cells, click the Home tab, click Conditional Formatting, and click Clear Rules from Selected Cells.

CHART
your data

To make your data appear more visually appealing, you can display it in chart form. Whether you are depicting rising or falling sales or actual costs compared to projected costs, charts can make it easy for others to interpret and understand your data.

The foundation of any chart is the worksheet data you use to create the chart. Called a *data series*, chart data is the content of a group of related cells, such as one row or column of data in your worksheet.

Using Excel, you can convert a data series into any one of a variety of types of charts, including column charts, line charts, pie charts, and bar charts. Each type of chart is composed of a variety of elements, called *objects*. These include legends, titles, axes, and so on.

When creating a chart, you can select from several predefined styles. You can then modify the chart as desired — for example, change the angle of text or adjust the colors or patterns used — and save it as a template for later use.

① Select the data series you want to chart.

   Note: Do not include subtotals or totals in your selection.

   Note: The cells that contain the data you want to include in your chart do not have to be adjacent to each other. To select noncontiguous cell ranges, click the first cell in the range and then press and hold down the Ctrl key on your keyboard while clicking additional cells.

② Click the Insert tab.

③ Click an item in the Charts group.

   A gallery of available chart designs opens.

④ Click the desired chart design.

   Note: For additional chart types, click the Charts dialog box launcher.

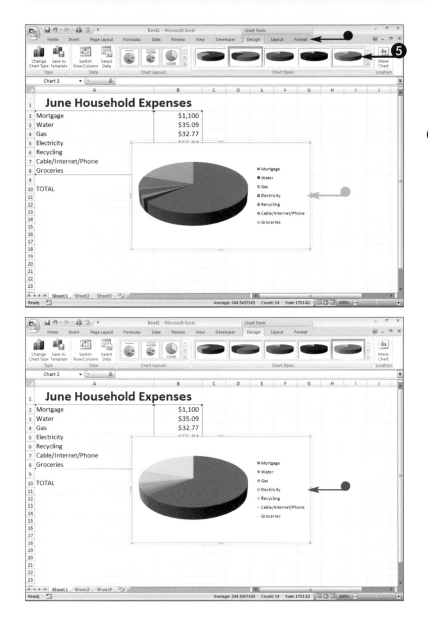

- The chart appears on your worksheet.

- Chart-related tabs (Design, Layout, and Format tabs) appear in the Ribbon.

⑤ To change the colors used in the chart, click an option in the Design tab's Chart Styles group.

- Excel updates the chart to reflect your selection.

TIPS

Did You Know?

If you find you use a particular chart type more often than not, you can set it as the default type. To do so, launch the Create Charts dialog box by clicking the diagonal arrow in the bottom-right corner of the Charts group; then click Set As Default Chart. Thereafter, when you open the Create Charts dialog box, that chart subtype is selected by default.

Try This!

To move the chart to the desired location in a sheet, click an empty area in the window containing the chart and drag the chart to the preferred spot. Alternatively, move the chart to its own sheet by clicking Move Chart on the Design tab and clicking New Sheet.

Customize your chart with
CHART OBJECTS

One way that charts make data easier to interpret and understand is through the use of chart objects.

These include legends, which convey what each data series in your chart represents; the chart title, which looks like a headline for your chart (as outlined here); the plot area, which is the background area of your chart; the value axis, which is the axis listing values for the data series; the value axis title, which is a headline identifying the value axis; the category axis, which lists the categories for the data series; the category axis title, which is a headline identifying

the category axis; and the data series, which is the data plotted on the chart.

If the predefined chart style you applied to your data series does not include a particular chart object, you can add it manually from the Layout tab.

Whether an object in your chart appears by default or was applied manually, you can format it to suit your needs — for example, change the font or color of the object.

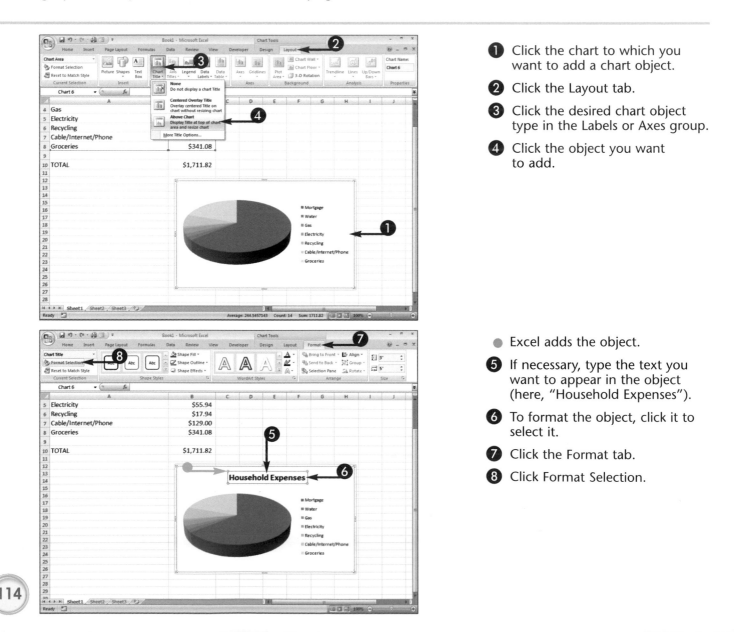

1 Click the chart to which you want to add a chart object.

2 Click the Layout tab.

3 Click the desired chart object type in the Labels or Axes group.

4 Click the object you want to add.

● Excel adds the object.

5 If necessary, type the text you want to appear in the object (here, "Household Expenses").

6 To format the object, click it to select it.

7 Click the Format tab.

8 Click Format Selection.

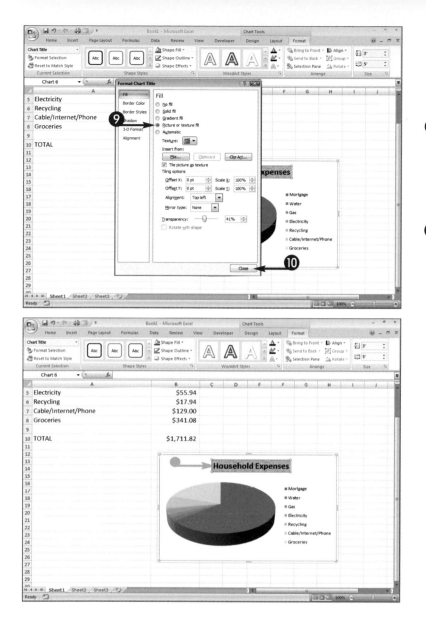

A format dialog box appears. Depending on the chart object you want to edit, the options offered will vary.

❾ Make the desired changes to the chart object.

In this example, a fill pattern is applied to the object.

❿ Click Close.

● Excel applies your changes to the chart.

TIPS

Try This!

If a chart object involves text or numbers, you can change the font used by selecting it in the object and then applying the tools in the Home tab's Font group. Alternatively, apply a Word Art design to your text by selecting the object containing the text, clicking the Format tab, and clicking an option in the WordArt Styles group.

Did You Know?

To print a chart — but not other data that appears on the same sheet — click the chart to select it, click the Office button, and click Print. A dialog box appears; click Selected Chart and click OK. If the chart is on its own sheet, you can simply click the Quick Print button in the Quick Access toolbar.

Reveal trends with
TRENDLINES

You are not limited to using charts to illustrate existing data; you can also chart forecasts using trendlines, which are used primarily in line, area, bar, and scatter charts. A *trendline* is a graphic representation of a trend in a data series.

For example, suppose you have created a chart showing your monthly household expenditures for the preceding year. You can add a trendline to your chart to show the projected expenditures for upcoming months. You can also add trendlines to

show the general trend (that is, upward or downward) of the existing data series, or add a line to represent a moving average, as shown here. A *moving average* is a sequence of averages computed from parts of a data series. Moving averages are helpful for smoothing the fluctuations in data to more clearly reveal the general pattern or trend.

Excel enables you to format various aspects of the trendline, such as its color, width, and so on.

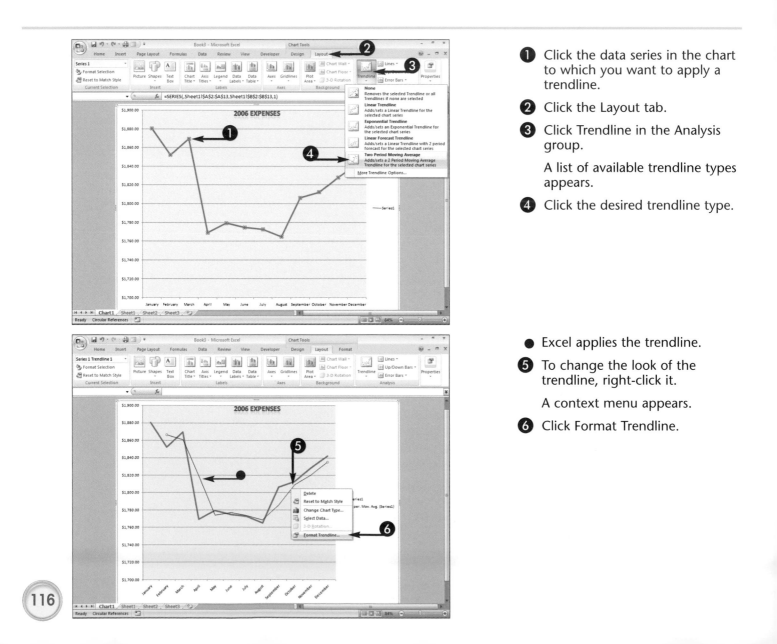

❶ Click the data series in the chart to which you want to apply a trendline.

❷ Click the Layout tab.

❸ Click Trendline in the Analysis group.

A list of available trendline types appears.

❹ Click the desired trendline type.

● Excel applies the trendline.

❺ To change the look of the trendline, right-click it.

A context menu appears.

❻ Click Format Trendline.

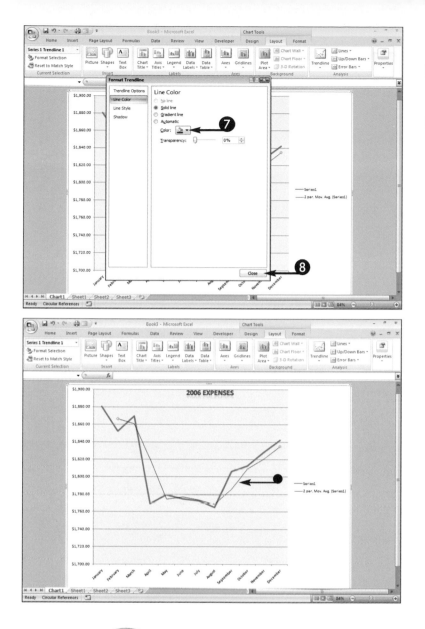

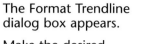

The Format Trendline dialog box appears.

7 Make the desired changes to the trendline.

8 Click Close.

DIFFICULTY LEVEL

● Excel applies the format changes to the trendline.

2006 EXPENSES

TIP

Customize It!

You can customize your trendline by changing the various input parameters. For example, if you opted for a moving average trendline, you can change the number of periods averaged to determine line placement. You can make this and other changes to the trendline from the Trendline Options screen of the Format Trendline dialog box. (Open the dialog box by right-clicking an existing trendline and clicking Format Trendline or by clicking Trendline in the Layout tab and clicking More Trendline Options.)

Align
CELL DATA

You can control the alignment of data in your worksheet cells. By default, Excel automatically aligns text data to the left and number data to the right. Data is also aligned vertically to sit at the bottom of the cell. You can change horizontal and vertical alignment of cell data to improve the appearance of your worksheet data. You align cell data using the various buttons in the Home tab's Alignment group.

In addition to aligning cell data, you can also indent it. To do so, click the cell or cells containing data you

want to indent, click the Home tab, and click the Increase Indent button in the Alignment group. To decrease the indent, click the Decrease Indent button.

If you need to rotate the data in a cell, Excel can accommodate you. Indeed, you can flip cell data sideways or print it from top to bottom instead of from left to right. You might rotate long column headers to manage the widths of your columns.

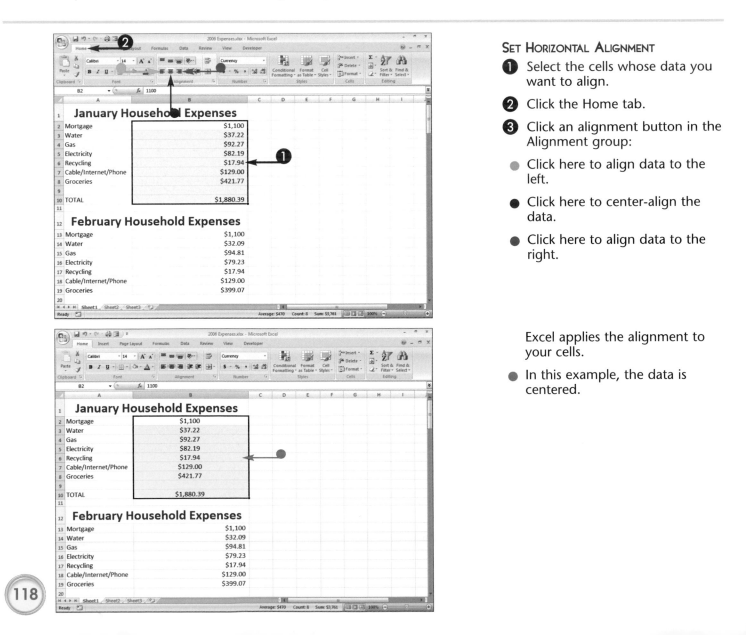

SET HORIZONTAL ALIGNMENT

1 Select the cells whose data you want to align.

2 Click the Home tab.

3 Click an alignment button in the Alignment group:

● Click here to align data to the left.

● Click here to center-align the data.

● Click here to align data to the right.

Excel applies the alignment to your cells.

● In this example, the data is centered.

118

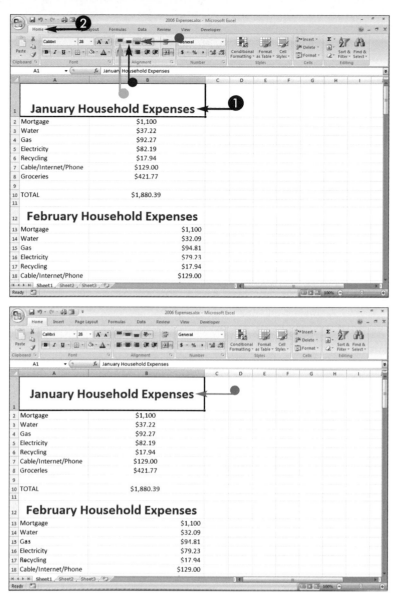

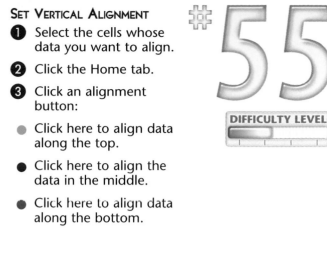

SET VERTICAL ALIGNMENT

1 Select the cells whose data you want to align.

2 Click the Home tab.

3 Click an alignment button:

● Click here to align data along the top.

● Click here to align the data in the middle.

● Click here to align data along the bottom.

Excel applies the alignment to your cells.

● In this example the data is middle-aligned.

TIPS

More Options!

To justify cell data, select the cells whose data you want justified and then click the diagonal arrow in the bottom-right corner of the Alignment group. In the Format Cells dialog box that appears, click the Alignment tab, and then click the Horizontal drop-down button and click Justify. Finally, click OK to apply the setting.

More Options!

You can rotate text from within the Format Cells dialog box. Launch the dialog box as described in the preceding tip; then click the desired angle in the Orientation section or enter a value in the Degrees field. Finally, click OK to apply the setting.

WRAP TEXT
for easy reading

Especially if your worksheet contains cells with text, you may run into situations where the text you need to enter is wider than the cell meant to hold it.

By default, when the amount of data in a cell exceeds the cell's width, the data remains on one line. If the cells to the right of the cell in question are empty, this poses no problem, because the data simply stretches across subsequent cells. If, however, the cells to the right contain data, those cells will obscure any text that spans beyond the cell in

question. To view the data in its entirety, you must click the cell that contains the data and look at the Formula bar.

If you want to be able to see the data in its entirety within the cell, you can turn on Excel's Text Wrapping feature. When you do, data in the cell wraps to the next line, with the height of the row containing the cell increasing to make room.

---

1 Click to select the cell or cells that you want to edit.

2 Click the Home tab.

3 Click the Wrap Text button.

● Excel applies text-wrapping to the selected cell(s).

Set
PRINT PREFERENCES

DIFFICULTY LEVEL

Gridlines make it easier to read a worksheet. By default, gridlines appear onscreen, but not in printed versions of your worksheet. If you plan to print your worksheet, you might want to set up Excel to print it with the gridlines displayed. Doing so makes the printed worksheet a bit easier to read — although be aware that printing with gridlines takes a bit longer than printing without them.

In addition to specifying that gridlines be printed, you can choose other print-related options in Excel. For example, you can specify that comments be

printed, either where they appear on the worksheet or at the end of the sheet. You can also choose whether and how to display errors in cells. Finally, you can also choose to print your worksheets in black and white or to print draft-quality sheets to save ink; you can specify the order in which pages in your workbook print; and preview your print job before sending it to the printer.

---

① Click the Page Layout tab.

● If you want Excel to print gridlines, but do not wish to alter other print settings, click Print (☐ changes to ☑).

② Click the group Sheet Options.

The Page Setup dialog box opens with the Sheet tab displayed.

③ Click here to print the gridlines in your sheet (☐ changes to ☑).

④ Click here to print in black and white (☐ changes to ☑).

⑤ Click here to generate a lower-quality printout (☐ changes to ☑).

⑥ Click the order in which workbook pages should be printed (◯ changes to ◉).

⑦ Click here and specify whether/how comments should be printed.

⑧ Click here and choose whether/how cell errors should be printed.

⑨ Click OK.

Excel applies your changes. To print the worksheet, click the Office button and then click Print.

Chapter 6

Explore the Possibilities with PowerPoint

You can use PowerPoint to create presentations to convey all kinds of messages to an audience. For example, you might employ PowerPoint to present an idea to a prospective client, explain a concept or procedure to employees, or teach a class about a new subject. Your presentation can include words, graphics, media clips, charts, tables, and more.

When creating a presentation, you build an outline, with each first-level heading in the outline serving as the title of an individual slide. Second-level headings appear as bullet points; third-level headings appear as sub-bullets; and so on.

Once your presentation is set up, you can set a time length for the display of each slide, add narration, and insert action buttons and hyperlinks to link to other content. If, for example, you want the presentation to play back in a booth at a trade show, you can set it up to run automatically, such that it requires no external input or management. If, on the other hand, you are the presenter, you can print out speaker notes for your use during the show. To help your audience better follow along, you can also print out handouts, which contain the slides in your presentation.

If you intend to deliver your presentation using a different computer, you can copy the presentation to a CD. You can also publish your presentation to the Web, enabling you to widen your audience substantially.

CONVERT A WORD DOCUMENT into a presentation

DIFFICULTY LEVEL

Suppose you have invested significant time generating a document in Word, and your boss asks you to give a presentation about that document. Rather than retyping the information from the document into PowerPoint, you can import it.

When you import a Word document into PowerPoint, PowerPoint translates any text in the Word document that is represented in Word's Outline view into a PowerPoint outline. Any heading in the document

styled with Word's Heading 1 style appears as a slide title atop a new slide. Second-level headings become bullet points, third-level headings become second-level bullet points, and so on. Normal-style text between the headings is omitted.

You can edit a presentation generated from a Word document just as you would any other presentation: by selecting the slide you want to edit and making the necessary changes.

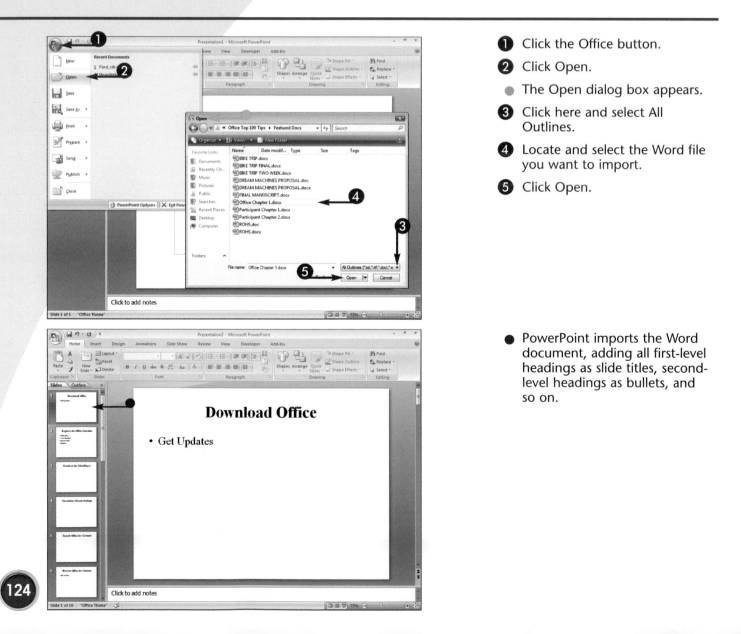

1. Click the Office button.
2. Click Open.
   - The Open dialog box appears.
3. Click here and select All Outlines.
4. Locate and select the Word file you want to import.
5. Click Open.

- PowerPoint imports the Word document, adding all first-level headings as slide titles, second-level headings as bullets, and so on.

SEND A PRESENTATION
to reviewers

#59

If your presentation involves a group effort, you likely need to share it with others before delivering it to your audience. An easy way to do so is to e-mail the presentation.

One way to e-mail a presentation is to simply send the presentation file as an attachment from within your e-mail program. If you prefer, however, you may be able to send the file from within PowerPoint assuming you use an e-mail program that is compatible, such as Outlook.

When others review your presentation, they can use PowerPoint's comment features to provide feedback quickly and easily. With these tools, reviewers can insert, edit, and delete comments, as well as opt to show or hide edits. These tools are available from the Comments group under the PowerPoint Ribbon's Review tab.

Before sharing your presentation with others, consider running a spell check. To do so, click the Spelling button in the Review tab's Proofing group.

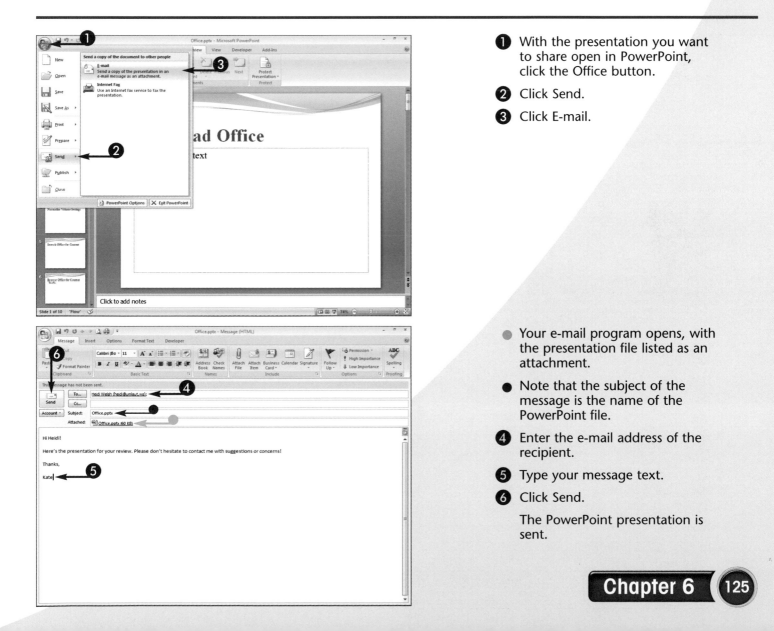

① With the presentation you want to share open in PowerPoint, click the Office button.

② Click Send.

③ Click E-mail.

● Your e-mail program opens, with the presentation file listed as an attachment.

● Note that the subject of the message is the name of the PowerPoint file.

④ Enter the e-mail address of the recipient.

⑤ Type your message text.

⑥ Click Send.

The PowerPoint presentation is sent.

Chapter 6 125

REUSE A SLIDE
from another presentation

Suppose you are working on a new presentation and you want to include information covered in an existing presentation. Rather than re-creating the content, you can insert the relevant slide from the existing presentation into the new one.

This is a great timesaver if, for example, you have created a slide with a highly detailed chart, table, or diagram because it saves you the trouble of reentering data and reformatting the object on the slide. When you insert a slide from a different presentation, the slide automatically adopts the

colors, fonts, graphics, and other formatting attributes of the new presentation (although you can opt to keep the original formatting if you prefer).

To reuse a slide from another presentation, you first locate the presentation containing the slide you want to reuse. This presentation might reside on your computer's hard drive, on a CD you insert in your CD drive, on a network to which your computer is attached, or in a Slide Library on a SharePoint Server. PowerPoint then displays the slides in the selected presentation in the Reuse Slides task pane.

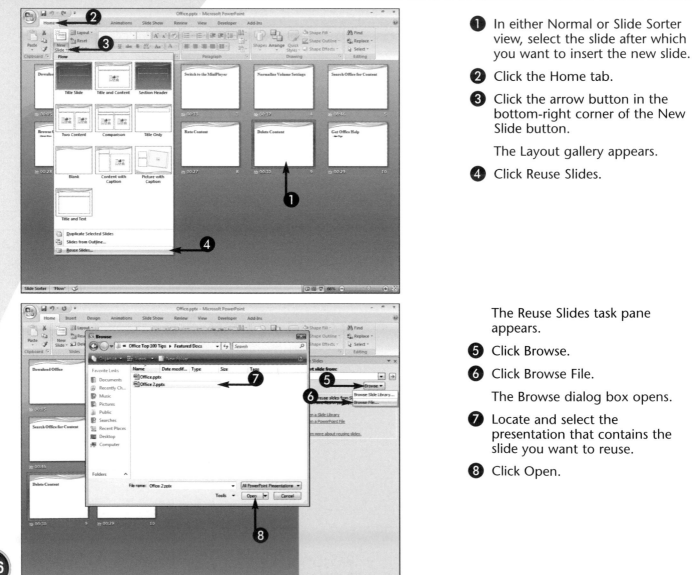

❶ In either Normal or Slide Sorter view, select the slide after which you want to insert the new slide.

❷ Click the Home tab.

❸ Click the arrow button in the bottom-right corner of the New Slide button.

The Layout gallery appears.

❹ Click Reuse Slides.

The Reuse Slides task pane appears.

❺ Click Browse.

❻ Click Browse File.

The Browse dialog box opens.

❼ Locate and select the presentation that contains the slide you want to reuse.

❽ Click Open.

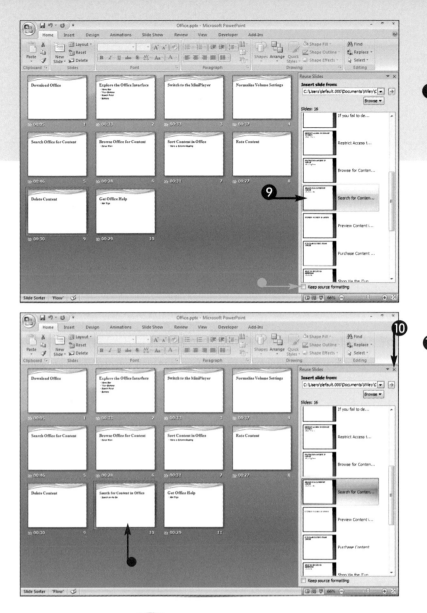

The slides in the selected presentation appear in the Reuse Slides task pane.

❾ Click the slide you want to reuse.

● To retain the slide's original formatting, click the Keep source formatting check box (☐ changes to ☑).

● The slide appears in the presentation.

❿ Click the Close button to close the Reuse Slides task pane.

TIPS

Try This!
To get a better look at the slides in the Reuse Slides task pane, hover the mouse pointer over the slide thumbnail rather than the slide title. When you do, an enlarged version of the thumbnail pops up, providing enhanced visibility and readability.

More Options!
If the slide you are looking for is not in the presentation you selected in the Browse dialog box, click the Browse button in the Reuse Slides task pane and choose Browse File to relaunch the Browse dialog box. Then locate and select the correct presentation file to reveal the presentation's slides in the Reuse Slides task pane.

Rehearse
TIMING

When delivering a presentation, you typically advance the slides manually by clicking the mouse button. You can, however, set up your presentation to advance the slides automatically. That way, you are free to move as you speak instead of being tethered to your laptop throughout the presentation.

If you opt for automatic slide advancement, you must rehearse the timing of your presentation to ensure that the slides advance at the correct time. To do so, use the Slide Timing feature to record the

amount of time you need for each slide. PowerPoint then uses the times you record during the presentation to determine when to advance from one slide to the next.

Note that the Slide Timing feature also works well for creating a self-running presentation — that is, a presentation that runs without narration (for example, in a kiosk at a trade show).

① With the slide show you want to rehearse open in PowerPoint, click the Slide Show tab.

② Click Rehearse Timings.

PowerPoint switches to full-screen view.

● The Rehearsal toolbar appears.

● Click the Pause button to pause the timer.

● The timer for the current slide appears here.

● Click the Start Over button to restart the timer for the current slide.

● The timer for the presentation appears here.

③ Rehearse your speech for the current slide.

④ When you are finished speaking, click the Next button.

Repeat steps **3** and **4** for each remaining slide.

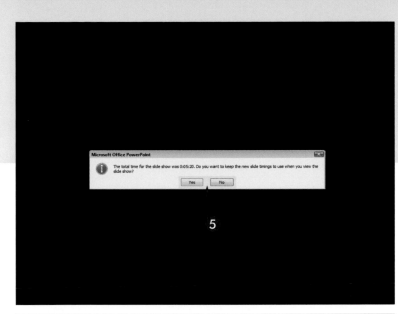

When you click the Next button after rehearsing the last slide, PowerPoint informs you of the total time for the presentation, and asks whether you want to keep the new slide timings you created.

5 Click Yes if you are satisfied with the slide timings. If you want to change the slide timings, click No and make the desired changes to the presentation.

● PowerPoint displays the slides in the show in Slide Sorter view, with the timing for each slide noted.

![TIPS]

Try This!

You can apply transition effects to your PowerPoint presentations. When you do, PowerPoint plays a special effect when advancing from one slide to the next. For example, you can choose a wipe transition effect, where the next slide appears to wipe the current slide from the screen. You can also apply sound effects for transitions, and establish how quickly the transition should occur. You access these settings from the Animations tab's Transition to This Slide group.

Remove It!

If you decide you want to advance the slides manually rather than use the timings you set, disable the timings by deselecting the Use Rehearsed Timings check box in the Slide Show tab's Set Up group.

Record
NARRATION

If you do not intend to present your PowerPoint show live — for example, if you will show it at a kiosk or over the Web — you might want to record a narration that talks the viewer through your key points. When a presentation uses a recorded narration, it advances to the next slide automatically at the end of the previous slide's narration.

Before you record your narration, take time to jot down just what you want to say when each slide

appears. When recording the narration, speak slowly, and be sure to enunciate.

In order for PowerPoint to play back your narration with the presentation, open the Set Up Show dialog box (click the Slide Show tab and click Set Up Slide Show) and make sure the Show Without Narration check box is unchecked. Otherwise, your audience cannot hear the recorded narration.

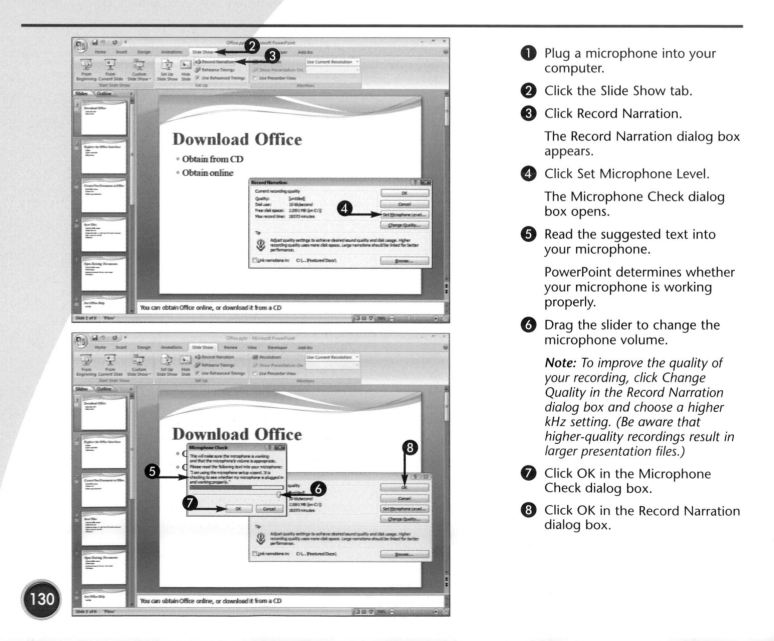

① Plug a microphone into your computer.

② Click the Slide Show tab.

③ Click Record Narration.

The Record Narration dialog box appears.

④ Click Set Microphone Level.

The Microphone Check dialog box opens.

⑤ Read the suggested text into your microphone.

PowerPoint determines whether your microphone is working properly.

⑥ Drag the slider to change the microphone volume.

Note: To improve the quality of your recording, click Change Quality in the Record Narration dialog box and choose a higher kHz setting. (Be aware that higher-quality recordings result in larger presentation files.)

⑦ Click OK in the Microphone Check dialog box.

⑧ Click OK in the Record Narration dialog box.

The presentation begins.

9 Speak your narration into your microphone, pressing the space bar to advance to the next slide as needed.

10 When you finish the presentation, press Esc.

A message appears asking whether you want to save the timings.

11 Click Save.

The presentation appears in Slide Sorter view.

● The timing appears beneath each slide and reflects the length of its recorded narration.

Note: To listen to a narration, click the sound icon on the slide, click the Options tab that appears in the Ribbon, and click Preview.

TIPS

Try This!

To rerecord a slide's narration, switch to Normal view, select the slide whose narration you want to rerecord, click the Slide Show tab, and click Record Narration. Click OK in the dialog box that appears, click Current Slide, recite the narration, and press Esc to stop the recording.

More Options!

If sound files are bloating your presentation file, link the audio files to your slides instead of embedding them. Select the Link Narrations In check box in the Record Narration dialog box and choose the folder in which the sound files should be stored. (Be sure to copy both the presentation and any linked files when you burn the presentation to CD or use another computer to run the presentation.)

ACTION BUTTONS

DIFFICULTY LEVEL

Action buttons enable you to quickly jump to related content while delivering a slide show. You might insert an action button that leads to another slide in your presentation, to another presentation altogether, to a Word document, to a program, or to a Web page. Alternatively, clicking an action button might result in the playing back of a sound file. (Note that the item to which the action button is linked must reside on the computer you are using to conduct your presentation. If the item is a Web page, then the computer must be connected to the Internet.)

PowerPoint offers several pre-designed action buttons from which to choose; alternatively, you can create your own custom button. After you select the button type, you then choose what action will occur when the button is clicked during a show.

Action buttons are especially handy for self-running presentations (that is, presentations that do not use a presenter, which are often played back at a booth or kiosk). They enable the audience to access additional materials or simply navigate the presentation.

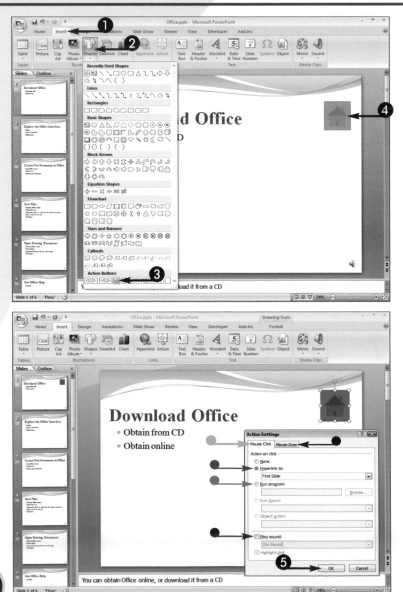

① Click the Insert tab.

② Click Shapes.

   The Shapes Gallery appears.

③ Click a button type in the Action Buttons group.

   The mouse pointer turns into a crosshair.

④ Click in the slide and drag diagonally to insert the action button.

   PowerPoint inserts the action button and displays the Action Settings dialog box.

● If you want the action button to engage when clicked, click the Mouse Click tab.

● To engage the action button when the mouse is over the button, click the Mouse Over tab.

● Click Hyperlink (◎ changes to ◉) to link the action button to another slide in your presentation; click the arrow button to choose the target slide.

● To link to an external item, click Run Program (◎ changes to ◉); then click Browse to launch a dialog box from which you can select the target item.

● To play a sound, select the Play Sound check box (☐ changes to ☑) and click the arrow button to select the sound file.

⑤ Click OK.

Insert a
HYPERLINK

DIFFICULTY LEVEL

In addition to inserting action buttons, you can insert hyperlinks. These are similar to action buttons in that clicking them enables you to direct the viewer to another slide in your presentation, another presentation altogether, a Word document, a program, a Web page, or a sound file. Like action buttons, hyperlinks are especially handy for self-running presentations.

Unlike action buttons, however, hyperlinks do not clutter up your slide. Instead, you can use the text on your slide as a hyperlink. Then, you need only click the text to engage the link.

Note that you can remove the hyperlink from text in a slide by selecting the text and clicking the Hyperlink button in the Insert tab. Then, in the dialog box that appears, click Remove Hyperlink.

The item to which the hyperlink is linked must be stored on the computer on which you are giving your presentation or, if the item is a Web page, then the computer must be connected to the Internet.

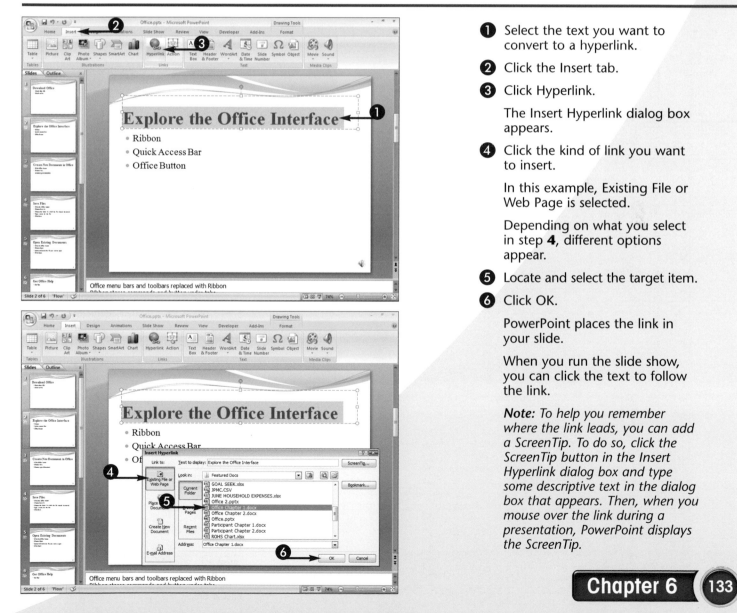

❶ Select the text you want to convert to a hyperlink.

❷ Click the Insert tab.

❸ Click Hyperlink.

The Insert Hyperlink dialog box appears.

❹ Click the kind of link you want to insert.

In this example, Existing File or Web Page is selected.

Depending on what you select in step **4**, different options appear.

❺ Locate and select the target item.

❻ Click OK.

PowerPoint places the link in your slide.

When you run the slide show, you can click the text to follow the link.

Note: To help you remember where the link leads, you can add a ScreenTip. To do so, click the ScreenTip button in the Insert Hyperlink dialog box and type some descriptive text in the dialog box that appears. Then, when you mouse over the link during a presentation, PowerPoint displays the ScreenTip.

Create a
SELF-RUNNING PRESENTATION

#65

DIFFICULTY LEVEL

If your presentation is destined for playback at, for example, a booth at a trade show, you can set it up to be a self-running show, with no presenter required. Alternatively, you might burn a self-running presentation to CD and send it to prospective clients.

Your self-running presentation can include hyperlinks or action buttons to enable your audience to navigate the presentation; alternatively, you can set up the show to advance from slide to slide automatically.

You can also include voice narration in your self-running presentation. (Follow the steps in "Task 62".) If you like, you can set up your show to *loop* — that is, run over and over again from beginning to end. (This is handy if your presentation is running at a trade-show booth.) You set up a presentation to be self-running from the Set Up Show dialog box.

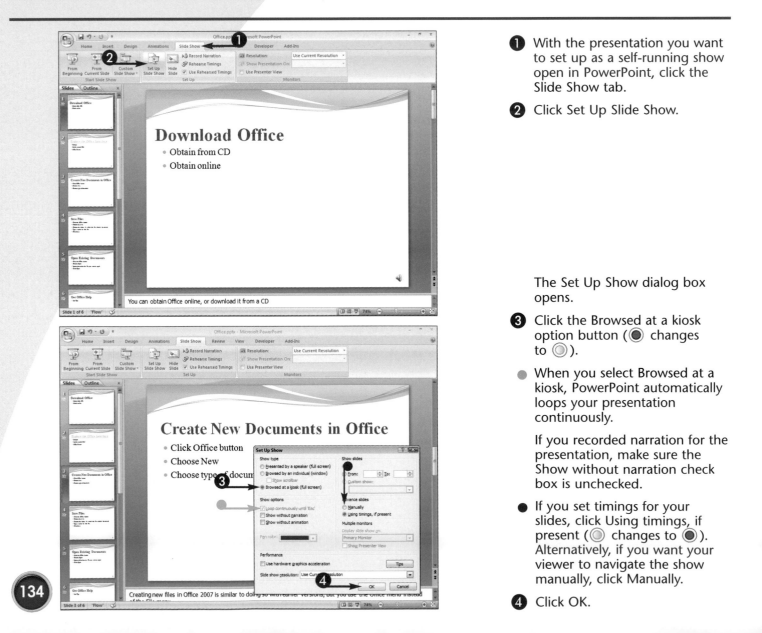

① With the presentation you want to set up as a self-running show open in PowerPoint, click the Slide Show tab.

② Click Set Up Slide Show.

The Set Up Show dialog box opens.

③ Click the Browsed at a kiosk option button (◉ changes to ◎).

● When you select Browsed at a kiosk, PowerPoint automatically loops your presentation continuously.

If you recorded narration for the presentation, make sure the Show without narration check box is unchecked.

● If you set timings for your slides, click Using timings, if present (◎ changes to ◉). Alternatively, if you want your viewer to navigate the show manually, click Manually.

④ Click OK.

WRITE ON A SLIDE
during a presentation

PowerPoint enables you to use a technology called *ink* to draw freehand on your screen during a presentation. For example, you might use ink to highlight or annotate an important point or to jot down ideas contributed by your audience.

You can choose the style and color used; options include Ballpoint Pen, Felt Tip Pen, and Highlighter. If you like, you can also change the color of the ink. To do so, right-click on a slide, click Pointer Options,

click Ink Color, and select a color from the palette that appears.

DIFFICULTY LEVEL

To delete any annotations made during a presentation, right-click the slide, click Pointer Options, and choose Erase All Ink on Slide from the menu that appears. Alternatively, choose the Eraser option; then drag the pointer over the annotations you want to erase. (When you are finished, click Eraser on the Pointer menu again to turn it off.)

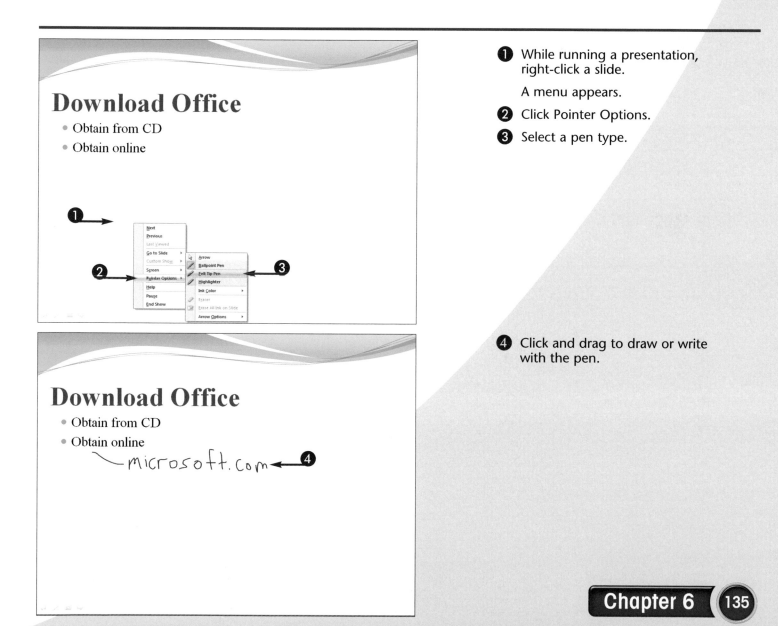

① While running a presentation, right-click a slide.

A menu appears.

② Click Pointer Options.

③ Select a pen type.

④ Click and drag to draw or write with the pen.

Create
SPEAKER NOTES

When giving a presentation, having a cheat sheet with additional facts, or with answers to questions the audience may ask, is handy. To create just such a cheat sheet, you can enter notes into PowerPoint slides, and then print them out. When you print out the notes you enter, the printout includes a small version of the slide to which the notes refer.

If you like, you can use PowerPoint's Notes master to control how printouts of your notes are laid out. For example, you can use the Notes master to change where the image of the slide appears, as well as to

add placeholders for headers, footers, the date, or slide numbers. To use the Notes master, switch to Notes Master view (click Notes Master in the View tab). Then use the various tools available on the Notes Master tab to add or remove placeholders, change the fonts or colors used, and so on.

To print speaker notes, click the Office button, choose Print, click the Print What drop-down arrow, choose Notes Pages, and then click OK.

DIFFICULTY LEVEL

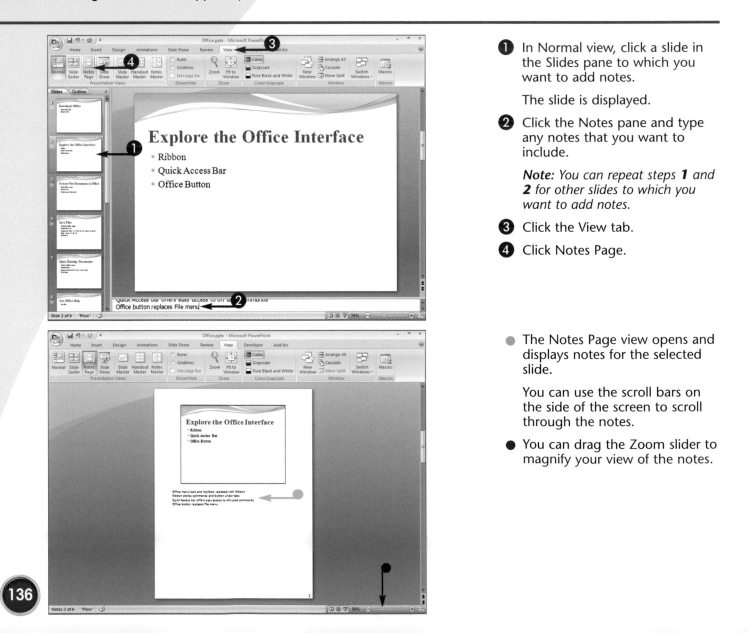

① In Normal view, click a slide in the Slides pane to which you want to add notes.

The slide is displayed.

② Click the Notes pane and type any notes that you want to include.

*Note: You can repeat steps **1** and **2** for other slides to which you want to add notes.*

③ Click the View tab.

④ Click Notes Page.

● The Notes Page view opens and displays notes for the selected slide.

You can use the scroll bars on the side of the screen to scroll through the notes.

● You can drag the Zoom slider to magnify your view of the notes.

Print
HANDOUTS

To help your audience follow along as you perform your presentation, as well as provide a place for them to take notes for future reference, you can print presentation handouts. These handouts can contain one, three, five, six, or nine slides per page. (Printing several slides per page can help you save paper when printing handouts for a lengthy presentation.)

You can use PowerPoint's Handout Master to control how your presentation handouts are laid out. For example, you can use the Handout Master to change

where the images of the slides appear, as well as to add placeholders for headers, footers, the date, slide numbers, a company logo, and so on. To use the Handout Master, switch to Handout Master view (click Handout Master in the View tab). Then use the various tools available on the Handouts Master tab to add or remove placeholders, change the fonts or colors used, and so on.

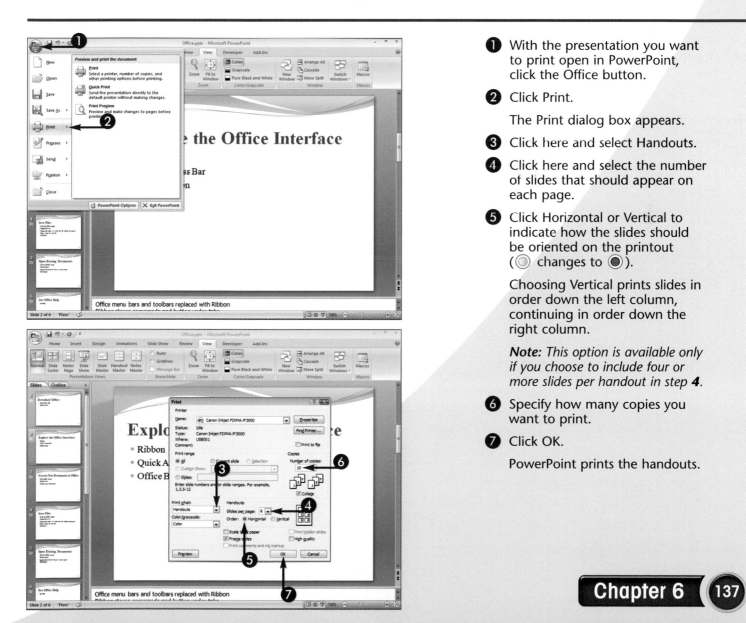

① With the presentation you want to print open in PowerPoint, click the Office button.

② Click Print.

The Print dialog box appears.

③ Click here and select Handouts.

④ Click here and select the number of slides that should appear on each page.

⑤ Click Horizontal or Vertical to indicate how the slides should be oriented on the printout (◉ changes to ◉).

Choosing Vertical prints slides in order down the left column, continuing in order down the right column.

Note: This option is available only if you choose to include four or more slides per handout in step 4.

⑥ Specify how many copies you want to print.

⑦ Click OK.

PowerPoint prints the handouts.

COPY A PRESENTATION #69
to CD

DIFFICULTY LEVEL

If you know you will give your presentation using a computer other than your own, you can copy it onto a CD. Then, you can simply insert the CD containing your presentation into whatever computer is available and run it from there. (Note that as yet, PowerPoint does not support direct burning to DVD.)

When you copy your presentation to CD, the computer also copies any files to which that presentation links by default. For example, if you set up an action button in your presentation to launch a program or document when clicked, the computer

also saves the target program or document on the CD with your presentation.

In the event the computer on which you plan to run your presentation does not have PowerPoint installed, PowerPoint includes a copy of PowerPoint Viewer when you burn a presentation to CD. You can then use the CD to install PowerPoint Viewer on the machine on which the presentation will run.

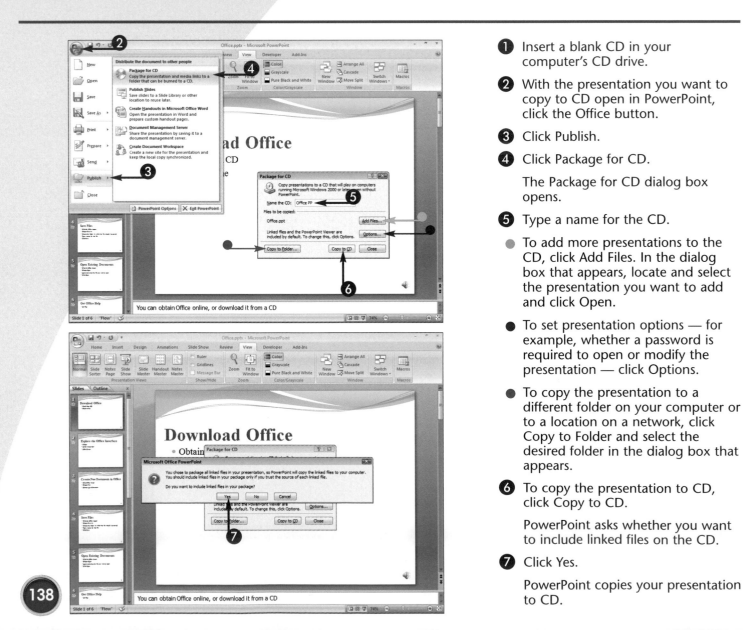

① Insert a blank CD in your computer's CD drive.

② With the presentation you want to copy to CD open in PowerPoint, click the Office button.

③ Click Publish.

④ Click Package for CD.

The Package for CD dialog box opens.

⑤ Type a name for the CD.

● To add more presentations to the CD, click Add Files. In the dialog box that appears, locate and select the presentation you want to add and click Open.

● To set presentation options — for example, whether a password is required to open or modify the presentation — click Options.

● To copy the presentation to a different folder on your computer or to a location on a network, click Copy to Folder and select the desired folder in the dialog box that appears.

⑥ To copy the presentation to CD, click Copy to CD.

PowerPoint asks whether you want to include linked files on the CD.

⑦ Click Yes.

PowerPoint copies your presentation to CD.

138

PUBLISH
a Web presentation

DIFFICULTY LEVEL

By placing your PowerPoint presentation online, you can maximize your audience. You can publish your presentation as a static Web page or as an interactive Web site.

To save your presentation for use on the Web, you need not employ a Web publishing program. Instead, you can publish the presentation to the Web from within PowerPoint. When you do, you essentially save the presentation in a Web file format — namely, hypertext markup language (HTML). You then post the presentation on a Web server. Note that you need to find a hosting service to house your

presentation online. If your presentation is for work, confer with your IT department for details. Otherwise, contact your ISP for information. They can tell you what Web address to use, and whether a user name and password is required.

When you publish your presentation, PowerPoint enables you to accommodate various types of browsers to ensure the presentation appears consistently regardless of what browser your computer uses to display it.

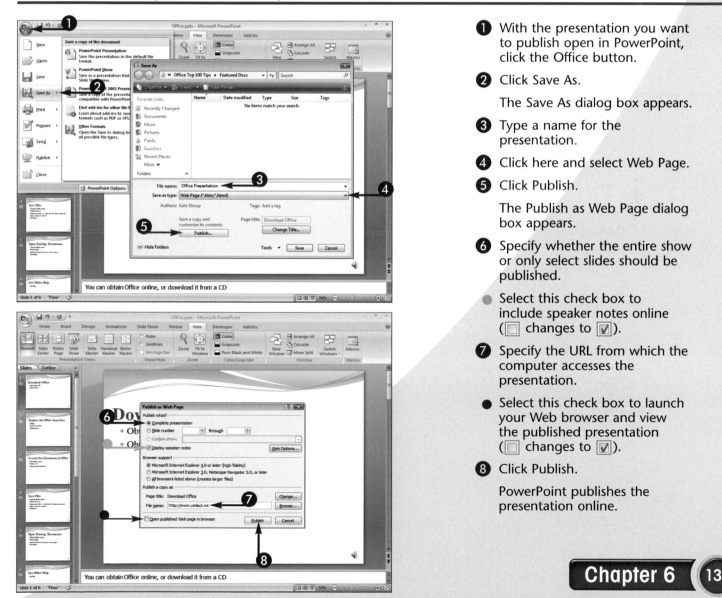

① With the presentation you want to publish open in PowerPoint, click the Office button.

② Click Save As.

The Save As dialog box appears.

③ Type a name for the presentation.

④ Click here and select Web Page.

⑤ Click Publish.

The Publish as Web Page dialog box appears.

⑥ Specify whether the entire show or only select slides should be published.

● Select this check box to include speaker notes online (☐ changes to ☑).

⑦ Specify the URL from which the computer accesses the presentation.

● Select this check box to launch your Web browser and view the published presentation (☐ changes to ☑).

⑧ Click Publish.

PowerPoint publishes the presentation online.

Chapter 7

Express Yourself through Presentations

Whatever your presentation's message, PowerPoint is designed to enable you to convey it in the most interesting way possible. To that end, the program offers countless features for enhancing your presentation visually.

When you create a presentation, PowerPoint enables you to select from several pre-designed slide layouts as well as create your own custom layouts. (A slide's layout determines how the title, text, graphics, and other visual elements appear.)

In addition to selecting the slide layout, you can apply themes to your slides. A theme is a set of colors, fonts, placeholder positions, graphic elements, backgrounds, effects, and other formatting attributes. Applying a theme enables you to streamline the look and feel of your presentation.

Of course, you are not limited to including text-based content in your slides. PowerPoint enables you to insert any number of objects, such as images, video, sound, and SmartArt graphics. (SmartArt graphics are ideal for creating organizational charts and illustrating other hierarchical concepts.) For added interest, you can animate these objects — for example, you might set up your slide show to fly in an image from the upper-left portion of the screen, landing it in the bottom-right corner. In moderate doses, animation can go a long way toward keeping your audience engaged.

If your presentation focuses more on images than on text, you can use PowerPoint's special Photo Album feature to create a special photo album presentation. This feature provides special tools for arranging your images just so.

Top 100

Choose a
SLIDE LAYOUT

When you open a new presentation, it contains a single slide with placeholders for a title and subtitle. This arrangement of placeholders is called the slide's *layout*, and determines where the slide's title, text, graphics, and other visual elements appear.

In addition to this default layout, you can choose from among several built-in slide layouts in PowerPoint. For example, the Title and Content slide layout, used by default when you insert new slides into your presentation, includes placeholders for title text and content such as images, tables, bulleted

lists, and so on. Other available layouts include Section Header, Two Content, Comparison, Title Only, Blank, Content with Caption, and Picture with Caption. You choose a slide's layout from the Layouts Gallery.

In addition to choosing different layouts, you can edit the placeholders in a slide's layout. For example, you can resize a placeholder, move it to another location on your slide, or delete it. You can also add placeholders to a slide. For more information, see "Task #72."

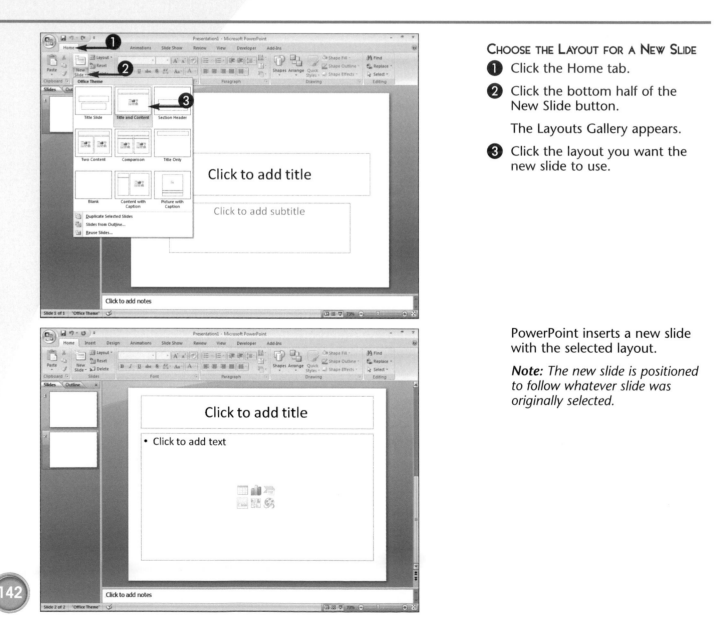

CHOOSE THE LAYOUT FOR A NEW SLIDE

① Click the Home tab.

② Click the bottom half of the New Slide button.

The Layouts Gallery appears.

③ Click the layout you want the new slide to use.

PowerPoint inserts a new slide with the selected layout.

Note: The new slide is positioned to follow whatever slide was originally selected.

142

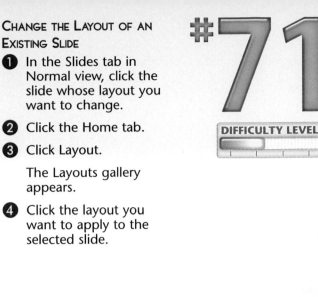

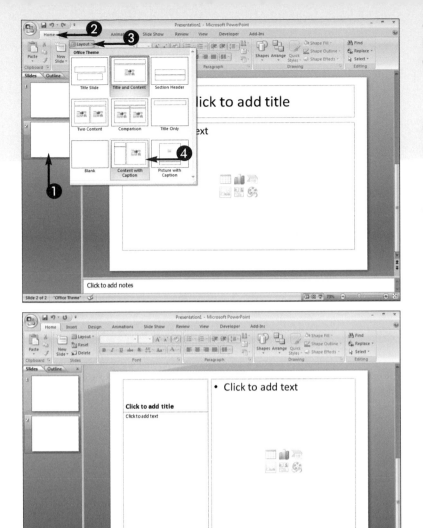

CHANGE THE LAYOUT OF AN EXISTING SLIDE

① In the Slides tab in Normal view, click the slide whose layout you want to change.

② Click the Home tab.

③ Click Layout.

The Layouts gallery appears.

④ Click the layout you want to apply to the selected slide.

71

DIFFICULTY LEVEL

PowerPoint changes the slide's layout.

TIPS

More Options!
Another way to change the layout of a slide is to right-click an empty area in the slide (that is, outside a placeholder), click Layout, and select a layout from the list that appears.

Did You Know?
If you apply a layout to an existing slide that does not include a placeholder for an item you added using the original layout — for example, a chart — PowerPoint retains that element on the slide, even with the new layout.

Did You Know?
By default, clicking the top portion of New Slide inserts a slide with the Title and Content layout. If you add a slide that uses a different layout, that layout becomes the default layout.

Create a
CUSTOM SLIDE LAYOUT

If none of the standard layouts available in PowerPoint's Layouts gallery quite suits your needs, you can create a new layout from scratch. You create new layouts from within Slide Master view. (You can learn more about this view in the next task.) When you create a new layout, you add the necessary text- and object-specific placeholders.

Whether working with a predefined layout or a custom one, you can edit the placeholders in a slide's layout. For example, you can resize a placeholder,

move it to another location on your slide, or delete it. You can also add placeholders to a slide.

You can save your new layout as a template. By doing so, you make the custom layout available in the Layouts gallery. To save a layout as a template, click the Office button, click Save As, type a name for the template in the File Name field, click the Save As Type drop-down arrow and choose PowerPoint Template, and click Save.

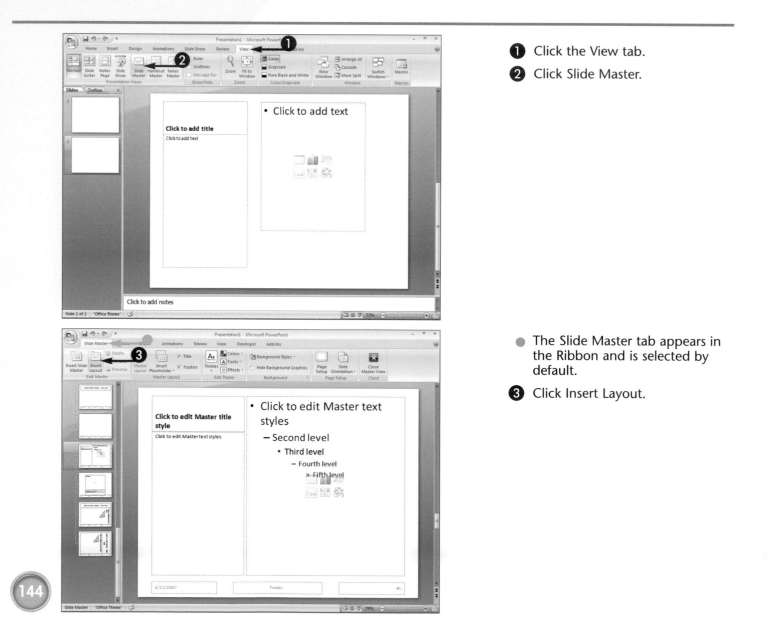

① Click the View tab.

② Click Slide Master.

● The Slide Master tab appears in the Ribbon and is selected by default.

③ Click Insert Layout.

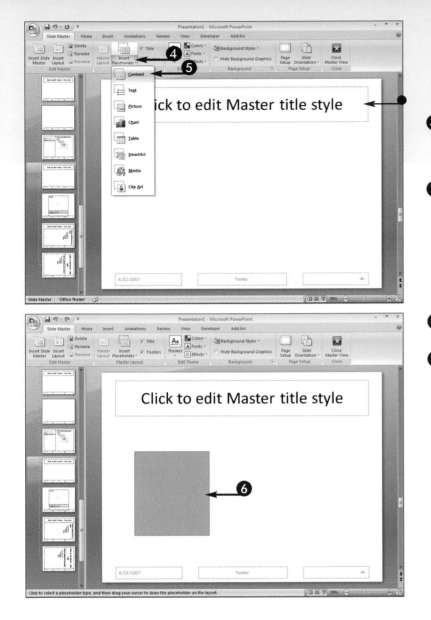

● Remove any unwanted default placeholders by clicking the border of the placeholder and pressing Delete on your keyboard.

④ To add a placeholder, click the bottom half of the Insert Placeholder button.

⑤ Choose the type of placeholder you want to insert.

⑥ Click in the slide and drag to draw the placeholder.

⑦ Repeat steps **4** to **6** to add more placeholders as needed.

TIPS

Try This!

To resize a placeholder, first click in the placeholder. Then place your mouse pointer over a sizing handle on the placeholder. The mouse cursor changes to a two-headed arrow; click and drag inward or outward to change the size of the placeholder. (Note: To preserve the aspect ratio of the placeholder — that is, the ratio of the height and width — drag one of the corner sizing handles.)

Try This!

To move a placeholder, place your mouse cursor over the placeholder's bounding box (that is, the box surrounding the placeholder). The mouse cursor changes to a four-headed arrow; click and drag to relocate the placeholder.

Insert a
CUSTOM SLIDE MASTER

A *slide master* determines the positioning of the various placeholders in the slide, such as the positioning of the slide title, any content in the slide, and so on.

When you apply a theme to a presentation, that theme includes predefined slide masters. If you make a change to a slide master, such as increasing the font size for slide titles or adding a footer or graphic, that change is applied to every slide in the

presentation. This saves you time and gives your presentation a consistent look and feel.

You work with the slide master in Slide Master view. You can use the tools on this Ribbon tab to delete, create, preserve, or rename masters, or change the placeholders contained in the master layout. (To close Slide Master view, click Close Master View in the Slide Master tab.)

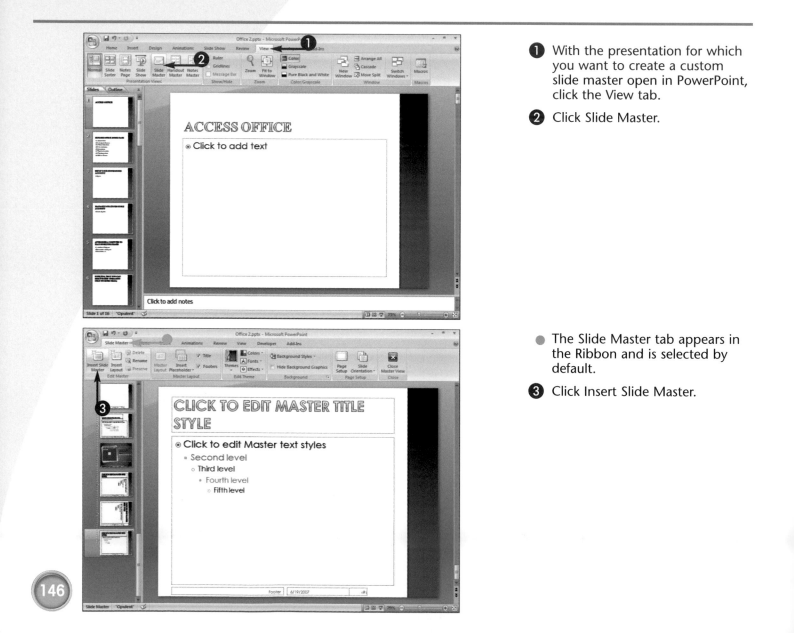

1 With the presentation for which you want to create a custom slide master open in PowerPoint, click the View tab.

2 Click Slide Master.

● The Slide Master tab appears in the Ribbon and is selected by default.

3 Click Insert Slide Master.

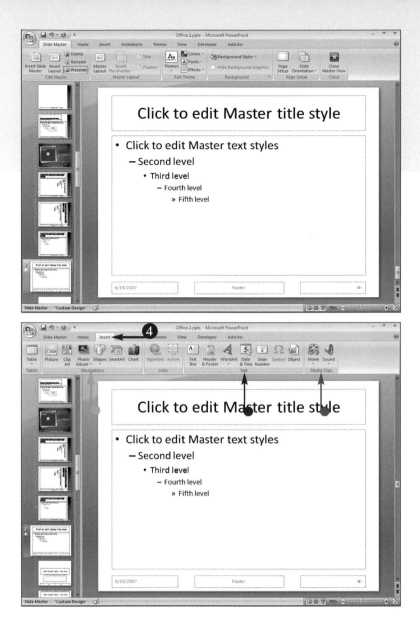

A new slide master appears.

73

④ To insert elements into the slide master, such as footers, a date, slide numbers, graphics, or what have you, click the Insert tab.

● Click a button in this group to insert a photo, clip art image, or other type of illustration.

● Click a button in this group to insert a text box, footer, date/time field, slide number, or other text item.

● Click a button in this group to insert a media item such as a movie or sound-clip file.

TIP

Try This!

In addition to inserting footers, images, and other items into slide masters, you can also insert placeholders. A placeholder reserves space in a slide for a particular type of element, such as a picture. You can then replace the placeholder with the specific picture you want to use. In this way, you can use a different picture on each slide, even though the same master is applied. To insert a placeholder, click the Slide Master tab, click Insert Placeholder, and choose the type of placeholder you want to insert.

Streamline your presentation with
THEMES

Although it is possible to manually format the slides in your presentation one by one — applying backgrounds, fonts, colors, graphics, and so on — an easier way to streamline the look and feel of the slides in your presentation is to apply a *theme*. Doing so applies specific colors, fonts, placeholder positions, graphic elements, backgrounds, effects, and other formatting to the slides in the presentation in one quick, easy operation. Slide masters determine the positioning of the placeholders and objects for the current theme.

You can apply one theme to all the slides in a presentation to lend a consistent, professional look. Alternatively, you can apply different themes to certain slides. Note that if you do opt to apply a different theme to certain slides, be sure it complements the design used on other slides. Otherwise, the transition from one theme to another as you move from slide to slide can be jarring to viewers.

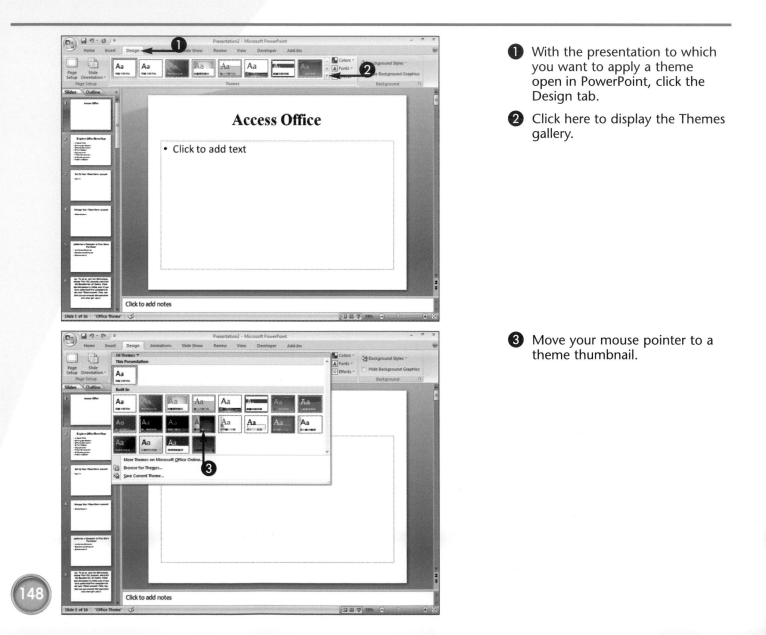

1 With the presentation to which you want to apply a theme open in PowerPoint, click the Design tab.

2 Click here to display the Themes gallery.

3 Move your mouse pointer to a theme thumbnail.

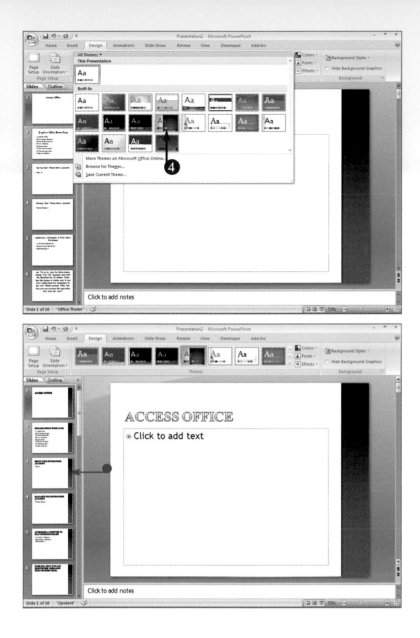

PowerPoint enables you to preview the new design in the Slide pane.

④ When you find a theme you want to apply, click its thumbnail.

● PowerPoint applies the theme to all the slides in the presentation.

TIPS

Did You Know?

Generally, dark-colored backgrounds with light-colored text work better in darker spaces, such as hotel conference rooms. Lighter backgrounds are easier to read in brighter, smaller spaces, such as small meeting rooms. Be warned: People may grow weary of looking at bright colors such as oranges or reds.

More Options!

As mentioned, you can apply different themes to certain slides. To do so, switch to Slide Sorter view and select the slides to which you want to apply the different theme. (Hold down the Ctrl key as you click to select noncontiguous slides in the presentation.) Then open the Themes gallery, right-click the theme you want to apply to the selected slides, and choose Apply to All Slides.

CUSTOMIZE
a theme

If you apply a theme to your presentation, but decide that you would prefer to use different colors or fonts with that theme, you can easily change them by selecting a different color theme or font theme. A *color theme* controls the colors automatically applied to text and objects such as tables and SmartArt diagrams. The font theme dictates the font formatting for all text.

Changing the color theme or font theme can give your presentation an entirely fresh look, even as other theme attributes are retained. Choosing

different color and font themes can also help make your presentation more attractive — not to mention readable — when it is displayed onscreen or in printout form.

In addition to applying a new predefined color theme or font theme to your presentation, you can also create your own custom color and font themes.

You can apply a different color theme to selected slides in your presentation or to the entire show. The font theme, however, must be applied to the presentation in its entirety.

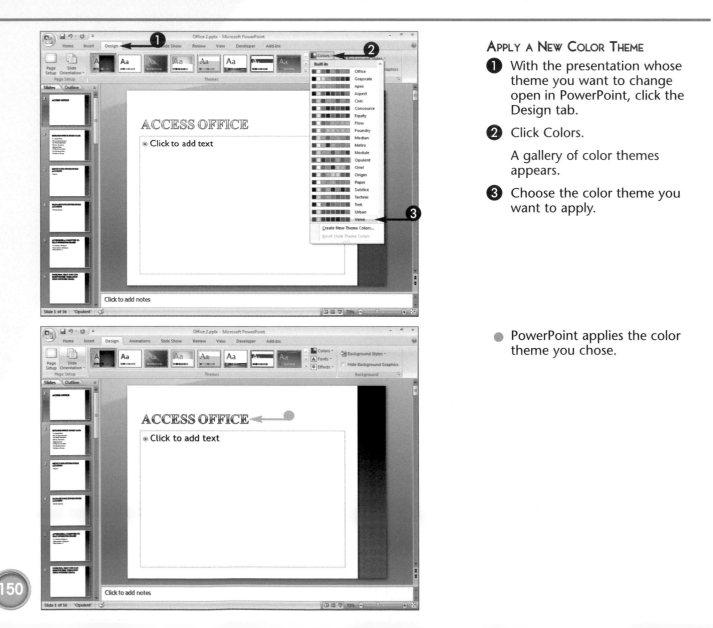

APPLY A NEW COLOR THEME

1 With the presentation whose theme you want to change open in PowerPoint, click the Design tab.

2 Click Colors.

A gallery of color themes appears.

3 Choose the color theme you want to apply.

● PowerPoint applies the color theme you chose.

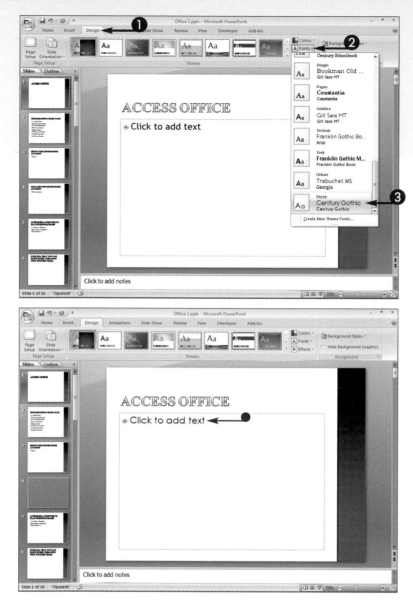

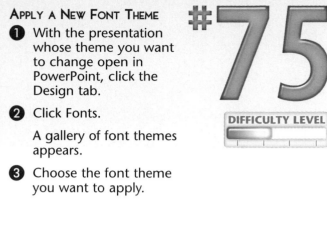

APPLY A NEW FONT THEME

#75

DIFFICULTY LEVEL

① With the presentation whose theme you want to change open in PowerPoint, click the Design tab.

② Click Fonts.

A gallery of font themes appears.

③ Choose the font theme you want to apply.

● PowerPoint applies the font theme you chose.

TIP

Try This!

You can create your own custom color theme or font theme by clicking Colors or Fonts and clicking Create New Theme Colors/Create New Theme Fonts. In the dialog box that appears, select the desired colors or font, type a name for the custom color or font theme, and click Save. You can then apply the custom color or font theme just as you would a built-in one.

SAVE
your own theme

If you opt to apply formatting to your slides manually, or if you customize an existing theme, you can save your formatting choices as a new theme. Doing so enables you to apply the same formatting settings to other presentations in the same way you would apply any other theme.

If you like, you can make the theme you save — or any other theme, for that matter — the default theme. PowerPoint then automatically applies that theme to any new presentations you create. To make

a theme the default theme, click the Design tab, click the arrow button, right-click the theme you want to set as the default, and choose Set as Default Theme.

In addition to saving themes you create for reuse, you can save presentations you create as templates on which subsequent presentations can be based. The template file includes both the presentation design (that is, the theme) and content, such as bulleted lists.

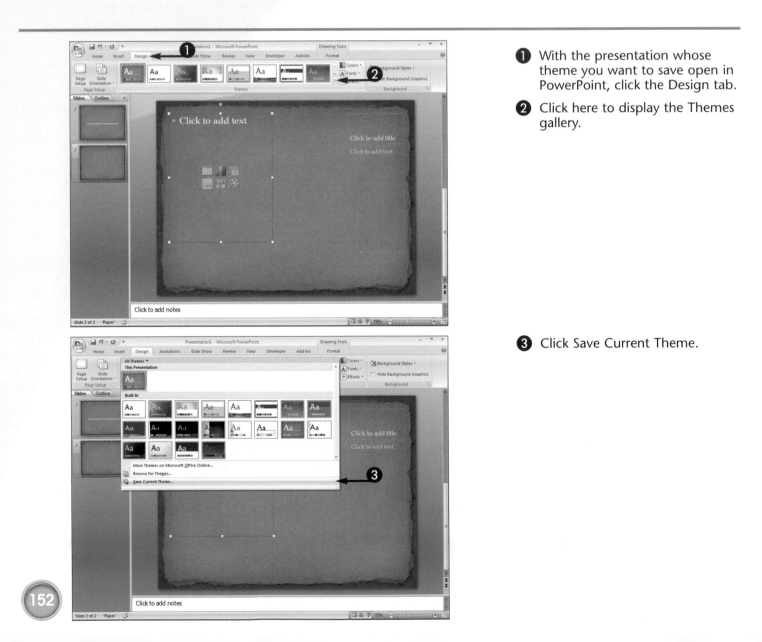

❶ With the presentation whose theme you want to save open in PowerPoint, click the Design tab.

❷ Click here to display the Themes gallery.

❸ Click Save Current Theme.

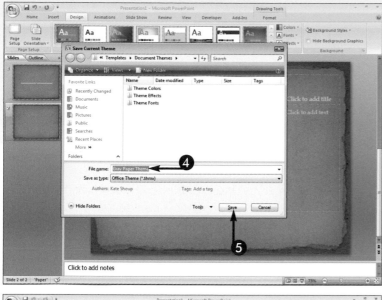

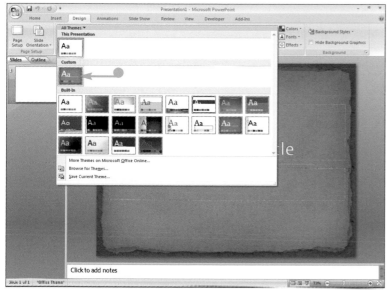

The Save Current Theme dialog box appears.

④ Type a filename.

Note: Do not change the folder in which the theme is saved. Using the default location ensures that the custom theme will appear in the Themes gallery.

⑤ Click Save.

● PowerPoint adds the theme to the gallery in a special section labeled Custom.

TIPS

Try This!
In addition to saving themes you create, you can also save a presentation as a template. To save a presentation as a template, click the Office button, click Save As, type a name for the template, click the Save As File Type drop-down arrow, choose PowerPoint Template, and click Save.

More Options!
If none of PowerPoint's themes suits your needs, and you do not want to take the time to create and save a new theme, you can obtain additional themes online. To do so, click the Design tab, click the More arrow button, and choose More Themes on Microsoft Office Online.

ADD A PICTURE
to your presentation

Adding graphic elements, such as clip art (as outlined here) or your own personal photos or other images (for example, a company logo), to your slides can enhance the slide's appearance. Graphic elements can be placed anywhere on your slide, inside or outside placeholders.

After you insert a picture into your slide, you can move and resize it as needed. To move a picture, click it in the slide, rest your mouse pointer over the box surrounding it, click, and drag it to the desired location. Resize a picture by clicking it, and then

clicking and dragging any of the resizing handles that appear inward or outward. You can also rotate and flip pictures. To do so, click the object to select it, click the Format tab, click Rotate, and select the desired option.

To otherwise edit a picture — for example, change the image's brightness, contrast, or color tone; crop it; apply a picture style; add a border; and so on — click the picture to select it, click the Format tab, and use any of the various tools that appear.

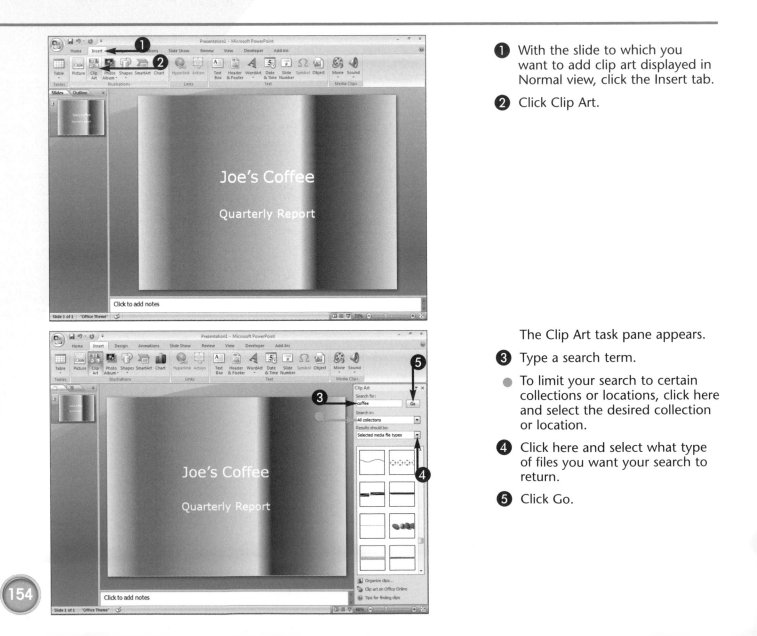

① With the slide to which you want to add clip art displayed in Normal view, click the Insert tab.

② Click Clip Art.

The Clip Art task pane appears.

③ Type a search term.

● To limit your search to certain collections or locations, click here and select the desired collection or location.

④ Click here and select what type of files you want your search to return.

⑤ Click Go.

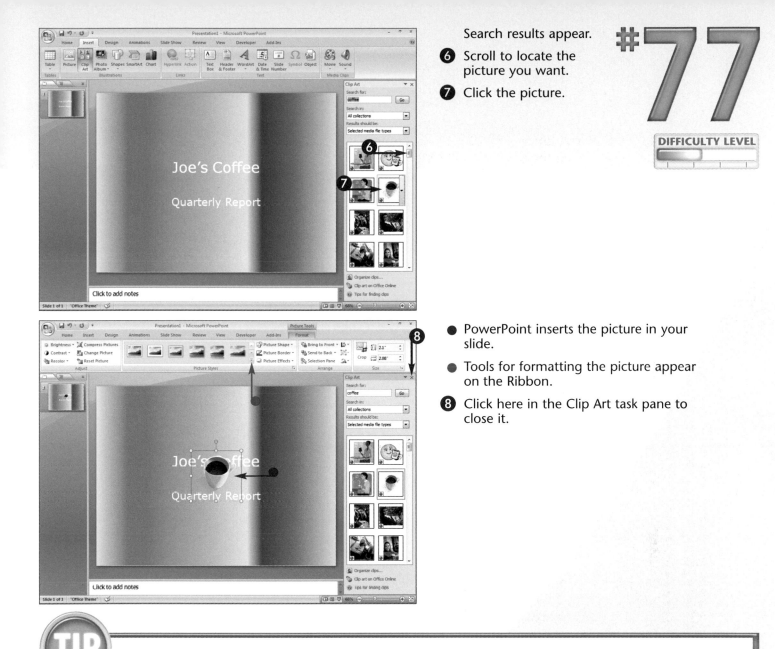

Search results appear.

6 Scroll to locate the picture you want.

7 Click the picture.

● PowerPoint inserts the picture in your slide.

● Tools for formatting the picture appear on the Ribbon.

8 Click here in the Clip Art task pane to close it.

TIP

More Options!

In addition to inserting clip art, you can insert images stored on your own computer. Here's how:

1 With the slide to which you want to add a photo displayed in Normal view, click the Insert tab.

2 Click Picture.

The Insert Picture dialog box appears.

3 Locate and select the folder in which your image is stored.

4 Click the image you want to insert.

5 Click Insert.

The image appears on your slide.

Insert a
SMARTART GRAPHIC

You can insert a new SmartArt graphic or diagram to illustrate a process, hierarchy, cycle, or relationship. For example, a diagram can show the workflow in a procedure or the hierarchy in an organization, as illustrated in this section. Using SmartArt graphics, you can create designer-quality graphics that beautifully convey your message with a few clicks of the mouse. PowerPoint offers dozens of SmartArt graphic layouts. Simply insert the graphic you want to use and add any necessary text.

When you insert a SmartArt graphic into your presentation, it has the same visual characteristics (that is, the color, style, and so on) of other content in the presentation. You can, however, change the style or color of the SmartArt graphic, or add effects such as glows or 3-D effects. You can even animate your SmartArt graphic. To remove any formatting changes you make to a SmartArt graphic, click the Design tab and click Reset Graphic.

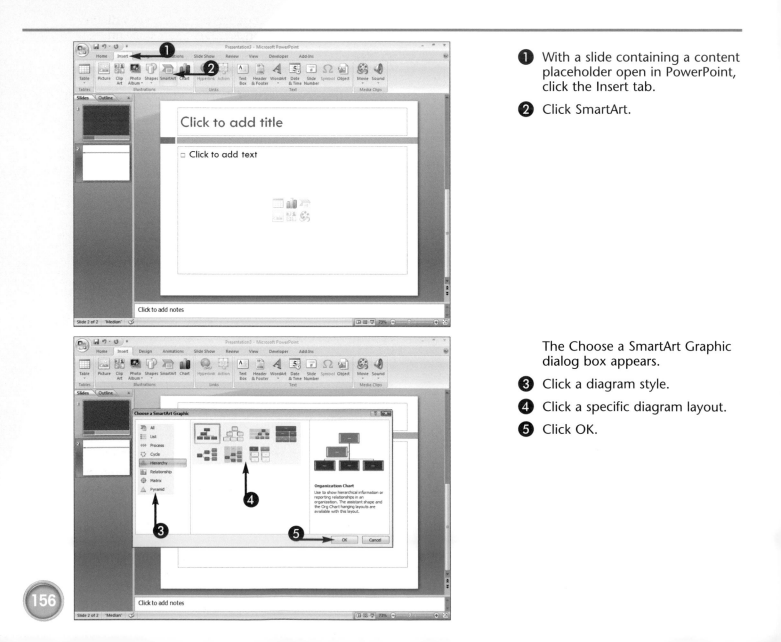

① With a slide containing a content placeholder open in PowerPoint, click the Insert tab.

② Click SmartArt.

The Choose a SmartArt Graphic dialog box appears.

③ Click a diagram style.

④ Click a specific diagram layout.

⑤ Click OK.

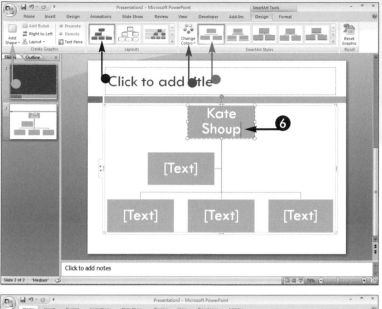

The dialog box closes and the diagram appears on the slide, ready for editing.

6 Click in a shape in the diagram and type the desired text.

● To add more shapes to the diagram, click the shape to which the new shape should be related, click the bottom half of Add Shape, and select where the new shape should appear.

● Click an option in the Layouts group to change the layout of the SmartArt graphic.

● Click Change Colors to choose a different set of colors for the SmartArt diagram.

● Choose a new style for the SmartArt graphic from the SmartArt Styles group.

7 Repeat step **6** for the remaining diagram elements.

8 Click outside the diagram to finish creating your diagram.

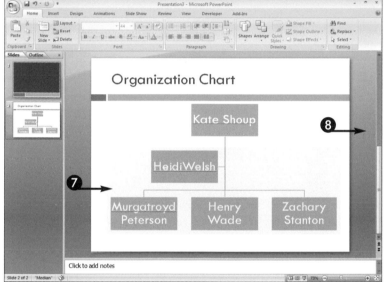

TIPS

Did You Know?

PowerPoint automatically resizes the text you type to fit the diagram. The more text you type, the smaller it will be.

Try This!

If your slide already contains the text you want to appear in your SmartArt graphic, you can convert it. To do so, click in the placeholder that contains the text you want to convert to a SmartArt graphic. Then click the Home tab and, in the Paragraph group, click Convert to SmartArt Graphic. (Alternatively, right-click the placeholder that contains the text you want to convert and choose Convert to SmartArt.) A gallery of SmartArt graphic layouts appears; click the one you want to use.

ADD VIDEO OR SOUND
to your presentation

To enhance your presentation, you can add movie clips to it. For example, if you have composed a presentation for an alumni association meeting, you might include a clip showing the campus. You can set up PowerPoint to play back your movie automatically; alternatively, you can choose to play it manually by clicking it. Supported movie file formats include AVI (Audio Video Interleave), MPEG (Moving Picture Experts Group), and WMV (Windows Media Video).

Movie files are always linked to, rather than embedded in, PowerPoint presentations to reduce the

size of the presentation file. For this reason, it is wise to first copy the movie file into the same folder in which your PowerPoint presentation is stored; this ensures that your presentation can locate the file when necessary.

You can also insert sound clips into your presentation. When you do, PowerPoint adds a small speaker icon to the selected slide. (If this icon clashes with your slide design, and if you have set up the sound to play automatically, you can hide the speaker icon by clicking it, clicking the Options tab, and selecting the Hide During Show check box.)

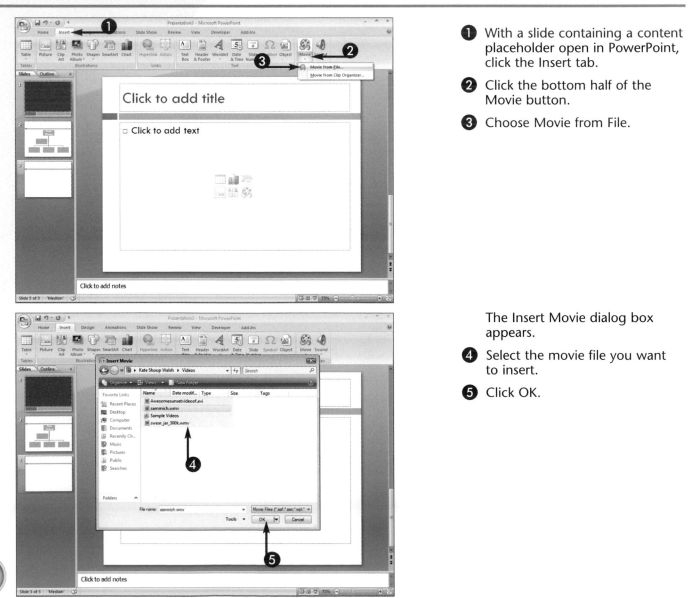

① With a slide containing a content placeholder open in PowerPoint, click the Insert tab.

② Click the bottom half of the Movie button.

③ Choose Movie from File.

The Insert Movie dialog box appears.

④ Select the movie file you want to insert.

⑤ Click OK.

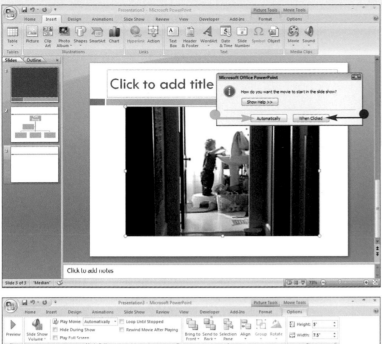

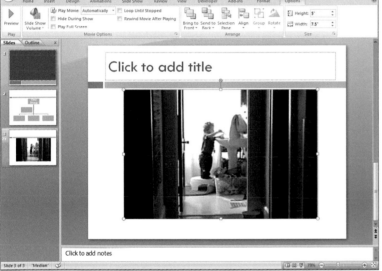

#79

DIFFICULTY LEVEL

A dialog box appears asking how you want to start the media clip when you run a show.

● Click Automatically to play the media clip when the slide appears.

● Click When Clicked to play the sound when you click an icon that appears on the slide.

The clip, or an icon for the clip, appears on the slide.

Note: *Click Preview on the contextual Ribbon tab that appears to preview the clip.*

TIPS

More Options!

To add sound, open a slide containing a content placeholder, click the Insert tab, click the bottom half of the Sound button, and choose from the menu that appears. After you select a sound, specify whether it plays automatically or when clicked.

More Options!

If you want to look for media clips to insert, rather than inserting a clip of your own, click the bottom half of Movie in the Insert tab and choose Movie from Clip Organizer. The Clip Art task pane opens; type a keyword describing the type of clip you want to find and click Go. To preview a clip, place your mouse over it, click the down arrow that appears, and choose Preview/Properties.

ANIMATE
your slides

By default, items you add to your slides remain static. To add interest, you can animate the items on PowerPoint slides — that is, apply motion to the text or objects in your slide, such as images, bulleted lists, and the like. For example, you might animate a table on your slide to slide in from the top of the screen.

The Ribbon's Animations tab contains options for setting up and working with animations in your presentation. You simply select the item in your presentation you want to animate, and then choose

the desired animation effect from the tab. PowerPoint previews the animation for you right after you apply it. Another option is to create a custom animation, as outlined here.

Be warned: You should avoid overusing animations. Otherwise, your presentation may seem too busy. Excessive use of animations can overshadow the message of your presentation. By using animations sparingly, you ensure they serve as effective attention grabbers rather than distractions.

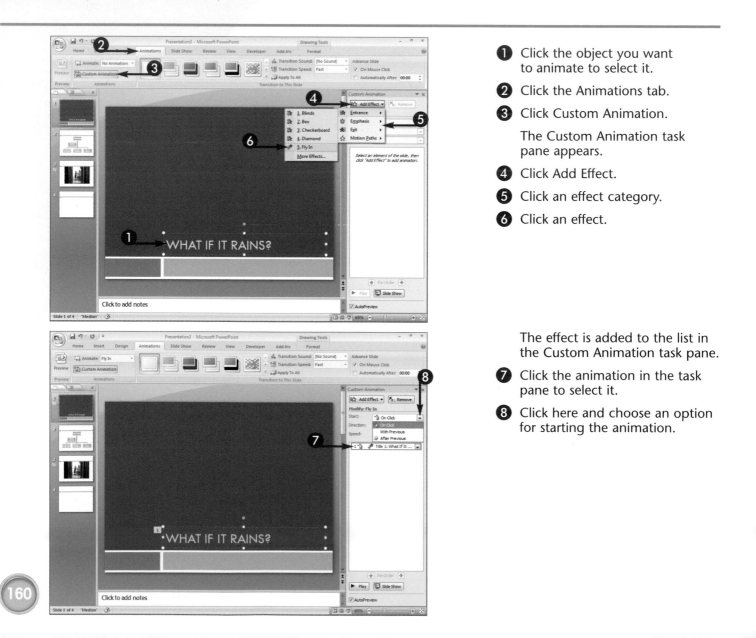

❶ Click the object you want to animate to select it.

❷ Click the Animations tab.

❸ Click Custom Animation.

The Custom Animation task pane appears.

❹ Click Add Effect.

❺ Click an effect category.

❻ Click an effect.

The effect is added to the list in the Custom Animation task pane.

❼ Click the animation in the task pane to select it.

❽ Click here and choose an option for starting the animation.

#80

DIFFICULTY LEVEL

⑨ Click here and choose a direction or path option.

⑩ Click here and choose a speed option. PowerPoint applies your settings.

● To preview your settings, click Play.

TIPS

Try This!
You can apply multiple animations to an object. If you do, you can then specify the order in which the animations should occur. To change the order, click an animation you want to move in the Custom Animation task pane and then click the up and down arrow buttons along the bottom of the pane to move it up or down, respectively.

Did You Know?
If you select a complex object — for example, a SmartArt diagram — you can apply animation to each of its individual parts. Simply select the part and apply the animation as normal.

Try This!
To change an animation you have applied, click it in the Custom Animation task pane, click Change, and choose the desired options.

Create a
PHOTO ALBUM PRESENTATION

Some presentations — for example, presentations that illustrate a process — should rely more on pictures than on text, tables, and graphs. If yours is one such presentation, consider using PowerPoint's Photo Album feature to set it up.

Using Photo Album, you can select the photos you want to include in your presentation and specify the order in which they should appear, as well as select a layout. Your choices include displaying one, two, or four pictures per slide. You can improve the appearance of your slideshow by choosing a frame shape for your photos and applying a theme.

If you think you need more than just photos to communicate your message, you can add picture captions. They can serve as descriptive or humorous labels. Alternatively, they might convey important information about the photos, such as the step or operation a photo depicts. For more extensive textual information, you can insert a text box; text boxes can also be used to insert a blank space in the slide — useful if you want to move the next photo in the album from one slide to the next.

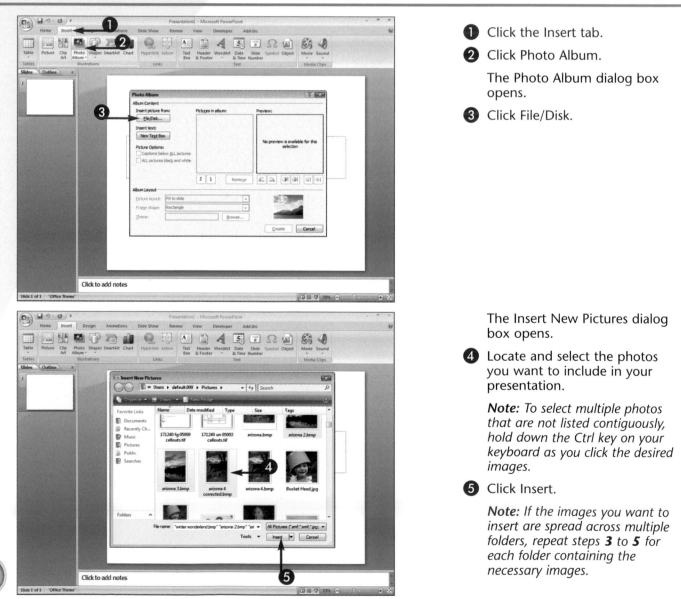

① Click the Insert tab.

② Click Photo Album.

The Photo Album dialog box opens.

③ Click File/Disk.

The Insert New Pictures dialog box opens.

④ Locate and select the photos you want to include in your presentation.

Note: To select multiple photos that are not listed contiguously, hold down the Ctrl key on your keyboard as you click the desired images.

⑤ Click Insert.

Note: If the images you want to insert are spread across multiple folders, repeat steps 3 to 5 for each folder containing the necessary images.

162

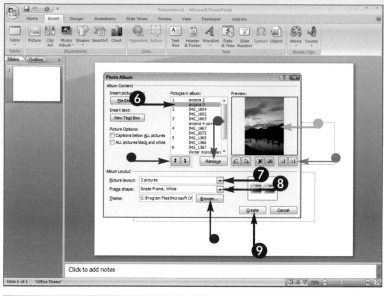

PowerPoint lists the images you selected.

6 Click an image in the list.

● A preview of the image appears.

● To change the order in which the selected image is listed, click here to move it up or down in the list, respectively.

● To remove the selected image, click Remove.

● Click on these buttons to adjust the appearance of the image.

7 Click here and select how many images should appear on each slide.

8 Click here and select a frame shape.

● To apply a theme, click Browse and select a theme from the dialog box that appears.

9 Click Create.

PowerPoint creates the photo album presentation.

TIPS

More Options!
You can edit a photo album presentation via the Edit Photo Album dialog box, which is identical to the Photo Album dialog box. To open it, click the bottom half of Photo Album and choose Edit Photo Album.

Try This!
To add captions to your photo album presentation, select the Captions below ALL pictures check box in the Photo Album dialog box. PowerPoint adds caption placeholders to the presentation slides; simply click a placeholder and type the desired text. To add a text box, click New Text Box in the Photo Album dialog box. PowerPoint inserts a text box placeholder after whatever image is currently selected in the Pictures in album list.

Make Your Data Work for You with Access

Microsoft Access 2007 is a program for creating databases to store business or personal information. You can use Access to create, retrieve, and manage large or small collections of information. To make it easier for you to create databases, Access provides several built-in templates, as well as additional templates online.

In Access, data is stored in tables. Each individual entry in a table is called a record. For example, in a Customers table, the information about each customer is a separate record. Each record is composed of one or more fields, which contain individual pieces of data. For example, a customer field might include a name, address, city, state, or ZIP code.

By default, tables appear as spreadsheet grids called datasheets, similar to the worksheets found in Excel. You can type directly into a datasheet. To make data entry more convenient, however, some people prefer to use forms, which are like dialog boxes that prompt for field entries. You can also import data from other programs such as Excel and Outlook.

You can filter the tables in a database to display only certain records, only certain fields, or both. You can run a one-time filter or you can create a query, which is like a saved filter. Tables and query results appear in plain datasheets, which are not very attractive when printed. In contrast, a report presents data from tables and queries in an attractive, customizable format.

Top 100

Save time with
TEMPLATES

To expedite the database-creation process, Access provides several built-in database templates. A *template* is a ready-to-use database that contains all the necessary components — tables, forms, reports, queries, macros, and relationships — to track a specific type of data. You can use a template database as is or customize it as needed.

You can also use templates available on Office Online. To download an Office Online template, click a template category under From Microsoft Office Online in the Getting Started with Microsoft Office Online screen, click the desired template from the list that

appears, and click Download on the right side of the screen.

In addition to creating databases with templates, you can create tables within a database by using a template. Each Access table template contains a pre-created set of fields, so you do not have to create fields manually. Templates work well when you need a standard table with common fields. To create a table from a template, click the Create tab in the Ribbon, click Table Templates, and choose from the list of table templates that appears.

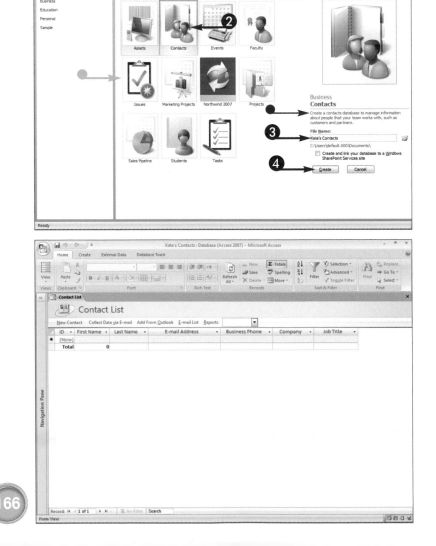

❶ In the Getting Started with Microsoft Access screen, click Local Templates.

Note: To display the Getting Started with Microsoft Access screen, click the Office button and click New.

● A list of templates available from within Access appears.

❷ Click the template you want to use.

● Information about the selected template appears here.

❸ Type a descriptive name for the new template.

❹ Click Create.

Access creates a new database based on the template you chose.

Import data from
EXCEL

DIFFICULTY LEVEL

Suppose you have an Excel worksheet that contains data you want to include in an Access database. You can import the worksheet right into Access, creating a new table. This table becomes part of the Access database; it does not retain any ties to Excel. (Note that in addition to importing the spreadsheet in its entirety, you can also import portions of it.)

For Excel data to import correctly into Access, it must be set up to mimic a datasheet in Access. Specifically, field names should appear in row 1;

each record should be on its own row; and no formulas or functions should be included.

You use the Import Spreadsheet Wizard to import Excel data into Access. When you do, the wizard asks you various configuration-related questions, such as whether fields in the table you are creating should be indexed and whether duplicates are okay. It also gives you the option to name the table.

① Click the External Data tab.

② In the Import group, click Excel.

   The Get External Data – Excel Spreadsheet dialog box opens.

③ Type the name and path (that is, the location) of the workbook that contains the worksheet you want to import in the File name box.

● If you are not sure of the path, click Browse to browse for the file.

④ Click Import the source data into a new table in the current database (◎ changes to ◉).

⑤ Click OK.

   The Import Spreadsheet Wizard starts.

⑥ Click Show Worksheets (◎ changes to ◉).

⑦ Click the worksheet you want to import.

● To select a range of data in the worksheet rather than an entire worksheet, click Show Named Ranges (◎ changes to ◉), and then select the named range in the list that appears.

   A preview of the worksheet (or named range) appears.

⑧ Click Next.

Import data from
EXCEL

As you step through the Import Spreadsheet Wizard, you are given the option to set a primary key. A *primary key* is a field or set of fields in a table that contains a unique identifier for every record. For example, if your table contains customer information, the primary key would likely be the field that contains a unique ID number for each customer. If none of the fields in your imported data contain information that is unique, then you can prompt the Import Spreadsheet Wizard to create a primary key

for you; when you do, a new field is added that contains a unique number for each record.

If the data you are importing will be regularly updated in Excel, it might be wise to link your Access database to the Excel worksheet rather than importing the spreadsheet into the database. That way, each time you open the linked worksheet in Access, it will contain the most recent data. To link a worksheet to an Access database, you use the Link Spreadsheet Wizard.

⑨ If the first row of the imported worksheet contains column headings, select First Row Contains Column Headings (☐ changes to ☑).

⑩ Click Next.

⑪ Click a field.

⑫ To change the name of the selected field, type a new name here.

⑬ To change a field's data type, click here and select a different data type from the list that appears.

⑭ To change the selected field's index settings, click here and choose the desired setting from the list that appears.

● To omit a field, click here.

Repeat steps **11** to **14** for any other fields you want to change.

⑮ Click Next.

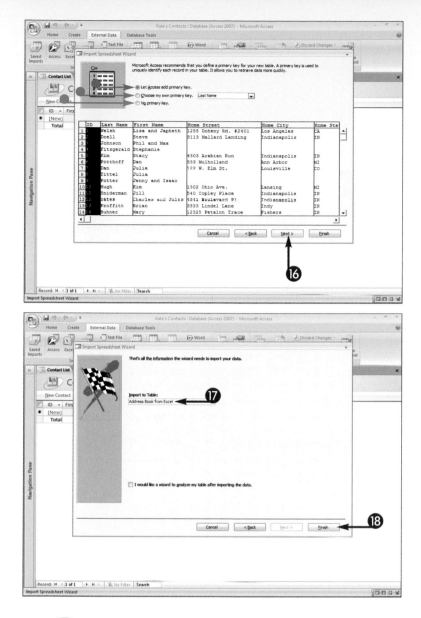

● Click here if the information you imported does not contain a field that would work well as a primary key.

● To choose a primary key from the fields in the imported worksheet, click here, and then select the desired field from the list that appears.

● To omit a primary key, click here.

⑯ Click Next.

⑰ Type a name for the table.

Note: The default name is the name of the tab from the worksheet.

⑱ Click Finish.

Excel prompts you to complete the import process.

⑲ Click Close.

The Excel worksheet is imported as a new table.

#83 CONTINUED

TIPS

More Options!

To link an Excel worksheet to your Access database rather than import it, use the Link Spreadsheet Wizard. To launch the wizard, choose the worksheet to which you want to link and then click Link to the Data Source by Creating a Linked Table in the Get External Data – Excel dialog box and follow the onscreen prompts.

Did You Know?

You can prompt Access to analyze your imported data by selecting the I would like a wizard to analyze my table after importing the data check box in the final screen of the Import Spreadsheet Wizard. When you click Finish, Access launches the necessary wizard to analyze your table.

COLLECT DATA
with Outlook

Suppose you want to conduct an e-mail survey and track the results using an Access database. In that case, you can create a data-entry form that can be e-mailed to others via Outlook 2007. When a recipient of your survey completes the data-entry form and returns it to you via e-mail, you can assimilate the data he or she has shared into your Access database the instant the message lands in your inbox. You create and distribute the data-entry form using the Collect data through e-mail messages Wizard. Note that the recipient of your e-mail need

not use Outlook in order to complete the data-entry form the e-mail contains; any e-mail program will do.

You have two options with regard to what types of forms to include in your e-mail message: HTML or InfoPath. If you are not certain whether all the recipients of your message have the necessary software to view and interact with InfoPath forms, opt for HTML.

Using Outlook as a data-collection tool also works well for gathering and tracking status reports and organizing an event.

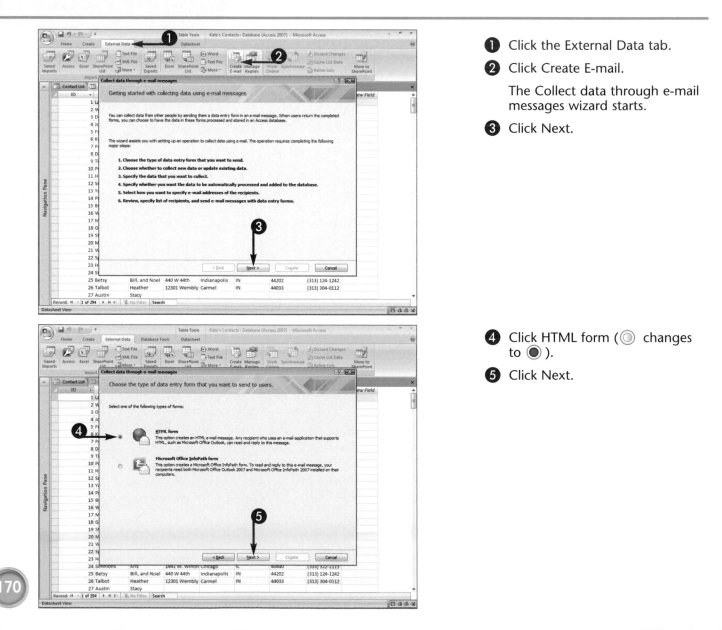

① Click the External Data tab.

② Click Create E-mail.

   The Collect data through e-mail messages wizard starts.

③ Click Next.

④ Click HTML form (◯ changes to ◉).

⑤ Click Next.

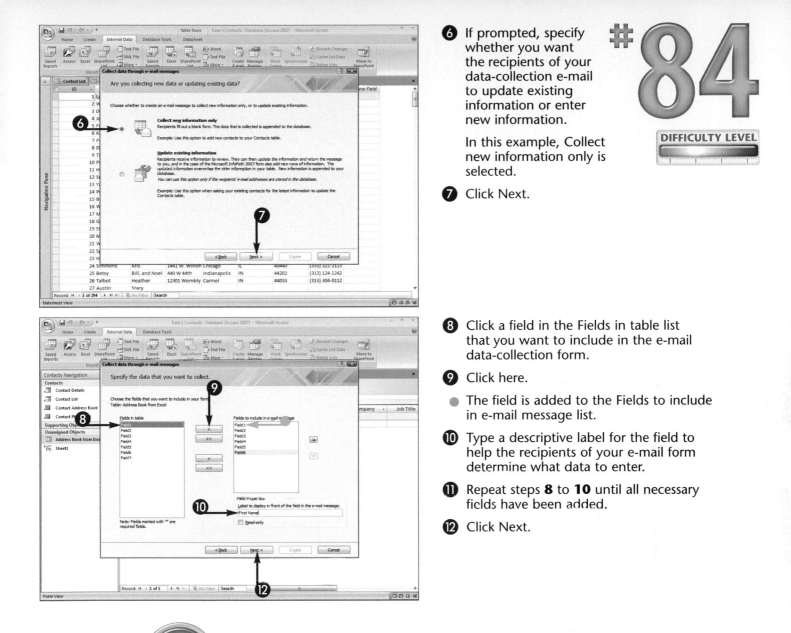

⑥ If prompted, specify whether you want the recipients of your data-collection e-mail to update existing information or enter new information.

In this example, Collect new information only is selected.

⑦ Click Next.

⑧ Click a field in the Fields in table list that you want to include in the e-mail data-collection form.

⑨ Click here.

● The field is added to the Fields to include in e-mail message list.

⑩ Type a descriptive label for the field to help the recipients of your e-mail form determine what data to enter.

⑪ Repeat steps **8** to **10** until all necessary fields have been added.

⑫ Click Next.

More Options!

If you know that all the recipients of your e-mail form have the necessary software to handle InfoPath forms (for example, if you are polling users in your company only, and your IT department has assured you that their computers have been configured to handle InfoPath forms), then you might prefer to use that type of e-mail form over HTML. InfoPath forms are generally easier to use, and provide a better data-entry and editing environment. In addition, InfoPath forms can be configured to validate the data submitted by the user when he or she clicks Send. If any of the entered data is deemed invalid, InfoPath enables the user to correct his or her responses before submitting the form.

COLLECT DATA
with Outlook

As you step through the Collect data through e-mail messages wizard, you are asked a series of questions. One is whether you want Access to automatically process replies to your e-mail when they arrive in your inbox and add the data those replies contain to your database. (Note that if you opt to process the data manually, you are not relegating yourself to tedious data entry; you simply launch the export operation that automatically transfers the collected data to your table by hand.)

You can also specify whether you want to enter the addresses of your recipients from within Outlook, or to use the addresses as they appear in your Access database. (Note that if you choose the latter, you will be asked to indicate the table and field from which you want to draw the e-mail addresses.) When prompted, you can type a subject for the form e-mail, as well as any message text you want the e-mail to contain.

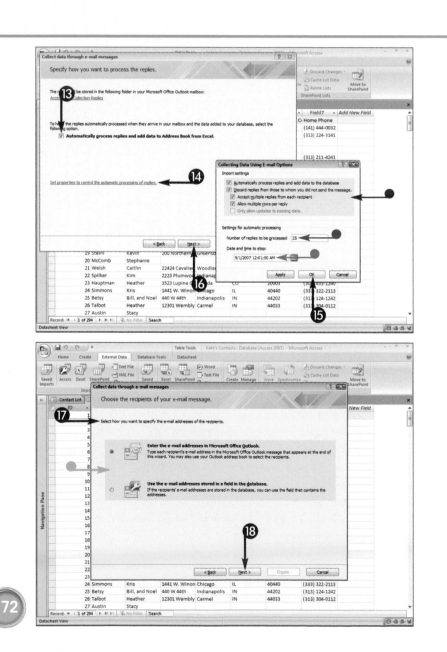

⑬ If you want Access and Outlook to automatically process replies to your e-mail, adding the data those replies contain to your Access database, click here.

⑭ To configure how Access and Outlook handle automatic processing of replies, click here.

  The Collecting Data Using E-mail Options dialog box opens.

● Change import settings here.

● Indicate the number of replies you want to have processed.

● Specify a stop date and time.

⑮ Click OK.

⑯ Click Next.

⑰ Indicate how you want to enter the recipients' e-mail addresses.

● You can choose to enter the e-mail addresses by using Outlook, or by using a field in the database.

⑱ Click Next.

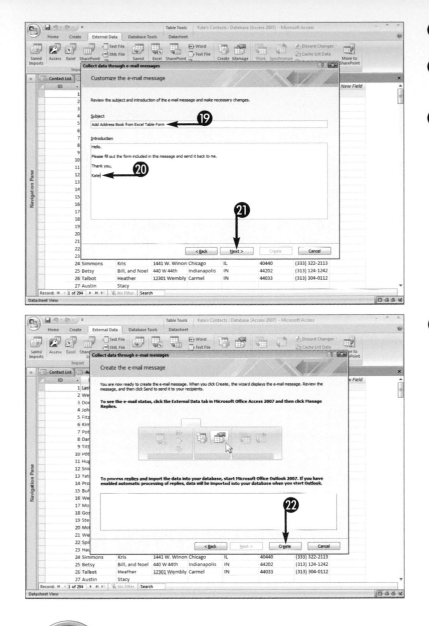

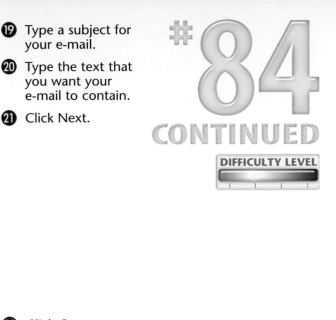

⑲ Type a subject for your e-mail.

⑳ Type the text that you want your e-mail to contain.

㉑ Click Next.

㉒ Click Create.

Access creates the e-mail form and launches an Outlook New Message window.

DIFFICULTY LEVEL

TIPS

Attention!

When someone receives your e-mail message containing a data-collection form, he or she can click Reply, respond to the prompts in the form, and then click Send. Depending on how you set up your form, either Outlook and Access will work together to automatically update your database with the submitted information, or you can manually launch an export operation from within Outlook to assimilate the data into your database. To do so, right-click the reply in your inbox that you want to process and click Export Data to Microsoft Office Access. Review the reply in the dialog box that opens and click OK.

Try This!

To resend a data-collection e-mail message, open the database containing the original message, click the External Data tab, and click Manage Replies in the Collect Data group. The Manage Data Collection Messages dialog box opens; click the message you want to resend, click Resend This E-mail Message, and follow the onscreen prompts.

IMPORT CONTACTS
from Outlook

If you are building a database of contacts, you can import any contacts you have already entered into Outlook 2007 from within Access. Doing so saves you the trouble of entering the contact information by hand — a real timesaver.

Before you add contacts from Outlook, you must have Outlook open and running on your PC before launching the import operation.

During the import process, you may see a dialog box informing you that a program is trying to access e-mail addresses you have stored in Outlook. Select the Allow Access For check box and type a value such as 5 in the corresponding field to instruct Outlook to allow access for five minutes. This will give you enough time to import the necessary contacts.

DIFFICULTY LEVEL

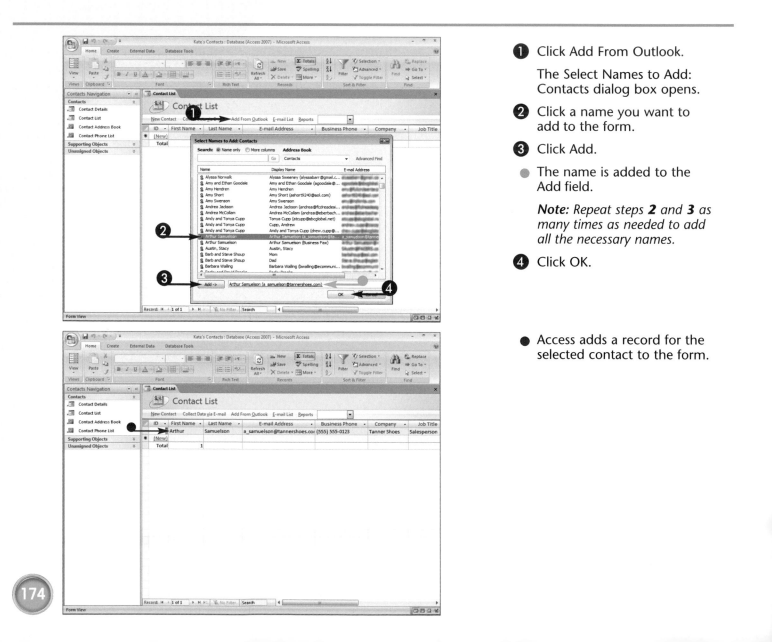

① Click Add From Outlook.

The Select Names to Add: Contacts dialog box opens.

② Click a name you want to add to the form.

③ Click Add.

● The name is added to the Add field.

Note: Repeat steps 2 and 3 as many times as needed to add all the necessary names.

④ Click OK.

● Access adds a record for the selected contact to the form.

TYPE LESS
with default values

#86

DIFFICULTY LEVEL

Suppose you are creating a form to record customers' contact information. If your business is limited to a certain state, you might make that state the default value in the State field. In this way, you can speed up data entry.

You can set default values for fields that use the following data types: Text, Memo, Number, Date/Time, Currency, Yes/No, and Hyperlink. If you do not set a default value, the field will remain blank until a value is entered.

Note that in order to set a default value, you must open the table containing the field for which you want to set the value in Design view. To do so, right-click the table in the Navigation pane and choose Design View from the menu that appears. Alternatively, if the table is already open in another view, right-click the table's tab and choose Design View.

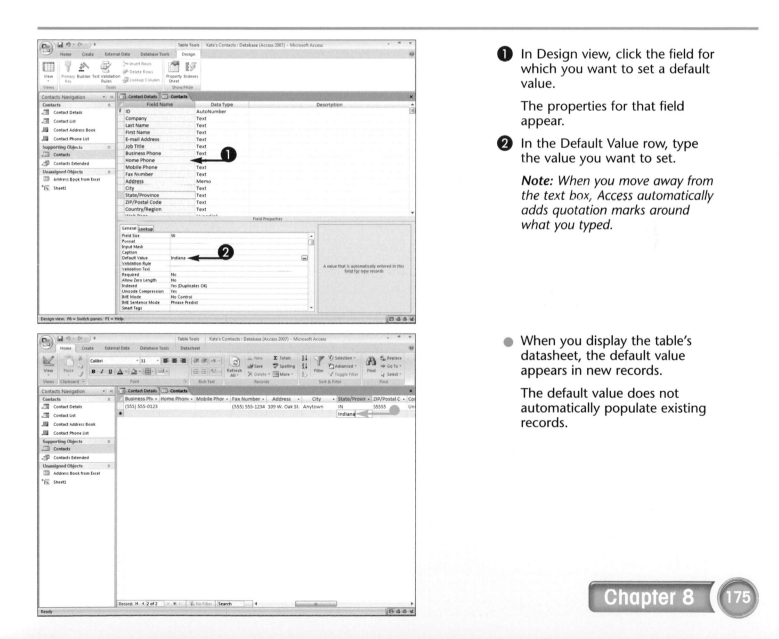

1 In Design view, click the field for which you want to set a default value.

The properties for that field appear.

2 In the Default Value row, type the value you want to set.

Note: When you move away from the text box, Access automatically adds quotation marks around what you typed.

● When you display the table's datasheet, the default value appears in new records.

The default value does not automatically populate existing records.

Make a
FIELD REQUIRED

#87

A primary key field is always required for each record. (As mentioned in an earlier task, a *primary key* is a field or set of fields in a table that contains a unique identifier for every record. For example, if your table contains customer information, the primary key would likely be a field that contains a unique ID number for each customer.)

You are not limited to making the primary key field required, however. You can also make other fields required as well. (Note that doing so does not change the primary key setting.) When a field is

required, Access does not enable users to move past it during data entry until they have entered a value in the field.

In order to set a field as required, you must open the table containing the field in Design view. To do so, right-click the table in the Navigation pane and choose Design View from the menu that appears. Alternatively, if the table is already open in another view, right-click the table's tab and choose Design View.

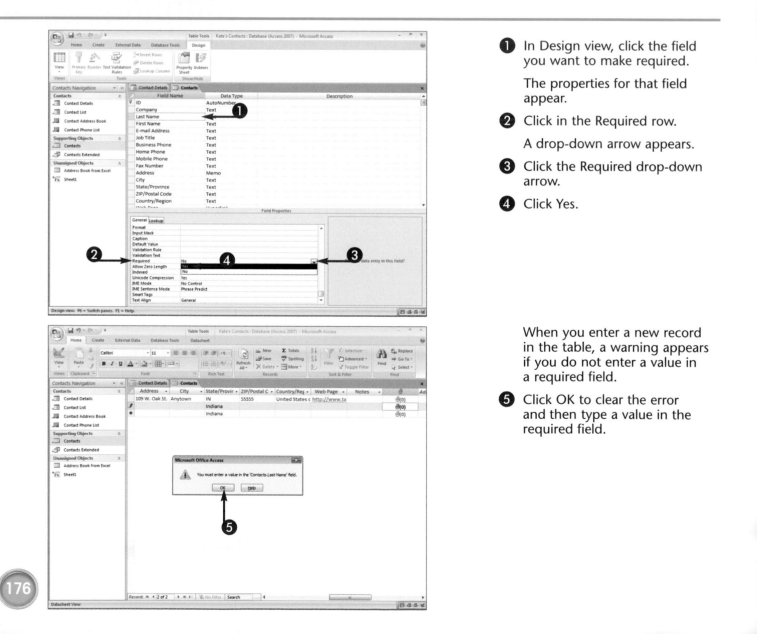

❶ In Design view, click the field you want to make required.

The properties for that field appear.

❷ Click in the Required row.

A drop-down arrow appears.

❸ Click the Required drop-down arrow.

❹ Click Yes.

When you enter a new record in the table, a warning appears if you do not enter a value in a required field.

❺ Click OK to clear the error and then type a value in the required field.

Set a
FIELD CAPTION

DIFFICULTY LEVEL

If a field in your table has an ambiguous or grammatically incorrect name, you can apply a caption to the field. For example, you might add the caption "Last Name" (note the space) to the LastName field. Captions appear in datasheet headings and on labels in forms and reports.

To apply a caption to a field, you must open the table containing the field in Design view. To do so,

right-click the table in the Navigation pane and choose Design View from the menu that appears. Alternatively, if the table is already open in another view, right-click the table's tab and choose Design View.

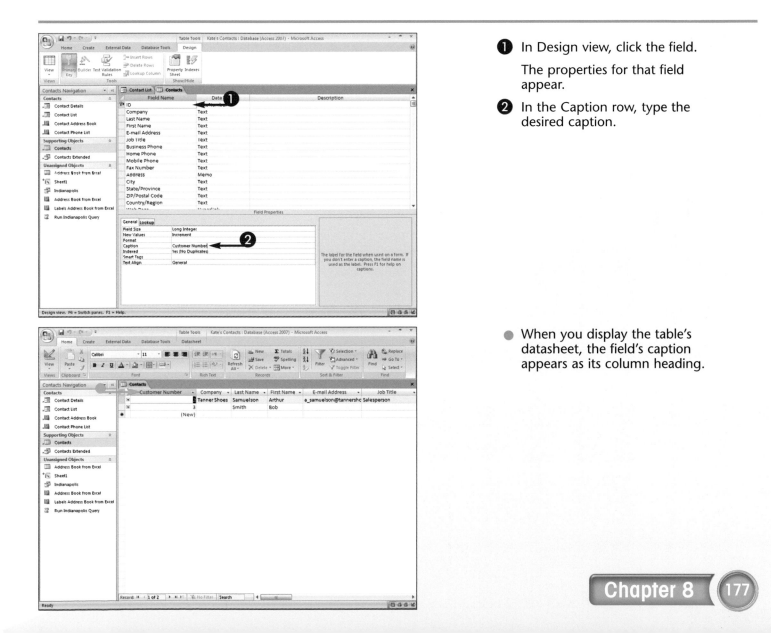

1 In Design view, click the field.

The properties for that field appear.

2 In the Caption row, type the desired caption.

● When you display the table's datasheet, the field's caption appears as its column heading.

Apply
INPUT MASKS

You can apply an input mask to a field to help minimize data-entry errors. Input masks help users enter the proper number and type of characters. They do so by providing a template for entering data in the field. For example, you might implement an input mask to include parentheses for the area code portion of a telephone number.

Access provides several predefined input masks from which you can choose. If none of these predefined input masks quite suits your needs, you can customize an input mask.

To apply an input mask to a field, you must open the table containing the field in Design view. To do so, right-click the table in the Navigation pane and choose Design View from the menu that appears. Alternatively, if the table is already open in another view, right-click the table's tab and choose Design View.

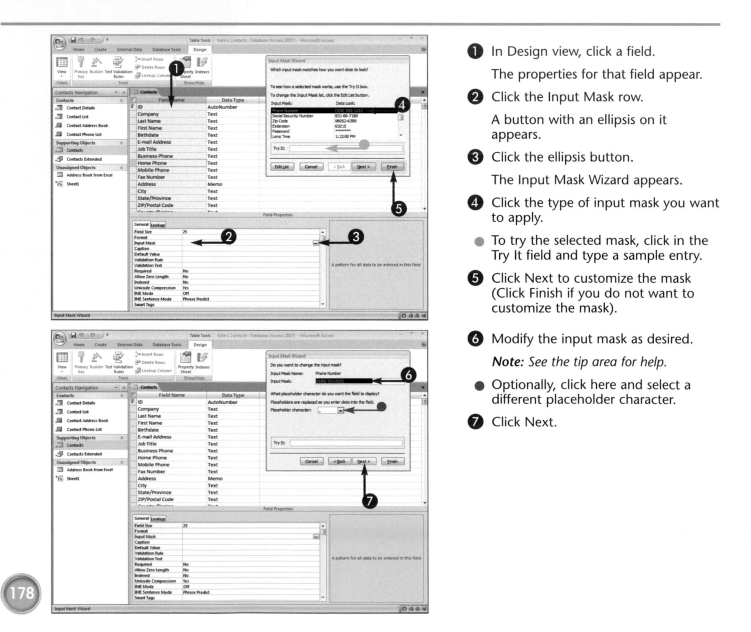

① In Design view, click a field.

The properties for that field appear.

② Click the Input Mask row.

A button with an ellipsis on it appears.

③ Click the ellipsis button.

The Input Mask Wizard appears.

④ Click the type of input mask you want to apply.

● To try the selected mask, click in the Try It field and type a sample entry.

⑤ Click Next to customize the mask (Click Finish if you do not want to customize the mask).

⑥ Modify the input mask as desired.

Note: See the tip area for help.

● Optionally, click here and select a different placeholder character.

⑦ Click Next.

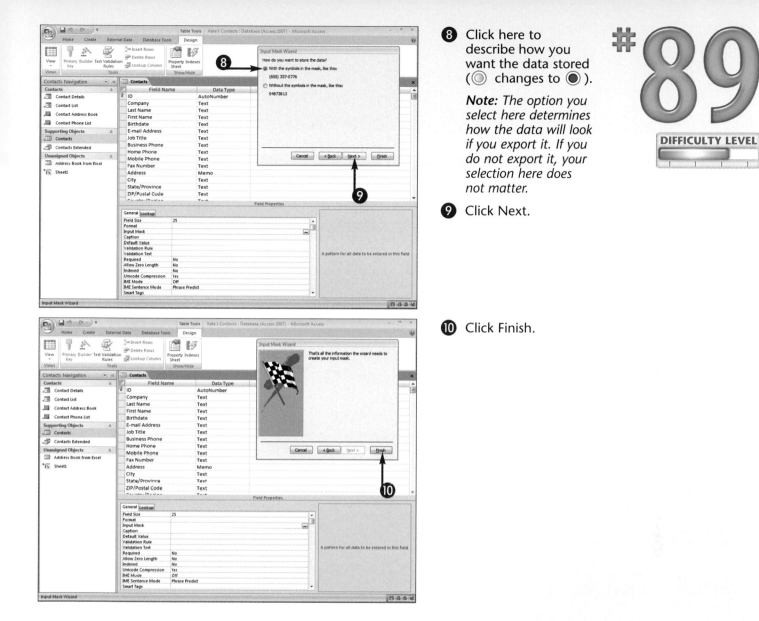

8 Click here to describe how you want the data stored (◉ changes to ●).

Note: The option you select here determines how the data will look if you export it. If you do not export it, your selection here does not matter.

9 Click Next.

10 Click Finish.

TIP

Attention!

Input masks use special characters to represent the types of data they can accept. You use these special characters to customize an input mask. The following table contains the most commonly used characters; for more information, look up "Input Mask Character Reference" in Access Help.

Character	Use
0	Single digit, required
9	Single digit, optional
#	A digit, space, plus sign, or minus sign
L	Single letter, required
?	Single letter, optional
A	Single letter or number, required
a	Single letter or number, optional
&	Any character or a space, required
C	Any character or a space, optional

Set
DATA-VALIDATION RULES

Input masks help users enter the proper number and type of characters, but they cannot restrict the field to certain entries based on logic. That is where data-validation rules come in. You can construct a validation rule that forces field entries to pass a logical test of their validity. For example, you could make sure that negative numbers are not entered into a numeric field. You can also create validation

text, a custom message that appears when the rule is violated.

You create data-validation rules using Expression Builder. It can guide you in determining the correct syntax for an expression. There are many types of expressions available in Expression Builder, including functions, constants, and operators.

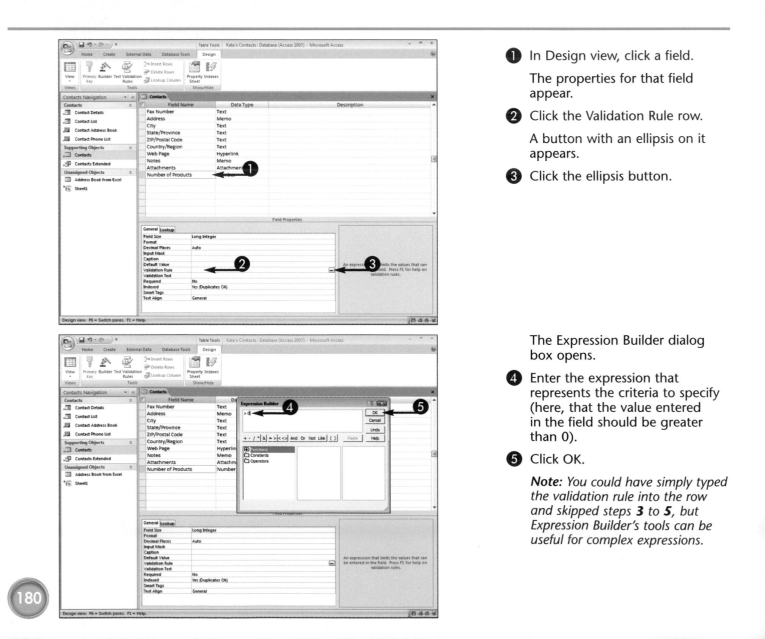

1 In Design view, click a field.

The properties for that field appear.

2 Click the Validation Rule row.

A button with an ellipsis on it appears.

3 Click the ellipsis button.

The Expression Builder dialog box opens.

4 Enter the expression that represents the criteria to specify (here, that the value entered in the field should be greater than 0).

5 Click OK.

Note: You could have simply typed the validation rule into the row and skipped steps 3 to 5, but Expression Builder's tools can be useful for complex expressions.

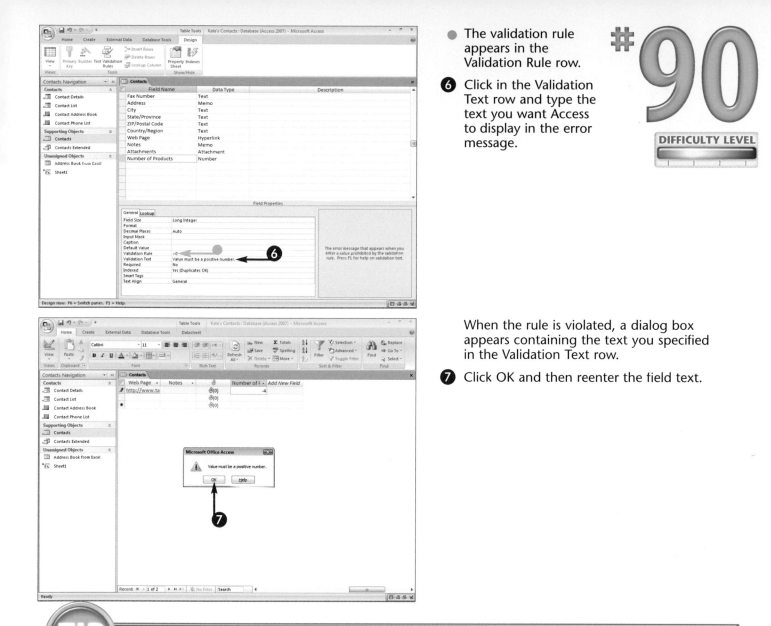

- The validation rule appears in the Validation Rule row.

6 Click in the Validation Text row and type the text you want Access to display in the error message.

When the rule is violated, a dialog box appears containing the text you specified in the Validation Text row.

7 Click OK and then reenter the field text.

TIP

More Options!

You can construct a record-level validation rule to create validation conditions that involve more than one field. For example, in an Employees table, you could make sure that the Hire date is before the Separation date because an employee cannot quit before being hired. To do so, follow these steps:

1 In Design view, click Property Sheet in the Ribbon.

2 The Property Sheet for the entire table appears. Click in the Validation Rule row and enter the desired expression.

3 Click in the Validation Text row and type the error message text.

4 Click Text Validation Rules in the Ribbon and follow the onscreen prompts.

ATTACH FILES
to records

Suppose you are maintaining a database of job candidates, and you want to attach each candidate's resume to her record. You can easily do so using Access. A single record can have multiple attached files of various types.

You can add an attachment to a record only if the table containing the record includes an Attachment field. To insert a field into a table, open the table in Design view, click the field above which the new field should appear, and click Insert Row. Type a name for the new field in the Name column; then click in the

Data Type column, click the drop-down arrow that appears, and choose Attachment.

To add an attachment to a record, the table containing the record must be open in Datasheet view. If it is not in Datasheet view, right-click the table's tab in the Access screen and choose Datasheet View in the menu that appears. Attachment fields are marked by a paperclip. The number in parentheses is the number of attachments the field currently contains.

① In Datasheet view, double-click the Attachment field in the record to which you want to add an attachment.

The Attachments dialog box opens.

② Click Add.

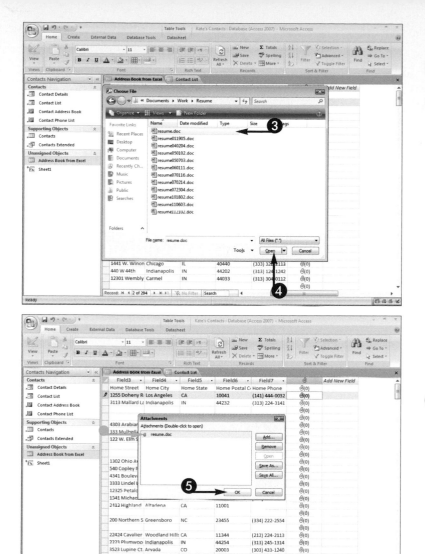

The Choose File dialog box opens.

③ Locate and select the file you want to attach.

④ Click Open.

● The file is added to the list of files in the Attachments dialog box.

You can repeat steps **2** to **4** to attach more files if necessary.

⑤ Click OK.

The file is attached to the record.

More Options!

After you have attached files to a record, you can open those files, save them as separate files outside of Access, or remove them from Access at any time. You do so from within the Attachments dialog box. To open the dialog box, double-click the Attachment field that contains the attachment you want to work with. Then click the attachment in the list and click Open, Save As, or Remove. Click Save All to save all files attached to the record to a new location; when you do, a Save Attachments dialog box appears, enabling you to either choose or create a folder in which to save the attached files.

Insert an
OLE OBJECT

Attaching a file to a database record works well if the file is static. If, however, it is dynamic — that is, it will be changed over time — you should insert the file as an OLE object rather than as an attachment. That way, the version of the file in the Access database will match the original, even if the original is changed in some way.

You can insert an OLE object into a record only if the table containing the record includes an OLE Object field. To insert a field into a table, open the table in

Design view, click the field above which the new field should appear, and click Insert Row. Type a name for the field in the Name column; then click in the Data Type column, click the drop-down arrow that appears, and choose OLE Object.

To insert an OLE object into a record, the table containing the record must be open in Datasheet view. If it is not in Datasheet view, right-click the table's tab in the Access screen and choose Datasheet View in the menu that appears.

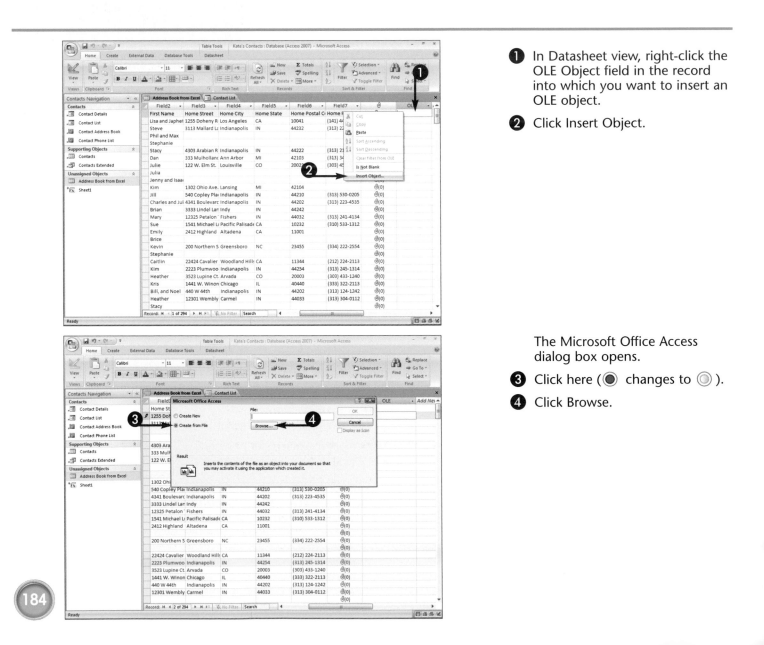

① In Datasheet view, right-click the OLE Object field in the record into which you want to insert an OLE object.

② Click Insert Object.

The Microsoft Office Access dialog box opens.

③ Click here (◉ changes to ◎).

④ Click Browse.

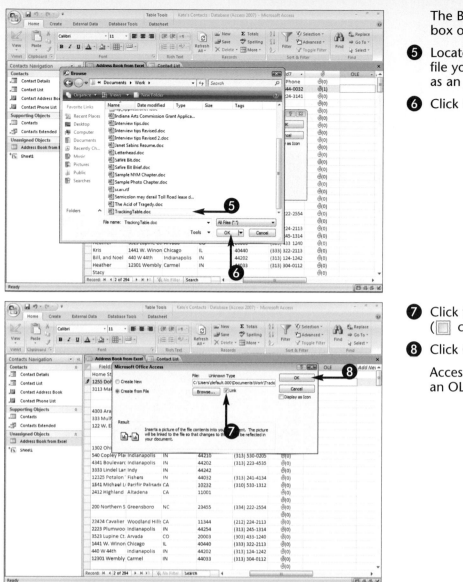

The Browse dialog box opens.

5 Locate and select the file you want to insert as an OLE object.

6 Click OK.

7 Click the Link check box to select it (☐ changes to ☑).

8 Click OK.

Access inserts the file into the record as an OLE object.

TIPS

More Options!

In addition to inserting an existing file into a record as an OLE object, you can also create a new object to insert. To do so, click Create New instead of Create from File, select the type of object you want to create, and click OK.

Try This!

After inserting a file as an OLE object, you can open the file and edit it from within Access. To do so, double-click the field containing the object; the file opens in its native application. Make any necessary edits and simply close the native application's window to save your changes. To remove an OLE object from a record, click the field containing the object, click the Home tab in the Ribbon, and click Delete.

SAVE A FILTER
as a query

DIFFICULTY LEVEL

You can use a filter to show only records that match criteria that you specify. For example, you can filter for records that are blank or nonblank, filter for records containing a specific value in a particular field, filter for multiple values, filter for a particular text string, filter by form, and so on.

If you filter by form, you can save your filter parameters. That way, you can rerun the Filter by Form filter at a later time. When you save a filter, a new query is created in the database. A *query* is something you use to display data from a table in

some modified way. Queries created from filters work just like any other query.

To create a Filter by Form filter, display the table you want to filter, click the Home tab, click Advanced, and click Filter by Form. Then click in the field by which you want to filter, click the drop-down arrow that appears, and choose the desired value. The results will display only those records that have the value you chose in the corresponding field.

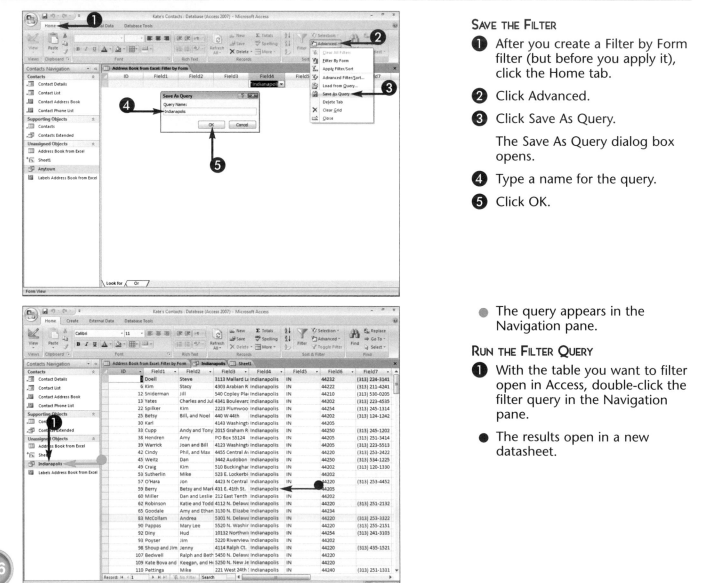

SAVE THE FILTER

1 After you create a Filter by Form filter (but before you apply it), click the Home tab.

2 Click Advanced.

3 Click Save As Query.

The Save As Query dialog box opens.

4 Type a name for the query.

5 Click OK.

● The query appears in the Navigation pane.

RUN THE FILTER QUERY

1 With the table you want to filter open in Access, double-click the filter query in the Navigation pane.

● The results open in a new datasheet.

Display
SUMMARY STATISTICS

#94

One reason people create reports and queries is to extract summary statistics about data, such as the sum or average of the values in certain fields. A new feature in Access 2007 is the ability to display such information directly on the datasheet, without having to create a query or report.

Available statistic types include Sum (this results in a total of the values in the selected column), Average (this averages the values in the selected column), Count (this totals up the number of rows in the selected column that contain a value), Maximum (this reveals the maximum value in the selected column), Minimum (this reveals the minimum value in the selected column), Standard Deviation (this measures how widely values in the selected column are dispersed from an average value), and Variance (this measures the statistical variance of all values in the selected column).

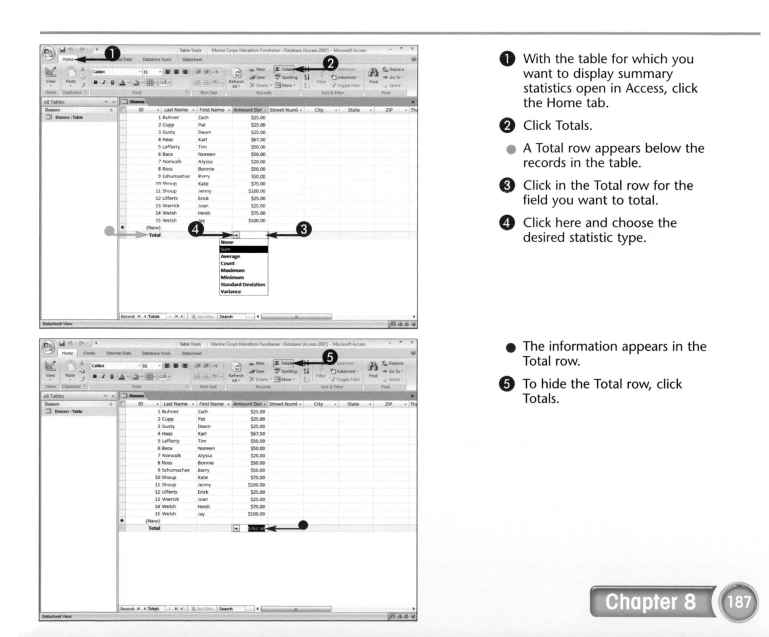

1 With the table for which you want to display summary statistics open in Access, click the Home tab.

2 Click Totals.

● A Total row appears below the records in the table.

3 Click in the Total row for the field you want to total.

4 Click here and choose the desired statistic type.

● The information appears in the Total row.

5 To hide the Total row, click Totals.

View
OBJECT DEPENDENCIES

#95

Access is a relational database. Relational databases are powerful because they can contain multiple related tables — for example, tables that share one or more fields.

In a complex database, relationships are often created among the various objects in the database. Indeed, very rarely would a table or similar object stand alone. Therefore, you should not delete an object until you understand what other objects are affected by that deletion. For example, if you delete a table on which a form is based, the form based on the table will be orphaned.

One way to view an object's dependencies is to use the Relationships window. To open this window, click the Database Tools tab and click Relationships. Another way is to use Access's Object Dependencies feature, which enables you to see all the dependencies of a particular object. (Note that to see all dependencies for all objects at once, you can use the Database Documenter feature, covered in the next task.)

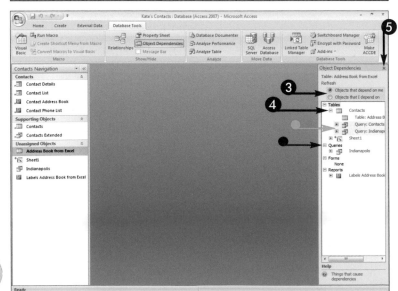

① With the table whose dependencies you want to examine displayed, click the Database Tools tab.

② Click Object Dependencies.

Note: Access may notify you that generating object-dependency information may take a few moments. If so, click OK.

The Object Dependencies task pane opens.

③ Click a type of dependency to view (◯ changes to ◉).

● Any queries, forms, or reports based on the table appear here.

④ Click here to view an object's dependencies.

● If any dependencies have a plus sign next to them, you can click it to expand it, too.

⑤ To close the Object Dependencies task pane, click here.

DOCUMENT
the database

Whereas Access's Object Dependencies feature enables you to view all the dependencies of a particular object, the program's Database Documenter feature allows you to see all dependencies for all objects in a database. Using this feature results in a full report of the database, including details about each object in the database and how it relates to other objects the database contains. Generating such a report might help another database designer understand the structure of your database.

When you run the Database Documenter feature, the feature launches the report it generates in Print Preview mode, enabling you to print out the report with the click of a mouse. Alternatively, you can export the report to an extensible markup language (XML) file or hypertext markup language (HTML) document, or even merge it with Microsoft Word. To export, rather than print, the report, simply click More in the Print Preview tab's Data group and select the desired output from the menu that appears.

❶ With the database you want to document open in Access, click the Database Tools tab.

❷ Click Database Documenter.

The Documenter dialog box opens.

❸ Click the All Object Types tab.

A list of all objects appears.

❹ Mark the check box for each object you want to include (☑ changes to ☐).

● Click here to include the database's properties in the generated report.

● Click here to include a Relationships diagram in the report.

❺ Click OK.

The information appears in a report in Print Preview mode.

❻ To zoom in on the report, click it. Click again to zoom out.

❼ Click Print.

The Print dialog box opens.

❽ Change printing options as needed.

● Click here to choose a different printer.

● Click here to increase the number of copies.

❾ Click OK.

The report prints.

EXPORT A REPORT
to Word

Reports are simply special views of your data, which are designed to be printed. Reports can be created with very basic formatting settings or can involve complex, custom layouts.

Access enables you to generate reports very easily, especially if you use the default settings. To create a report, click the table or query for which you want to generate a report in the Navigation pane, click the Create tab, and click Report.

After you have created the report, you can export it to Word. Doing so enables you to apply Word's full-

featured formatting functionality to the report. To export the report to Word, you launch the Export Wizard, which steps you through the process of converting the report to a Word document.

In addition to exporting reports to Word, you can also export other types of Access objects, such as tables and queries. As with reports, you launch the export operation from within Print Preview mode.

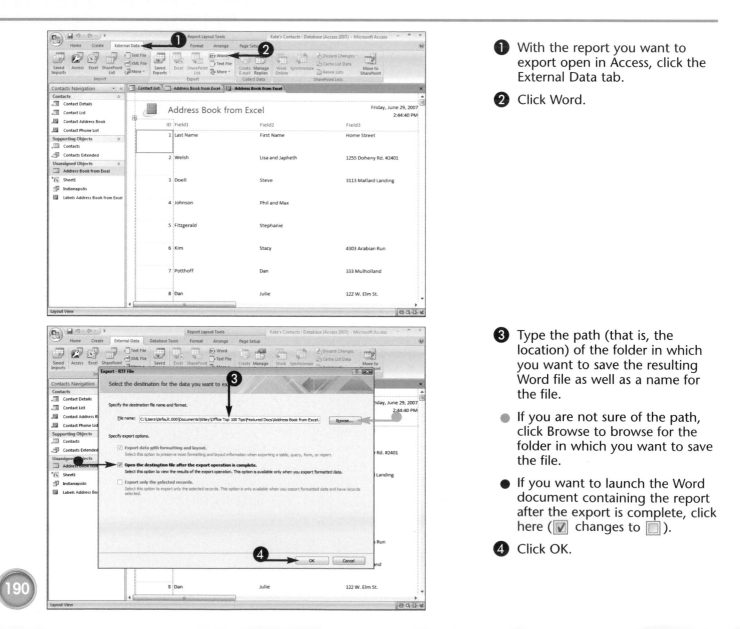

1 With the report you want to export open in Access, click the External Data tab.

2 Click Word.

3 Type the path (that is, the location) of the folder in which you want to save the resulting Word file as well as a name for the file.

● If you are not sure of the path, click Browse to browse for the folder in which you want to save the file.

● If you want to launch the Word document containing the report after the export is complete, click here (☑ changes to ☐).

4 Click OK.

Access exports the report to Word.

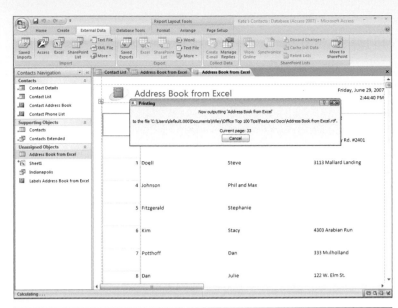

Access notifies you when the export is complete.

⑤ Click Close.

Did You Know?

If you will need to export this report to Word at some later date, you can save your export settings. Select the Save export steps check box in the Export Wizard's final screen. A series of additional fields appears; type a name for the export settings in the Save As field, type a description in the Description field, and click Save Export. (To automatically run the export operation at fixed intervals, such as once a week or once a month, select the Create Outlook Task check box before clicking Save Export; Access launches an Export Task dialog box, where you can set the necessary parameters.)

Create
MAILING LABELS

In addition to standard reports, Access can create mailing labels. This enables you to print labels without exporting the data first into a word-processing program and to set up reusable label definitions for recurring mailings.

Labels are a special type of report. They print multiple records per page, in a layout designed to correspond to self-stick labels that feed into your printer.

After choosing the size and formatting for the label, you set up the fields that should appear on it. These

come from the table or query that you selected before you started the wizard.

You can format the labels you create, changing the background color, adjusting the font and font color, and more. For additional formatting options, you can export the labels to Word. To do so, click the External Data tab, click Word, and follow the onscreen instructions.

1 Click the Create tab.

2 Click Labels.

The Label Wizard appears.

3 Click here and select the manufacturer of the labels you plan to use.

4 Click the product number.

5 Specify the unit of measure.

6 Indicate whether the label type is Sheet feed or Continuous.

7 Click Next.

8 Click here and choose a font for your labels.

9 Click here and choose a font size.

10 Click here and choose a font weight.

● Click a check box to make the label font italic (☑ changes to ☐) or underlined.

11 Click here to choose a text color.

● A Color dialog box opens.

12 Click the desired text color.

13 Click OK.

14 Click Next.

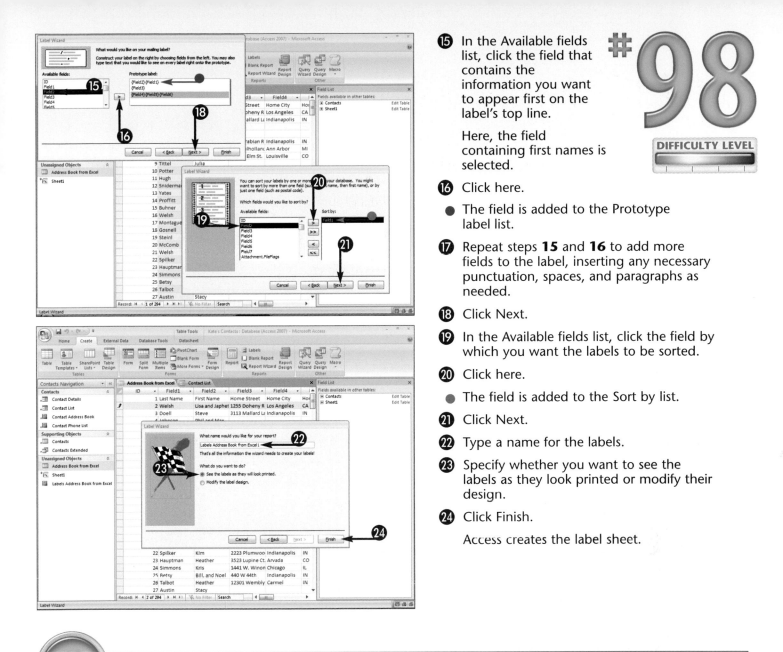

15 In the Available fields list, click the field that contains the information you want to appear first on the label's top line.

Here, the field containing first names is selected.

16 Click here.

● The field is added to the Prototype label list.

17 Repeat steps **15** and **16** to add more fields to the label, inserting any necessary punctuation, spaces, and paragraphs as needed.

18 Click Next.

19 In the Available fields list, click the field by which you want the labels to be sorted.

20 Click here.

● The field is added to the Sort by list.

21 Click Next.

22 Type a name for the labels.

23 Specify whether you want to see the labels as they look printed or modify their design.

24 Click Finish.

Access creates the label sheet.

98

DIFFICULTY LEVEL

TIP

Did You Know?

You can change the labels' formatting attributes, such as their font, color, and so on. To do so, follow these steps:

1 Click the label entry in the Navigation pane to display the labels.

2 Right-click the labels' tab and choose Design View.

3 Click the portion of the label you want to change. For example, to change the font used in the top line of text, click the box containing that line; alternatively, click outside the text fields to select the entire label.

4 Use the tools in the Ribbon's Design tab to make the desired changes.

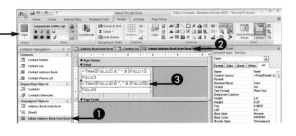

Automate Access tasks with
MACROS

If you frequently use Access to complete the same task — for example, to format the entries in a table a certain way — you can expedite the process by creating a macro. When you create a macro, you essentially record a series of actions. Then, you can run the macro you created to automatically perform the actions.

Unlike other Office programs, which enable you to "record" macros by essentially tracking the steps you take to complete a task, Access requires you to

select the actions, arguments, and other elements of a macro from a list. You create a macro in Access by using Macro Builder, listing the actions you want Access to carry out when the macro is run, and in what order.

Once a macro has been created, you can easily run it with the click of a button. Using macros can save you loads of time and effort, automating tasks that might normally require dozens of keystrokes or clicks.

① Click the Create tab.

② Click Macro.

The Macro Builder appears.

③ Click the first empty cell in the Action column.

A drop-down list appears.

④ Click here.

⑤ Choose the action you want the macro to take from the drop-down list (here, OpenQuery).

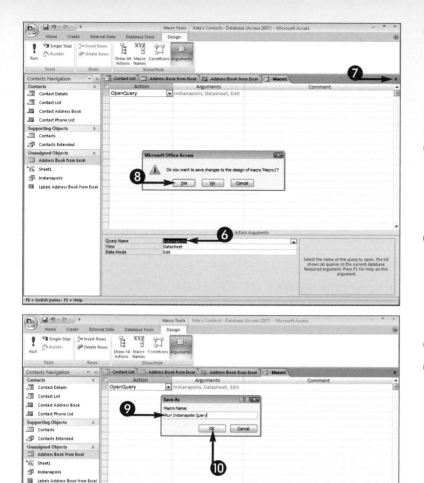

6 Set arguments for the macro.

In this case, because the selected action was OpenQuery, the query to be run must be selected.

7 Click here to close Macro Builder.

Access asks whether you want to save the macro.

8 Click Yes.

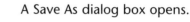

99

DIFFICULTY LEVEL

A Save As dialog box opens.

9 Type a name for the macro.

10 Click OK.

Access saves the macro and adds it to the Navigation pane.

TIP

Apply It!

To run a macro you have created, right-click it in the Navigation pane and choose Run from the menu that appears. Alternatively, click the Database Tools tab, click Run Macro, and, in the dialog box that appears, click the Macro Name drop-down arrow, choose the macro you want to run, and click OK.

Customize Your Database and Forms

To be sure, Access databases can hold volumes of data — so much so that it can sometimes be difficult to comprehend.

Fortunately, you can mitigate this difficulty by using Access's formatting tools. For example, you can auto-format your forms and reports to create a more polished and professional look, as well as add pictures to them. To expedite data entry, you can change the tab order of your forms — that is, the order in which the insertion point is moved from one field to another when the Tab key is pressed.

To draw attention to data that meets criteria you set, you can apply conditional formatting. For example, you might set a rule to highlight fields that contain values greater than, less than, equal to, or between a range of specified values. This enables you to detect problems, patterns, and trends at a glance.

Another way to display your data is in PivotTable or PivotChart form. A PivotTable is an interactive table that summarizes your data by using format and calculation methods you specify. PivotTables are useful in that they enable you to create many different views of your data rather than a fixed report. This way you can decide which one is most useful. A PivotChart is like a PivotTable, except it expresses the data graphically rather than as text and numbers.

To ensure that your data reaches others, you can save your reports as hypertext markup language (HTML) documents, which you can then upload to a Web server.

Top 100

AUTO-FORMAT
a form

#100

If you choose to create a form, you might reasonably want to format that form for added eye appeal. One way to do so would be to simply apply formatting changes to the form manually — for example, choosing a background color, border style, font, and so on from the Format tab on the Ribbon. An easier way, however, is to use Access's AutoFormat feature. Similar to the Theme feature found in other Office programs, AutoFormat enables you to apply a background color, fonts, borders, and so on to the form in a single operation.

Of course, before you can auto-format a form, you must create one. To create a form in Access, first display the table or query on which you want the form to be based in Access. (In this task, Layout view is used; you can also auto-format a form in Design view, although the steps for doing so are slightly different.) Then click the Create tab in the Ribbon and click the Form button. Access creates the form.

❶ With the form you want to format displayed in Access, click the Format tab.

❷ Click here in the AutoFormat group.

A gallery of AutoFormat choices appears.

❸ Click the desired AutoFormat option.

Note: You can tweak an AutoFormat option by clicking AutoFormat Wizard. In the dialog box that appears, click the AutoFormat option you want to apply, click Options, and deselect any of the check boxes to prevent Access from applying the selected AutoFormat's font, color, or border settings to the report.

Access auto-formats the form.

Change a form's TAB ORDER

If you have ever purchased anything on the Internet, chances are you have entered your billing and shipping information in an online form. You probably already realize, then, that you can move from one field of a form to the next by pressing the Tab key on your keyboard.

The order in which the insertion point is moved from one field to another when the Tab key is pressed is the form's *tab order*. By default, the tab order is the order in which fields are added to a form. You can

change this tab order, however, to any order you like. You might change a form's tab order if, for example, you added a field to the middle of your form at the last minute.

To change the tab order, you must display the form in Design view. To do so, right-click the form in the Navigation pane and choose Design view from the menu that appears.

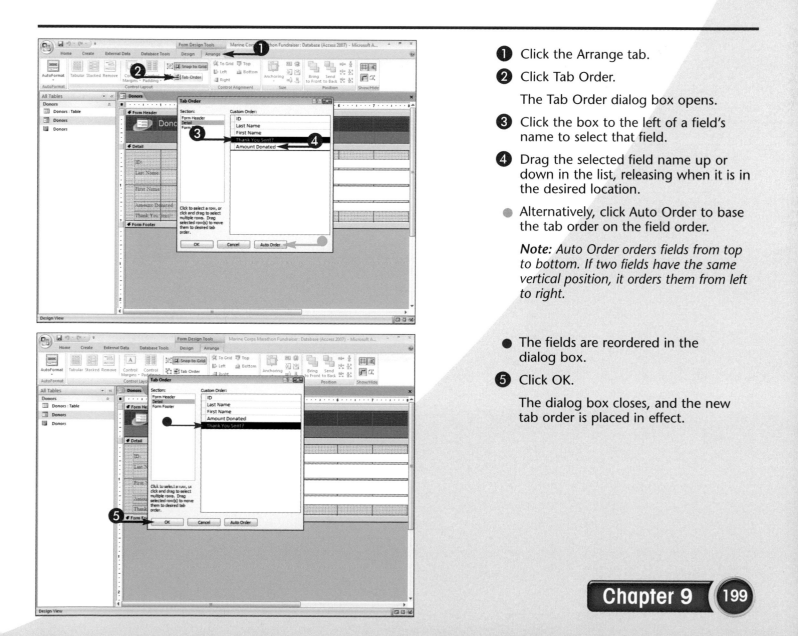

❶ Click the Arrange tab.

❷ Click Tab Order.

The Tab Order dialog box opens.

❸ Click the box to the left of a field's name to select that field.

❹ Drag the selected field name up or down in the list, releasing when it is in the desired location.

● Alternatively, click Auto Order to base the tab order on the field order.

Note: Auto Order orders fields from top to bottom. If two fields have the same vertical position, it orders them from left to right.

● The fields are reordered in the dialog box.

❺ Click OK.

The dialog box closes, and the new tab order is placed in effect.

AUTO-FORMAT
a report

If you choose to create a report about your data, you might reasonably want to format that report for added eye appeal. One way to do so would be to simply apply formatting changes to the report manually — for example, choosing a background color, border style, font, and so on from the Format tab on the Ribbon. An easier way, however, is to use Access's AutoFormat feature. Similar to the Theme feature found in other Office programs, AutoFormat, enables you to apply a background color, fonts, borders, and so on to the report in a single operation.

Of course, before you can auto-format a report, you must create one. To create a report in Access, first display the table or query on which you want the report to be based in Access. (In this task, Layout view is used; you can also auto-format a report in Design view, although the steps for doing so are slightly different.) Then click the Create tab in the Ribbon and click the Report button. Access creates the report.

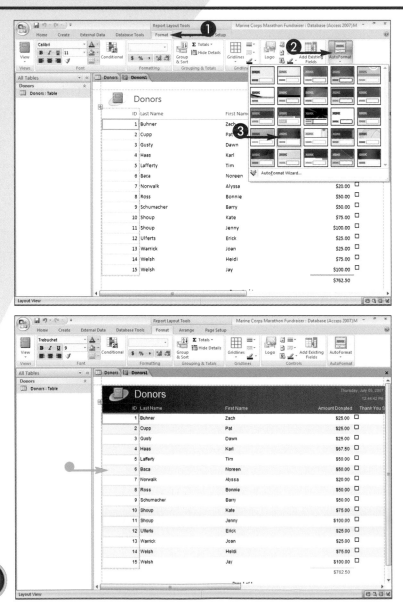

① With the report you want to format displayed in Access, click the Format tab.

② Click AutoFormat.

A gallery of AutoFormat choices appears.

③ Click the desired AutoFormat option.

Note: You can tweak an AutoFormat option by clicking AutoFormat Wizard. In the AutoFormat dialog box that appears, click the AutoFormat option you want to apply, click Options, and deselect any of the check boxes to prevent Access from applying the selected AutoFormat's font, color, or border settings to the report.

● Access auto-formats the report.

Save your report as a
WEB PAGE

DIFFICULTY LEVEL

If you have access to a Web server, you can share your Access reports with others by saving them as Web pages. In this way, you can share your Access reports with people who do not use Access.

When you save an Access report as a Web page, Access converts the document to an HTML file. This file contains all the necessary coding to be read by a Web browser such as Internet Explorer 7.

Of course, simply saving an Access report as an HTML document is not enough to share it with others

online. You also need to upload the HTML file to a Web server. That requires the use of a Web host.

You might have access to Web-hosting services through your Internet service provider; contact your provider to find out. If not, you can sign up with a Web-hosting service to place your Access reports online. For specific instructions on uploading your Access reports to the Internet, consult your provider.

---

① With the report you want to save as a Web page open in Access, click the External Data tab.

② Click More in the Export group.

③ Click HTML Document.

The Export – HTML Document Wizard appears.

④ Type the path (that is, the location) of the folder in which you want to save the resulting HTML file, as well as a name for the file.

● If you are not sure of the path, click Browse to browse for the folder in which you want to save the file.

⑤ Click OK.

The HTML Output Options dialog box appears.

⑥ Click Default encoding (◎ changes to ⦿).

⑦ Click OK.

⑧ Click Close.

Access creates an HTML version of your report.

Note: The HTML version of your report may not reflect any formatting you applied to your report in Access.

Jazz up your forms with
PICTURES

One way to make your forms more visually appealing is to insert an image in the form. For example, you might insert your company logo into a form, or an image that relates to the type of data the form requests.

After you insert an image, you can resize it as needed, either by dragging the image's corner handle or by opening its Property Sheet. (To open a picture's Property Sheet, right-click the picture, and choose

Properties. Change the sizing settings by clicking the Format tab and adjusting the Width and Height properties.) Images are inserted in the form's header by default; to change the placement of the image, drag it to the desired location on the form.

In addition to enabling you to insert pictures into forms, Access allows you to add images to reports. You add images to both forms and reports from Design view.

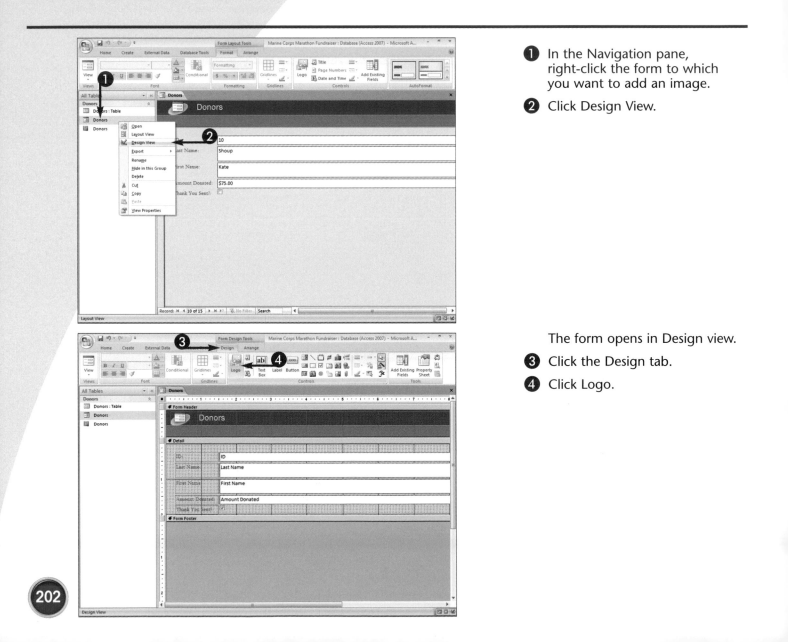

❶ In the Navigation pane, right-click the form to which you want to add an image.

❷ Click Design View.

The form opens in Design view.

❸ Click the Design tab.

❹ Click Logo.

The Insert Picture dialog box opens.

⑤ Locate and click the image you want to insert.

⑥ Click OK.

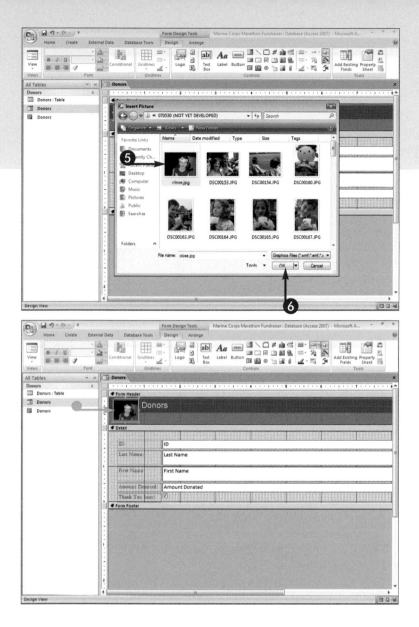

● Access inserts the image in the form's header.

TIPS

More Options!

As mentioned, you can insert images in reports. Simply open the report in Design view and follow the same basic steps you used to insert an image into a form: Click the Design tab, click Logo, locate and click the image you want to insert, and click OK.

More Options!

Another way to insert an image into a form or a report is to click the Image button (it features a sun setting behind some mountains) in the Design tab's Controls area. The Cursor changes to resemble the button; click in the form or report where you want to add the image and drag diagonally to establish the image's size. When you release the mouse button, Access launches the Insert Picture dialog box; locate and select the image you want to add and click OK.

Color-code your data with CONDITIONAL FORMATTING

You can use Access's conditional formatting functionality to assign certain formatting to fields in forms and reports when the value in a field meets a specified condition. For example, if you have a report with a Balance field, you might opt to present all negative values in that field in red text. This enables you to detect problems, patterns, and trends at a glance.

Access offers several predefined rules for conditional formatting. For example, you can set a rule to highlight data that is greater than, less than, equal to, or between a range of specified values; contains specific text; is a duplicate value; is among the top ten or bottom ten values; is above average or below average; and more. You can format data that meets conditions you set by changing the font or background.

You can apply conditional formatting from Design view or Layout view (as covered here), although the location of the Conditional Formatting button differs by view; it appears in the Design tab in Design view and in the Format tab in Layout view.

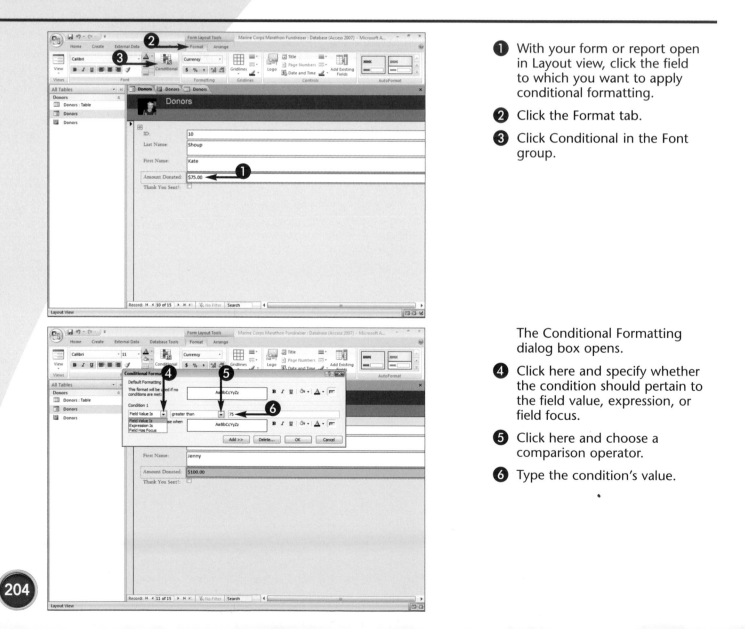

1 With your form or report open in Layout view, click the field to which you want to apply conditional formatting.

2 Click the Format tab.

3 Click Conditional in the Font group.

The Conditional Formatting dialog box opens.

4 Click here and specify whether the condition should pertain to the field value, expression, or field focus.

5 Click here and choose a comparison operator.

6 Type the condition's value.

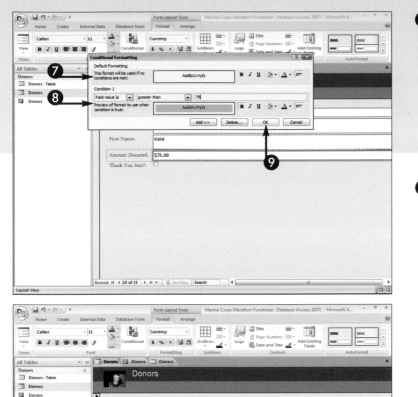

#105

7 Choose from various formatting options in the Default Formatting area to indicate how values that do not meet the condition should be formatted.

8 Choose from the various formatting options in the Condition area to indicate how values that do meet the condition should be formatted.

● Click the Enable/Disable button to enable or disable the conditional formatting. (This enables you to preserve the conditional settings, but opt out of applying the conditions when you don't want them used.)

9 Click OK.

● The conditional formatting is applied to any records whose field value meets the condition you set.

TIPS

Did You Know?
You are not limited to applying a single condition. To apply multiple conditions, click Add in the Conditional Formatting dialog box and repeat steps **4**, **5**, **6**, and **8**.

Remove It!
To remove the conditional formatting, click Delete beneath the condition you want to remove in the Conditional Formatting dialog box.

Summarize a datasheet with a
PIVOTTABLE

You can view your data using a PivotTable. A *PivotTable* is an interactive table that summarizes your data using format and calculation methods you specify. PivotTables are useful in that they enable you to create many different views of your data rather than a fixed report. This way you can decide which one is most useful.

You create a PivotTable by displaying the table or query containing the data you want to summarize in PivotTable view and then dragging the desired fields in the table or query to the blank PivotTable grid that appears.

After you have the PivotTable in place, you can enhance it by filtering by certain fields, or by certain values in a particular field. You can add fields to it specifically for the purpose of filtering, or you can exclude certain values from individual rows or columns.

If, after creating a PivotTable, you realize that it contains too many individual entries to be meaningful, you can group the entries into summary items.

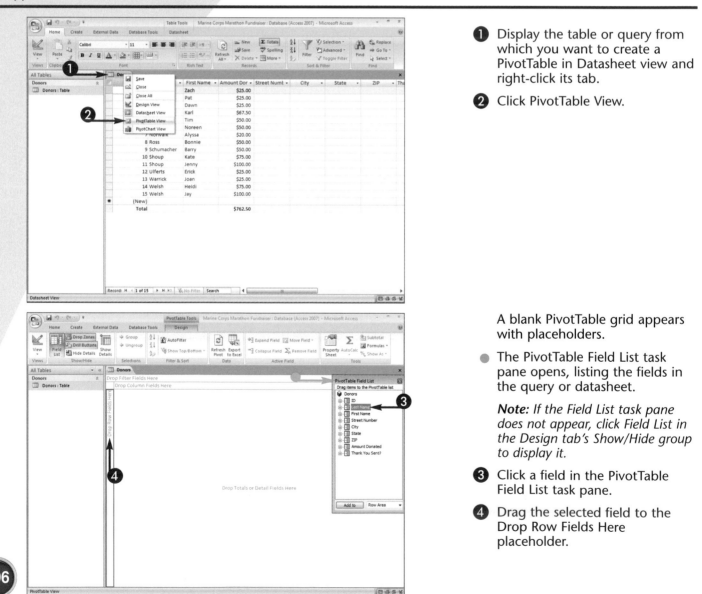

1 Display the table or query from which you want to create a PivotTable in Datasheet view and right-click its tab.

2 Click PivotTable View.

A blank PivotTable grid appears with placeholders.

● The PivotTable Field List task pane opens, listing the fields in the query or datasheet.

Note: If the Field List task pane does not appear, click Field List in the Design tab's Show/Hide group to display it.

3 Click a field in the PivotTable Field List task pane.

4 Drag the selected field to the Drop Row Fields Here placeholder.

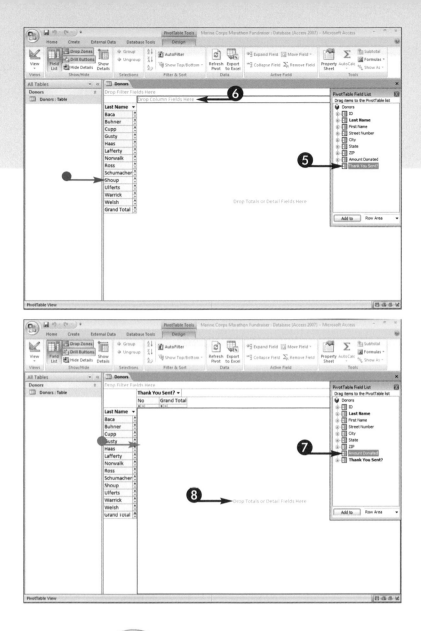

● Data from the selected field appears in a column at the left.

⑤ Click a field in the PivotTable Field List task pane.

⑥ Drag the field to the Drop Column Fields Here placeholder.

● Data from the selected field appears in a row along the top.

⑦ Click a field in the PivotTable Field List task pane.

⑧ Drag the field to the Drop Totals or Detail Fields Here placeholder.

The data appears in the center of the grid in the appropriate row and column.

Note: You can have multiple fields in the same placeholder area. If a field is already in the area, simply drag another one on top of it.

TIPS

More Options!
To filter your PivotTable, drag the field by which you want to filter to the Drop Filter Fields Here area, click the drop-down arrow to the right of the filter field, and clear the check boxes for any values you do not want. To filter for certain values in individual fields, click the drop-down arrow next to a field name, clear the check box for each value you do not want to include, and click OK.

More Options!
To group entries in a PivotTable, select the entries you want to group and click Group in the Details tab. To ungroup a grouped entry, select the group and click Ungroup.

Remove It!
To remove a PivotTable field, right-click it and choose Remove from the menu that appears.

Summarize a datasheet with a
PIVOTCHART

You can view your data using a PivotChart. A *PivotChart* is an interactive chart that summarizes your data using format and calculation methods you specify. PivotCharts are useful in that they enable you to create many different views of your data rather than a fixed report. This way you can decide which one is most useful.

A PivotChart is like a PivotTable, except it expresses the data graphically rather than as text and numbers. Indeed, PivotTables and PivotCharts are two different views of the same data, so you can switch freely

between them. (To do so, right-click the PivotTable or PivotChart's tab and choose PivotChart View or PivotTable View, respectively.) If you switch to PivotChart view while there are fields in PivotTable view, the fields carry over unless they are cleared first.

You create a PivotChart by displaying the table or query containing the data you want to summarize in PivotChart view and then dragging the desired fields in the table or query to the blank PivotChart that appears.

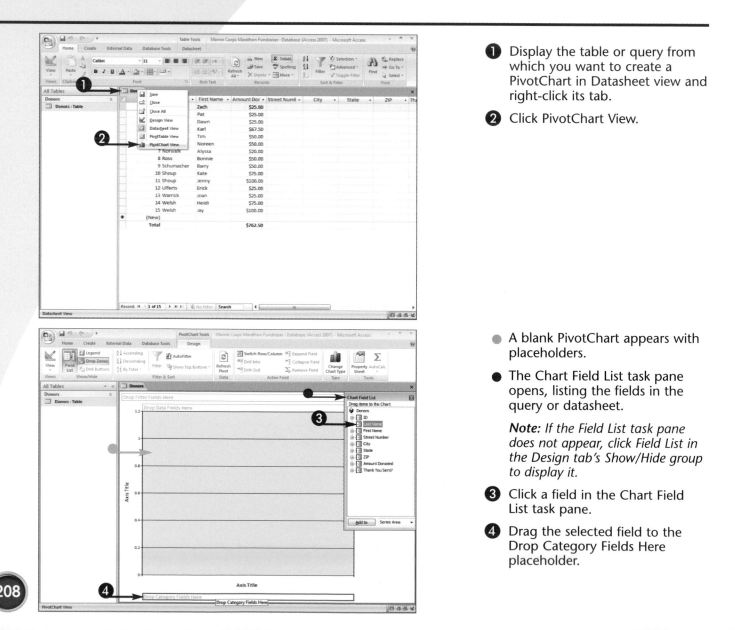

① Display the table or query from which you want to create a PivotChart in Datasheet view and right-click its tab.

② Click PivotChart View.

● A blank PivotChart appears with placeholders.

● The Chart Field List task pane opens, listing the fields in the query or datasheet.

Note: If the Field List task pane does not appear, click Field List in the Design tab's Show/Hide group to display it.

③ Click a field in the Chart Field List task pane.

④ Drag the selected field to the Drop Category Fields Here placeholder.

5 Click a field in the Chart Field List task pane.

6 Drag the selected field to the Drop Data Fields Here placeholder.

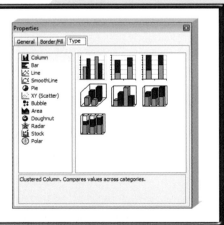

● The data is displayed as a PivotChart.

● You can also drag a field to the Drop Series Fields Here placeholder.

Note: The Chart Field List task pane covers the Drop Series Fields Here placeholder by default. To move the task pane, click its title bar and drag to the desired location.

TIP

More Options!

To change the chart type, right-click the PivotChart and select Change Chart Type. The chart's Properties dialog box appears with the Type tab displayed; choose a chart category from the list on the left, and then choose a specific chart type from the pane on the right.

Chapter 9: Customize Your Database and Forms

Chapter 10

Tap Outlook's Inner Power through E-mail

In the last several years, e-mail has become a primary method of communicating — so much so that many people are deluged with messages every day. Outlook's Mail component enables you to view, respond to, forward, and compose new e-mails, as well as create folders for organizing the e-mails you send and receive.

With these basics mastered, you can graduate to using Outlook's more advanced e-mail functions. For example, you can use Outlook to create distribution lists, which are useful if you frequently send e-mails to the same group of contacts — for example, to your team members at work — because they enable you to simply enter the name of the distribution list in the message's To field instead of adding each contact individually. You can also append a signature to the end of your messages, encrypt messages that contain sensitive data, recall messages sent in error, establish an automated message to be sent when you are out of the office, establish rules for managing messages, filter junk e-mail, archive e-mails to save space, and subscribe to RSS feeds.

Note that to use Outlook's Mail function, you must first set up an account with and obtain an e-mail address from an Internet service provider (ISP). Then, you can use Mail's Add New E-mail Account Wizard to automatically configure Mail to send and receive messages using that address.

Top 100

Create a
DISTRIBUTION LIST

Normally, to send an e-mail to multiple people, you must enter each name in the To or Cc field individually, either by typing it or by clicking the corresponding To or Cc button and selecting the recipients from the contacts listed in the Select Names dialog box that appears.

If you frequently send e-mails to the same group of contacts — for example, to your team members at

work — you can place those people in a *distribution list*. Then, any time you need to send a message to the group, you can simply type the name of the distribution list in the message's To or Cc field instead of adding each contact individually. Alternatively, click the To or Cc button in the message window and, in the Select Names dialog box that appears, click the list's name.

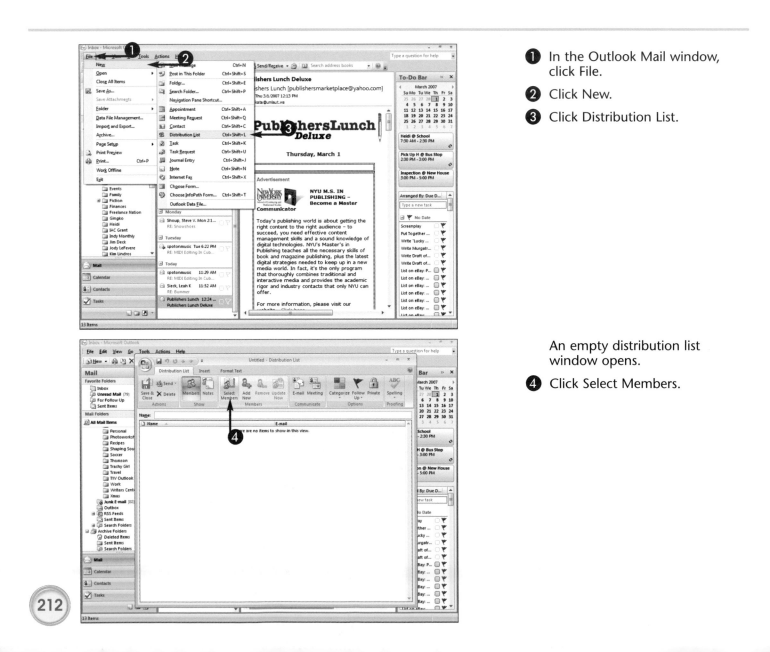

❶ In the Outlook Mail window, click File.

❷ Click New.

❸ Click Distribution List.

An empty distribution list window opens.

❹ Click Select Members.

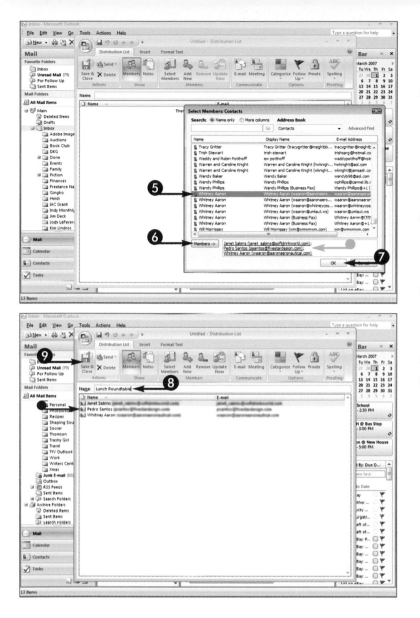

The Select Members: Contacts dialog box appears.

5 While holding down the Ctrl key on your keyboard, click each contact you want to include in your distribution list. (This is called *Ctrl+ clicking*.)

6 Click Members.

● The contacts you Ctrl+clicked appear in the Members field.

7 Click OK.

● The contacts you selected appear in the distribution list window.

8 Type a name for the distribution list.

9 Click Save & Close.

Outlook creates the distribution list.

TIPS

More Options!

If someone you want to include in your distribution list is not already listed in Contacts, click Add New in the Distribution List window and type the necessary information in the dialog box that appears. If you want to add the person to Contacts as well as to the distribution list, click the Add to Contacts check box.

More Options!

To edit a distribution list, locate the list's entry in your Outlook Contacts and double-click it to open it. To add more recipients to your list, follow steps **4** to **7** in this task. To remove a member, click his or her entry in the list and then click Remove. Clicking Update Now updates the list to reflect changes to contacts included in the list.

Customize an
E-MAIL SIGNATURE

You can use Outlook to create a *signature* — that is, a string of text that appears at the bottom of messages you send. This text might include your name, e-mail address, and other contact information; alternatively, it could spell out the name of your business, display a link to your Web site, or even include a picture.

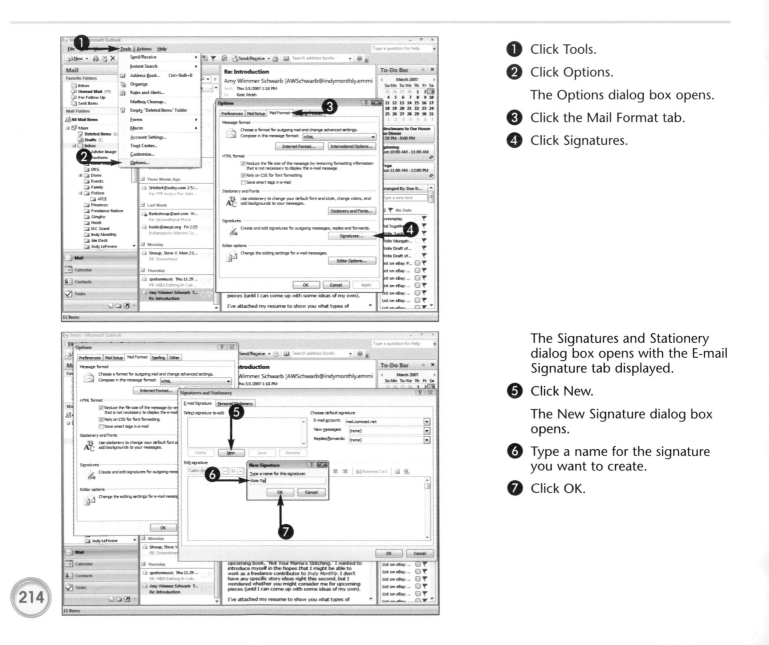

① Click Tools.

② Click Options.

The Options dialog box opens.

③ Click the Mail Format tab.

④ Click Signatures.

The Signatures and Stationery dialog box opens with the E-mail Signature tab displayed.

⑤ Click New.

The New Signature dialog box opens.

⑥ Type a name for the signature you want to create.

⑦ Click OK.

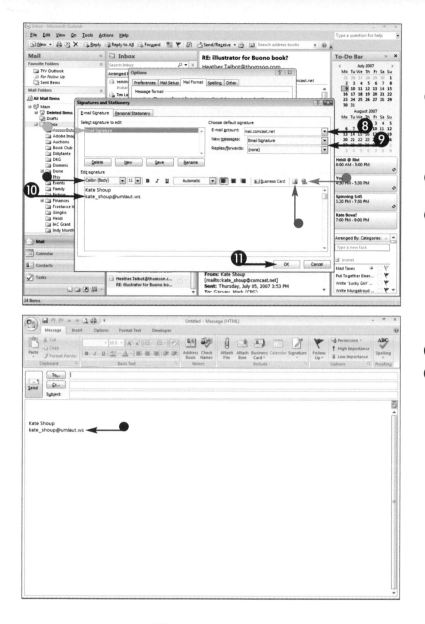

● The new signature's name appears selected in the list.

8 Click here and select the e-mail account to which the signature should apply.

9 Specify which messages should contain the signature.

10 Type the signature text.

● These controls enable you to customize the font and the text alignment.

● Click here if you want to add a picture to the signature.

● Click here to insert a hyperlink into the signature.

11 Click OK.

12 Click OK to close the Options dialog box.

● Messages you create will include the signature you established.

DIFFICULTY LEVEL

TIPS

Important!

To change your signature, simply open the Signatures and Stationery dialog box, click the signature you want to edit in the list, and make the necessary changes. When you're finished, click OK.

Try This!

To add your electronic business card to your signature, click the Business Card button in the Signatures and Stationery dialog box. In the Insert Business Card dialog box, click your contact entry to preview it, and click OK to add it to your signature. (You'll learn how to create an electronic business card in Chapter 11.)

ENCRYPT
a message

If your message contains highly sensitive information meant for the recipient's eyes only, you can encrypt it. When you encrypt a message, Outlook scrambles the text it contains. Only recipients with the necessary "keys" can decipher the message.

To share the necessary keys with the recipient, you must exchange certificates. (A *certificate* is a digital ID.) Once you have obtained a digital certificate, you can use it to digitally "sign" your encrypted message. The recipient can then save your information,

including the digital ID, to his or her contacts. For information about obtaining certificates and digitally signing your e-mail messages, see the tips at the end of this task.

You can opt to encrypt all messages you send out by default, or encrypt them on an as-needed basis. You encrypt single messages from the Security Properties dialog box; to encrypt all messages, you use the Trust Center's E-mail Security page.

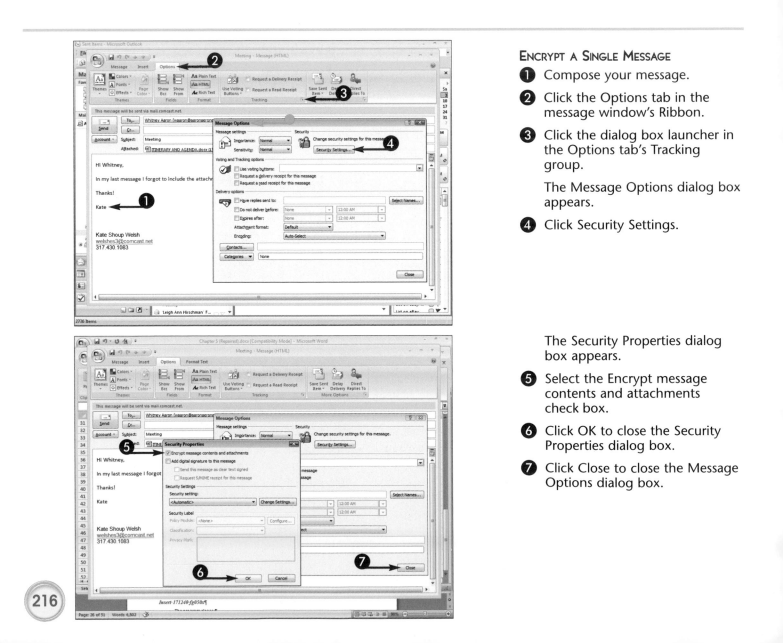

ENCRYPT A SINGLE MESSAGE

① Compose your message.

② Click the Options tab in the message window's Ribbon.

③ Click the dialog box launcher in the Options tab's Tracking group.

The Message Options dialog box appears.

④ Click Security Settings.

The Security Properties dialog box appears.

⑤ Select the Encrypt message contents and attachments check box.

⑥ Click OK to close the Security Properties dialog box.

⑦ Click Close to close the Message Options dialog box.

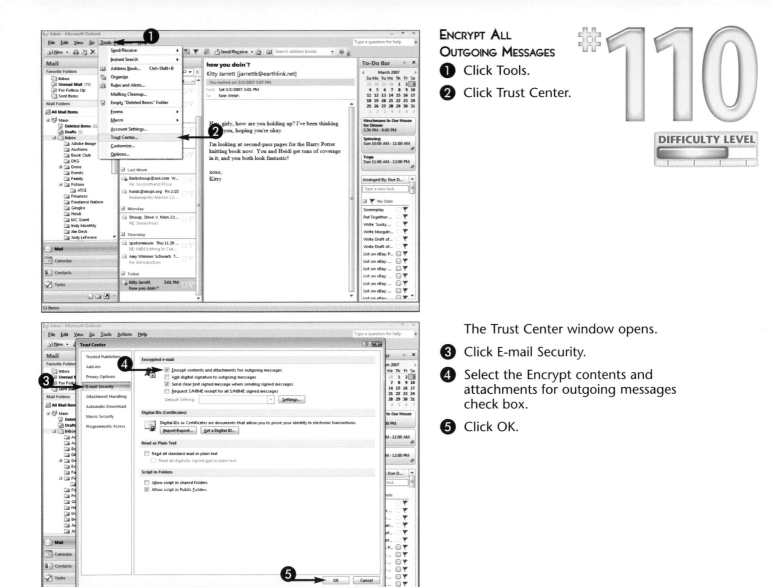

ENCRYPT ALL OUTGOING MESSAGES

#110

1 Click Tools.

2 Click Trust Center.

DIFFICULTY LEVEL

The Trust Center window opens.

3 Click E-mail Security.

4 Select the Encrypt contents and attachments for outgoing messages check box.

5 Click OK.

TIPS

Important!
To obtain a certificate, or digital ID, click Get a Digital ID in the Outlook Trust Center's E-mail Security screen. (To access this screen, follow steps **1** to **3** in the section "Encrypt All Outgoing Messages.") Doing so launches a special Web page with links to several organizations that issue certificates.

Important!
To digitally sign e-mail messages, select the Add digital signature to outgoing messages check box in the Trust Center's E-mail Security screen. (To access this screen, follow steps **1** to **3** in the section "Encrypt All Outgoing Messages.")

RECALL
a message

Suppose after sending your message you realize it contains an error. Assuming the message has not yet been received by the recipient, you may be able to *recall* it. When you recall a message, Outlook gives you the option of replacing it with an updated version.

Note that to recall or replace a sent message, you and the message's recipient must be using a Microsoft Exchange 2000, 2003, or 2007 account. If your account is a home or personal account,

chances are it is probably not an Exchange account.

To determine whether your Outlook account is a Microsoft Exchange account, hold down the Ctrl key on your keyboard as you right-click the Outlook icon in the notification area in the Windows taskbar; then click Connection Status. The Microsoft Exchange Connection Status window opens, indicating whether you are indeed using an Exchange account.

DIFFICULTY LEVEL

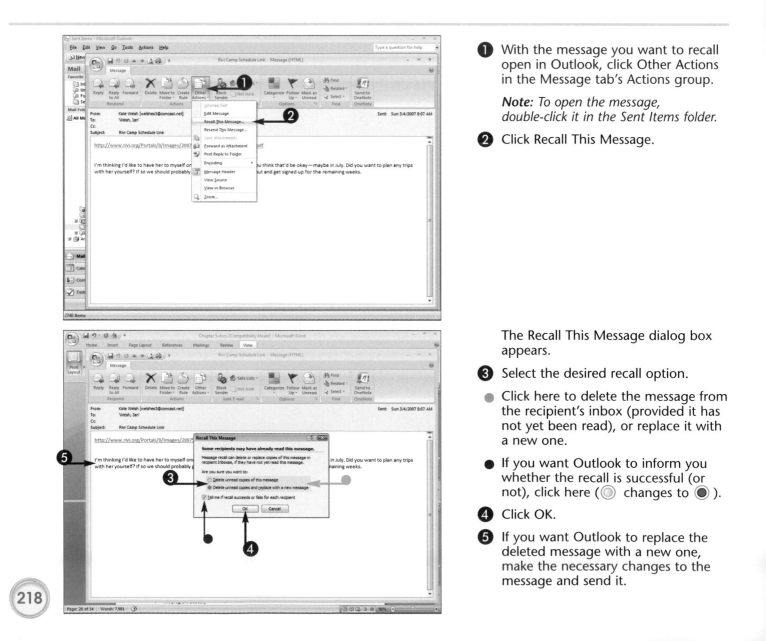

① With the message you want to recall open in Outlook, click Other Actions in the Message tab's Actions group.

   Note: To open the message, double-click it in the Sent Items folder.

② Click Recall This Message.

The Recall This Message dialog box appears.

③ Select the desired recall option.

● Click here to delete the message from the recipient's inbox (provided it has not yet been read), or replace it with a new one.

● If you want Outlook to inform you whether the recall is successful (or not), click here (◎ changes to ◉).

④ Click OK.

⑤ If you want Outlook to replace the deleted message with a new one, make the necessary changes to the message and send it.

OUT-OF-OFFICE REPLY #112

DIFFICULTY LEVEL

Suppose you will not have access to e-mail for a time — for example, if you are on vacation. You can configure Outlook to automatically send an out-of-office reply anytime you receive an e-mail during your absence, indicating that you do not have access to your account but will respond to the sender as soon as possible.

The first step when creating an out-of-office reply is to compose the message you want Outlook to send on your behalf and save it as a template. To compose the message, create a new message as

normal (click the New button in Outlook Mail). Then click the Options tab in the new message window's Ribbon, click Plain Text, and type the message you want to include in your out-of-office reply. Finally, click the Office button in the message window, click Save As, type a name for the message (such as "Out of Office Reply"), click Save as Type, choose Outlook Template (*.oft) from the list that appears, and then click Save. (Note: If the message window does not close automatically, click its Close button to close it.)

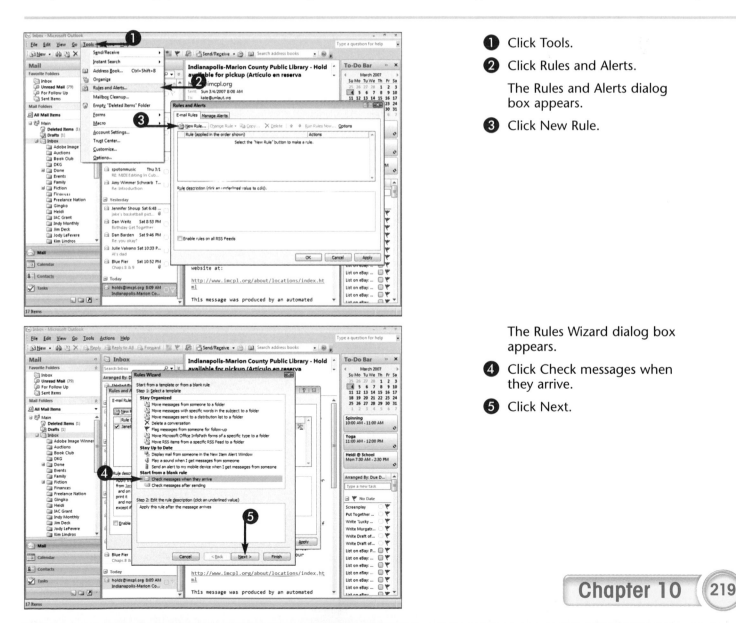

① Click Tools.

② Click Rules and Alerts.

The Rules and Alerts dialog box appears.

③ Click New Rule.

The Rules Wizard dialog box appears.

④ Click Check messages when they arrive.

⑤ Click Next.

Set up an
OUT-OF-OFFICE REPLY

The precise steps for setting up an out-of-office reply differ depending on what type of Outlook account you have. This task outlines how to set up an automatic reply for a Post Office Protocol (POP) or Internet Message Access Protocol (IMAP) account, a process that involves setting up a message template and then creating a rule that employs that template.

If you use an Exchange account rather than a POP or IMAP account, you follow a different — and, frankly, simpler — series of steps to set up an out-of-office reply. To begin, click Tools and then Out of Office Assistant, and follow the onscreen prompts.

Note that in order for Outlook to send your out-of-office reply, your computer must be on with Outlook running. In addition, Outlook must be set up to periodically check for incoming messages.

Even if you receive more than one message from a sender while you are away, Outlook sends your out-of-office reply only once — provided the program is not restarted during your absence, in which case it resets the list it keeps of senders to which it has responded.

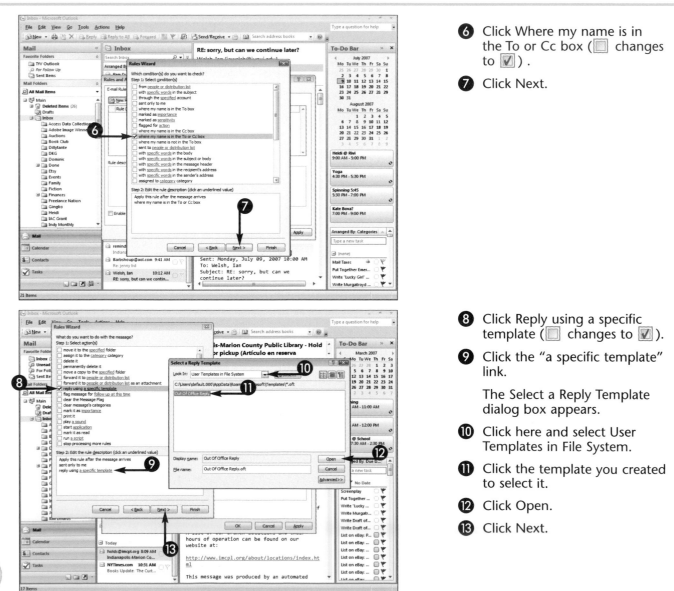

6 Click Where my name is in the To or Cc box (☐ changes to ☑) .

7 Click Next.

8 Click Reply using a specific template (☐ changes to ☑).

9 Click the "a specific template" link.

   The Select a Reply Template dialog box appears.

10 Click here and select User Templates in File System.

11 Click the template you created to select it.

12 Click Open.

13 Click Next.

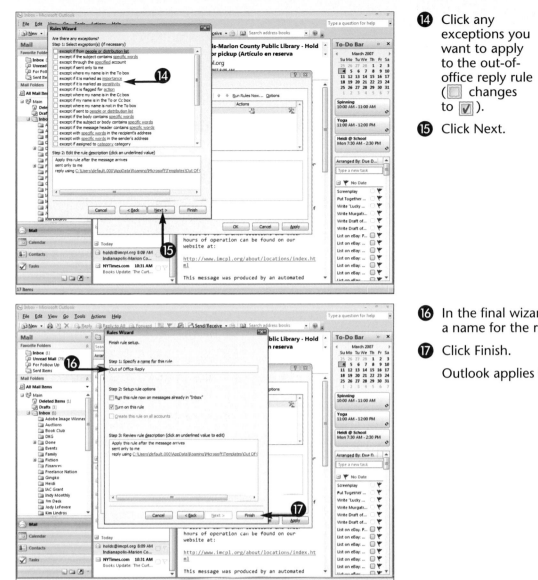

⑭ Click any exceptions you want to apply to the out-of-office reply rule (☐ changes to ☑).

⑮ Click Next.

⑯ In the final wizard page, type a name for the rule.

⑰ Click Finish.

Outlook applies the rule.

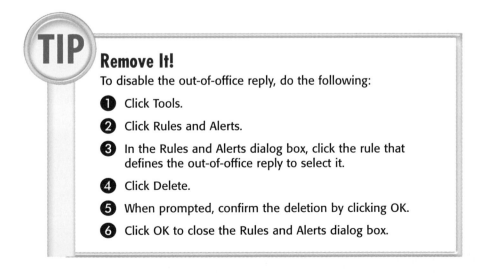

TIP

Remove It!

To disable the out-of-office reply, do the following:

❶ Click Tools.

❷ Click Rules and Alerts.

❸ In the Rules and Alerts dialog box, click the rule that defines the out-of-office reply to select it.

❹ Click Delete.

❺ When prompted, confirm the deletion by clicking OK.

❻ Click OK to close the Rules and Alerts dialog box.

MANAGE MESSAGES
using rules

Suppose you'd like all messages you receive from a specific sender to be filed in a particular folder automatically. To accomplish that, as well as many other automated Mail tasks, you can set up a *rule*. Any messages that meet the criteria defined in the rule will be handled in the manner you specify. To create rules in Outlook, you use the program's Rules Wizard.

In addition to creating rules based on predefined templates provided by Outlook, you can create them from scratch. Alternatively, if you established rules in an earlier version of Outlook, you can import those rules into this version.

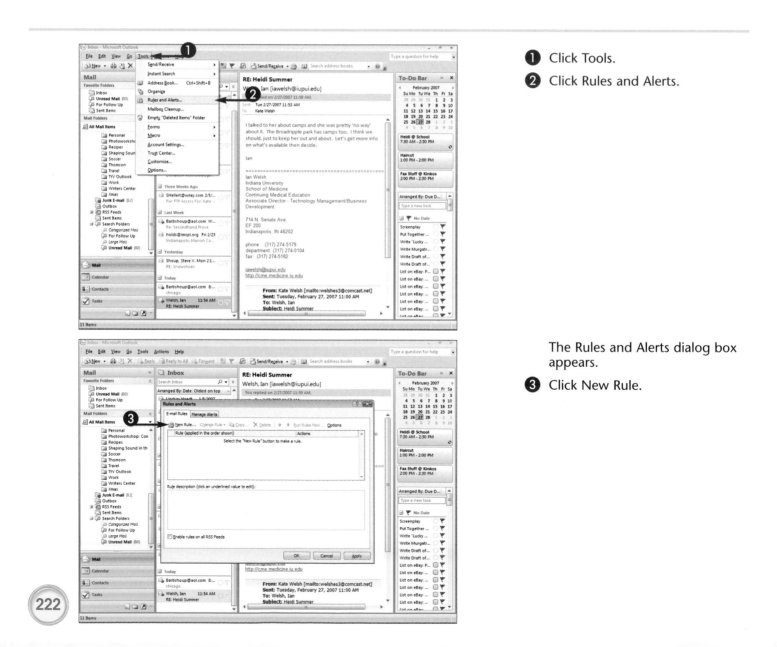

① Click Tools.

② Click Rules and Alerts.

The Rules and Alerts dialog box appears.

③ Click New Rule.

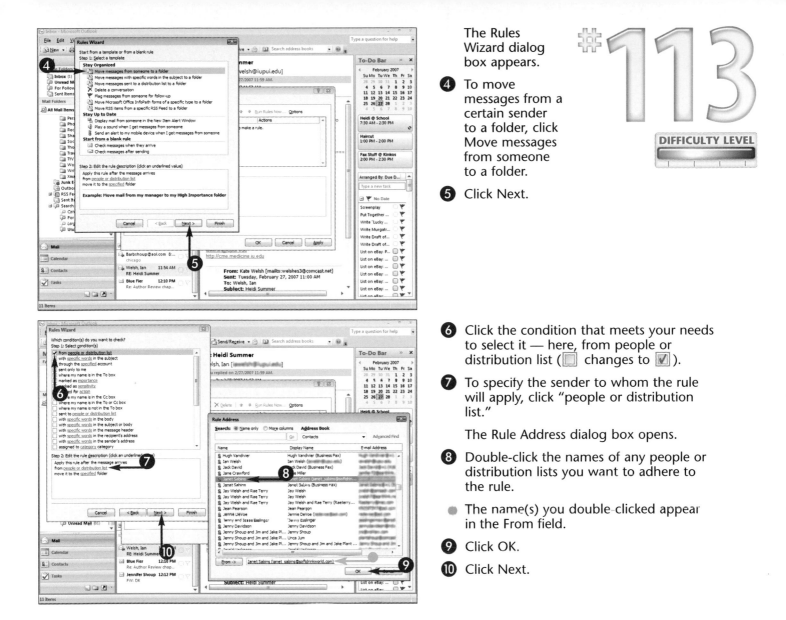

The Rules Wizard dialog box appears.

④ To move messages from a certain sender to a folder, click Move messages from someone to a folder.

⑤ Click Next.

⑥ Click the condition that meets your needs to select it — here, from people or distribution list (☐ changes to ☑).

⑦ To specify the sender to whom the rule will apply, click "people or distribution list."

The Rule Address dialog box opens.

⑧ Double-click the names of any people or distribution lists you want to adhere to the rule.

● The name(s) you double-clicked appear in the From field.

⑨ Click OK.

⑩ Click Next.

＃113

DIFFICULTY LEVEL

TIPS

More Options!

In addition to creating rules based on predefined templates provided by Outlook, you can create them from scratch. To do so, launch the Rules Wizard dialog box, choose the desired option under Start from a blank rule, click Next, and follow the onscreen prompts.

More Options!

If you established rules in an earlier version of Outlook, you can import those rules into this version. (Note that to import your rules from a previous version of Outlook, you must first *export* them from that earlier version.) To access the tools for importing and exporting rules, as well as for upgrading any rules you import for better performance in Outlook 2007, click Options in the Rules and Alerts dialog box.

MANAGE MESSAGES
using rules

You are not limited to creating rules that place messages from a certain sender in a specific folder. For example, you might create a rule that dictates that all messages from a particular sender (for example, your boss) be flagged for immediate attention. You can also set *exceptions* — that is, situations in which the rule you create is ignored. For example, you might specify that the rule be ignored when messages contain a certain word in the body text or subject line.

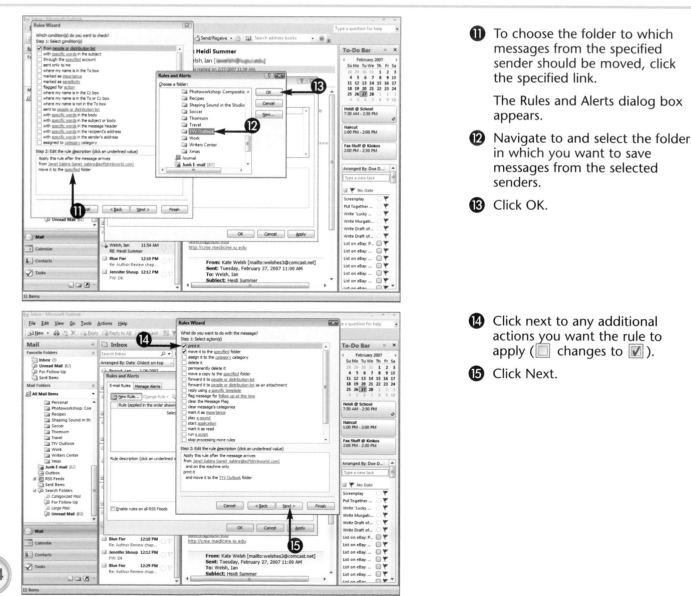

⑪ To choose the folder to which messages from the specified sender should be moved, click the specified link.

The Rules and Alerts dialog box appears.

⑫ Navigate to and select the folder in which you want to save messages from the selected senders.

⑬ Click OK.

⑭ Click next to any additional actions you want the rule to apply (☐ changes to ☑).

⑮ Click Next.

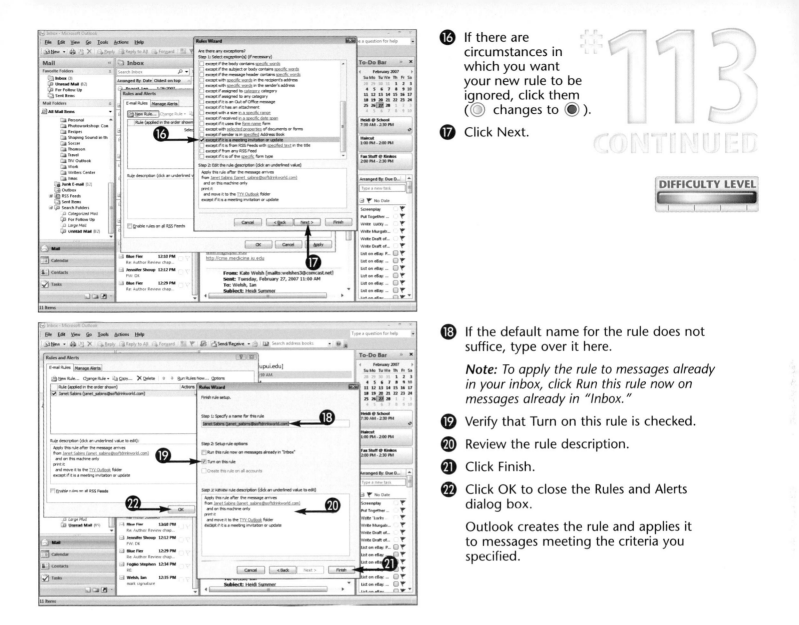

⑯ If there are circumstances in which you want your new rule to be ignored, click them (○ changes to ●).

⑰ Click Next.

DIFFICULTY LEVEL

⑱ If the default name for the rule does not suffice, type over it here.

Note: To apply the rule to messages already in your inbox, click Run this rule now on messages already in "Inbox."

⑲ Verify that Turn on this rule is checked.

⑳ Review the rule description.

㉑ Click Finish.

㉒ Click OK to close the Rules and Alerts dialog box.

Outlook creates the rule and applies it to messages meeting the criteria you specified.

TIP

Try This!

If you want to create a rule that applies to a certain sender, and it so happens you have a message from that sender in your message list, you can do the following to expedite the rule-creation process:

❶ Right-click a message from the sender to which you want to apply the rule and click Create Rule in the shortcut menu that appears.

❷ The Create Rule dialog box opens. Under When I get e-mail with all the selected conditions, click the check box next to the necessary conditions (here, the From check box).

❸ Under Do the Following, click the check box next to the actions you want Outlook to take when the conditions are met.

❹ Depending on what options you choose, Outlook may prompt you for additional information; respond as necessary.

❺ Click OK. Outlook creates the rule.

FILTER JUNK
e-mail

Using e-mail opens you up to a deluge of junk e-mail messages, called *spam*. Indeed, you probably sift through dozens of spam e-mails to locate "real" messages every day. You can use Outlook Mail's Junk E-mail Filter to automatically divert spam from your inbox into a Junk E-Mail folder.

By default, Outlook Mail applies a low level of protection from junk e-mail. To change the level of protection, click Actions, click Junk E-mail, and click Junk E-mail Options. The Junk E-mail Options dialog box opens; in it, you can specify the level of protection from junk e-mail that you want.

You should periodically check Outlook's Junk E-mail folder to ensure that no "authentic" messages have been diverted. If one is, you can mark it as "not junk"; this moves the message to the message list and, optionally, adds the sender to your Safe Senders list. On the flip side, if the Outlook filter fails to detect a junk e-mail message and allows it into your inbox, you can set up Outlook to block all e-mail from the message's sender.

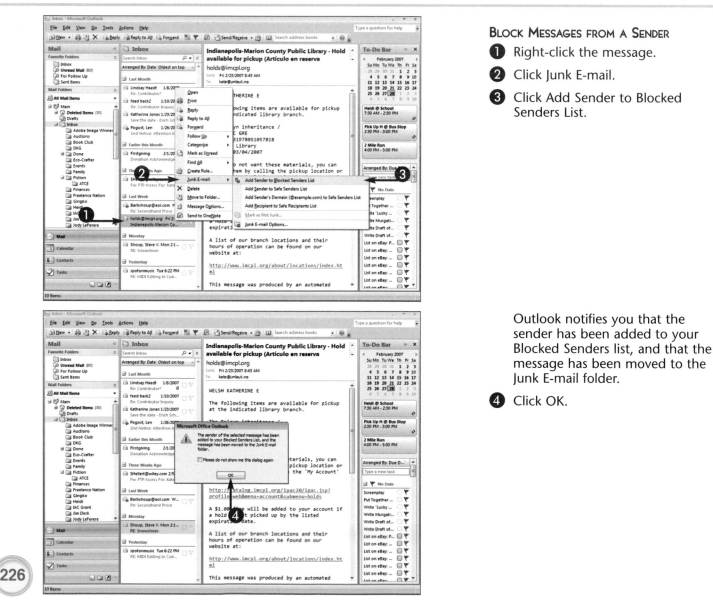

BLOCK MESSAGES FROM A SENDER

❶ Right-click the message.

❷ Click Junk E-mail.

❸ Click Add Sender to Blocked Senders List.

Outlook notifies you that the sender has been added to your Blocked Senders list, and that the message has been moved to the Junk E-mail folder.

❹ Click OK.

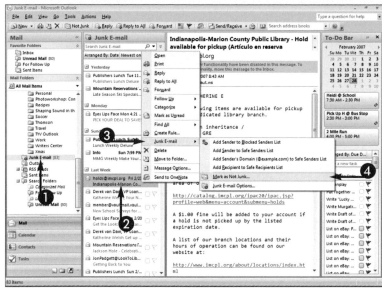

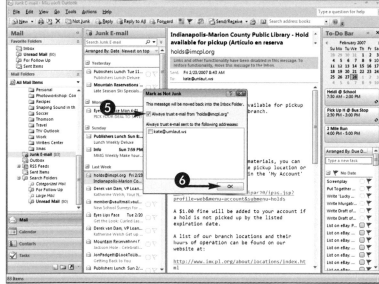

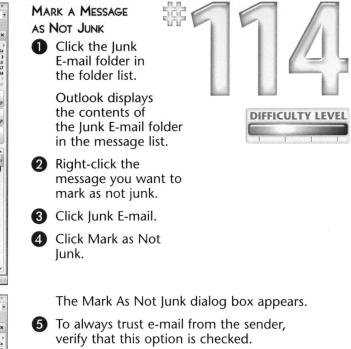

1 Click the Junk E-mail folder in the folder list.

Outlook displays the contents of the Junk E-mail folder in the message list.

2 Right-click the message you want to mark as not junk.

3 Click Junk E-mail.

4 Click Mark as Not Junk.

The Mark As Not Junk dialog box appears.

5 To always trust e-mail from the sender, verify that this option is checked.

6 Click OK.

Outlook moves the message to your inbox.

DIFFICULTY LEVEL

TIPS

Try This!

To ensure that any sender who is listed in Contacts is considered "safe" by the Junk E-mail Filter, open the Junk E-mail Options dialog box and, in the Safe Senders tab, verify that the Also trust e-mail from my Contacts check box is checked. Optionally, click the Automatically add people I e-mail to the Safe Senders list check box to select it. When you're finished, click OK.

Did You Know?

Phishing typically involves an e-mail message that appears to be from a legitimate source, such as a bank, informing the user that his or her account information must be updated. When the user clicks the link provided, however, he or she is directed to a bogus site designed to mimic a trusted site in order to steal personal information. Outlook's anti-phishing features help detect these fraudulent messages automatically, disabling any links in messages it deems suspicious and alerting you to the problem in the message window's InfoBar.

ARCHIVE E-MAILS
to create space

If you use Outlook with any regularity, you quickly discover that the sheer volume of e-mail messages, not to mention calendar entries and other Outlook items, can prove overwhelming. To mitigate this, Outlook automatically archives old files. If the default settings for this automatic operation do not suit you, you can change them.

In addition to changing Outlook's AutoArchive settings, as outlined here, you can also launch an archive operation manually. To do so, open Outlook's File menu, choose Archive, and select the desired option in the Archive dialog box that appears.

Alternatively, you may decide you want to disable Outlook's AutoArchive functionality altogether.
To do so, click Tools and then click Options. In the Options dialog box, click the Other tab, and click AutoArchive. Finally, in the AutoArchive dialog box, deselect the Run AutoArchive Every *x* Days check box. To prevent AutoArchive from running on a particular folder, right-click the folder in the folder list, click Properties, click the AutoArchive tab, and click Do Not Archive Items in This Folder.

DIFFICULTY LEVEL

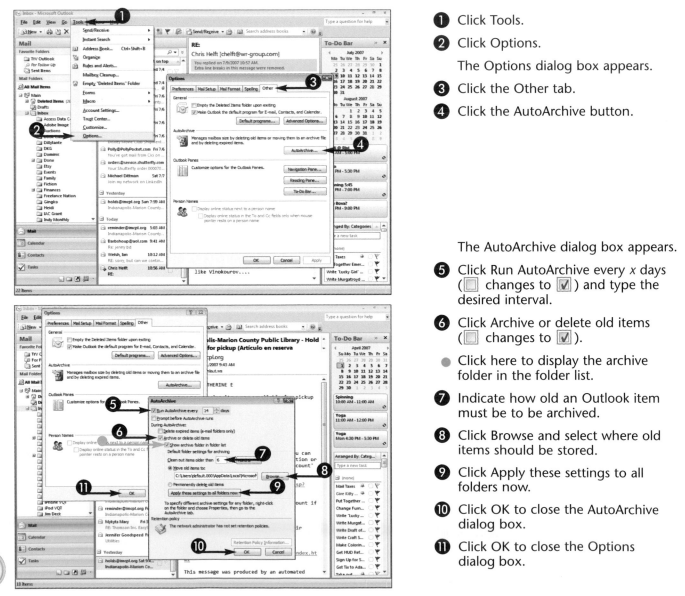

❶ Click Tools.

❷ Click Options.

The Options dialog box appears.

❸ Click the Other tab.

❹ Click the AutoArchive button.

The AutoArchive dialog box appears.

❺ Click Run AutoArchive every *x* days (☐ changes to ☑) and type the desired interval.

❻ Click Archive or delete old items (☐ changes to ☑).

● Click here to display the archive folder in the folder list.

❼ Indicate how old an Outlook item must be to be archived.

❽ Click Browse and select where old items should be stored.

❾ Click Apply these settings to all folders now.

❿ Click OK to close the AutoArchive dialog box.

⓫ Click OK to close the Options dialog box.

View
ARCHIVED E-MAILS

Just because an item has been archived does not mean you cannot view it if need be. You view archived items from the Archive Folders entry in your folder list.

In addition to viewing archived items, you can restore archived items back to their original folder or to a different folder, either individually or as a group. To restore an archived file, click Archive Folders in the folder list. (If the folder list is not displayed, click Go and then Folder List to open it.) Navigate to the folder that contains the message you want to restore

and click it to open it, click the item you want to restore, and drag the item to its original folder in the folder list.

To restore an entire archived folder, use the Import and Export Wizard. To launch the wizard, click File and then Import and Export; then select Import from Another Program or File, click Next, choose Personal Folder File (.pst), click Next, and follow the onscreen instructions.

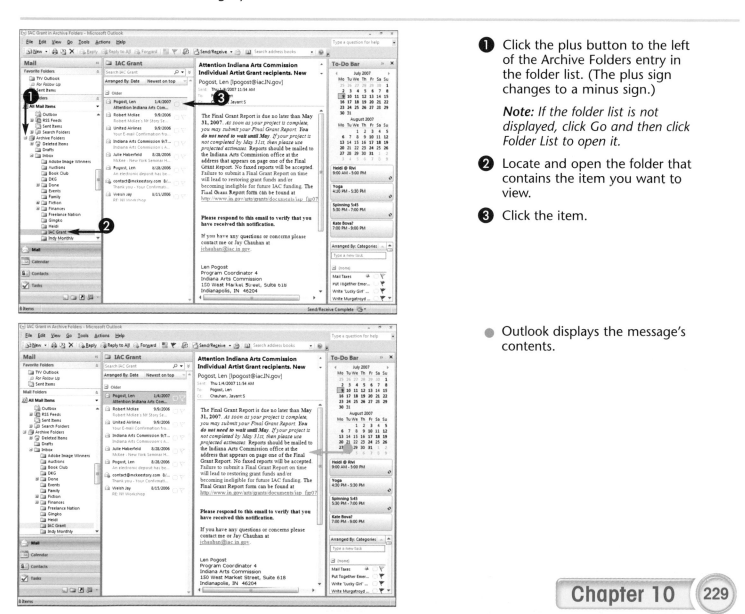

❶ Click the plus button to the left of the Archive Folders entry in the folder list. (The plus sign changes to a minus sign.)

Note: If the folder list is not displayed, click Go and then click Folder List to open it.

❷ Locate and open the folder that contains the item you want to view.

❸ Click the item.

● Outlook displays the message's contents.

Subscribe to
RSS FEEDS

Really Simple Syndication (RSS) is a technology that enables Web content to be *syndicated* — that is, converted to a Web feed. This content might include blogs, podcasts, news, and so on. When you use Outlook to subscribe to an RSS feed, Outlook automatically downloads new posts from those feeds. That means that rather than visiting several Web sites to stay informed, you can simply view these various feed posts in Outlook.

You can subscribe to a feed from the Web site that hosts the feed. (Note that if you use Internet

Explorer 7 to subscribe to a feed, you can then access and manage the feed from within Outlook 2007. Internet Explorer 7 indicates when it has detected an RSS feed by changing its RSS Feed button from gray to orange.

Alternatively, if you know the Web address, or URL, of the feed that interests you, you can subscribe to that feed from within Outlook. When you do, Outlook automatically checks for and downloads feed updates. Subscribing to a feed is typically free.

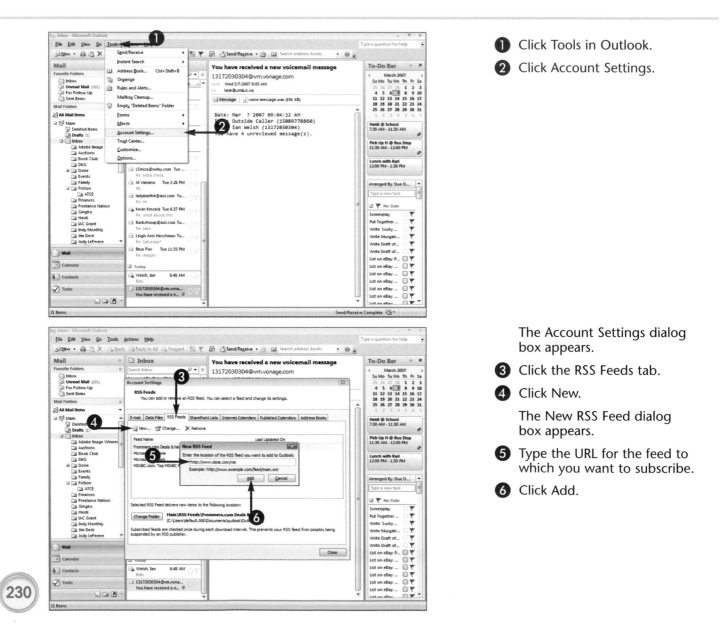

❶ Click Tools in Outlook.

❷ Click Account Settings.

The Account Settings dialog box appears.

❸ Click the RSS Feeds tab.

❹ Click New.

The New RSS Feed dialog box appears.

❺ Type the URL for the feed to which you want to subscribe.

❻ Click Add.

The RSS Feed Options dialog box appears.

- The name of the feed appears here.

- To change the folder in which feed updates are saved, click here.

- Click here to automatically download feed enclosures (☐ changes to ☑).

- The publisher of the feed to which you are subscribing likely limits how frequently you can check for new postings. Click here to ensure Outlook does not check more frequently than is permitted.

7 Click OK.

8 Click Close.

9 In Outlook Mail, double-click the RSS Feeds folder in the folder list.

- The feed to which you subscribed is listed.

Chapter 11

Manage Multiple Priorities with Outlook

Whether you are a seasoned user of earlier versions of Outlook or completely new to the program, you will appreciate Microsoft's efforts to streamline the program's interface. By default, the program displays the Mail component, consolidating it with your calendar, upcoming appointments, and tasks on a single screen.

In addition to enabling you to send and receive e-mails, Outlook is designed to help you keep track of appointments, manage your contacts, maintain a to-do list, keep a journal to track your time, and more.

Of course, Outlook contains many basic-level tools that are designed to make you more efficient. More advanced tools, however, can really help you stay organized. For example, you can categorize your Outlook items so you can color-code them. Outlook's automatic journal tools enable you to track the time you spend on a project. If you find yourself overloaded, you can delegate a task you create in Outlook to someone else. You can also forward Outlook items to your mobile phone to help you stay on track while you are on the go. And speaking of being on the go, you can use Outlook's Contacts map feature to pinpoint an address contained in a contact record.

With Outlook 2007, sharing your information with others has never been easier. For example, you can easily create an electronic business card, which you can exchange with others in much the same way paper-based cards are shared. In addition, you can send a snapshot of your calendar to another Outlook 2007 user.

Create an
ELECTRONIC BUSINESS CARD

Just as you likely exchange paper-based business cards with others, you can also exchange business cards created with Contacts. You can send your business card to others via e-mail, either as an attachment or as part of your e-mail message's signature.

The first step in creating an electronic business card is to create a contact entry in Outlook for yourself. To do so, click the Contacts button in Outlook's

Navigation pane, click New, and enter your contact information in the window that appears.

In addition to including vital information such as your name, phone number, e-mail address, and so on, your electronic business card can include a photo and/or a logo. You can also customize the design of your electronic business card.

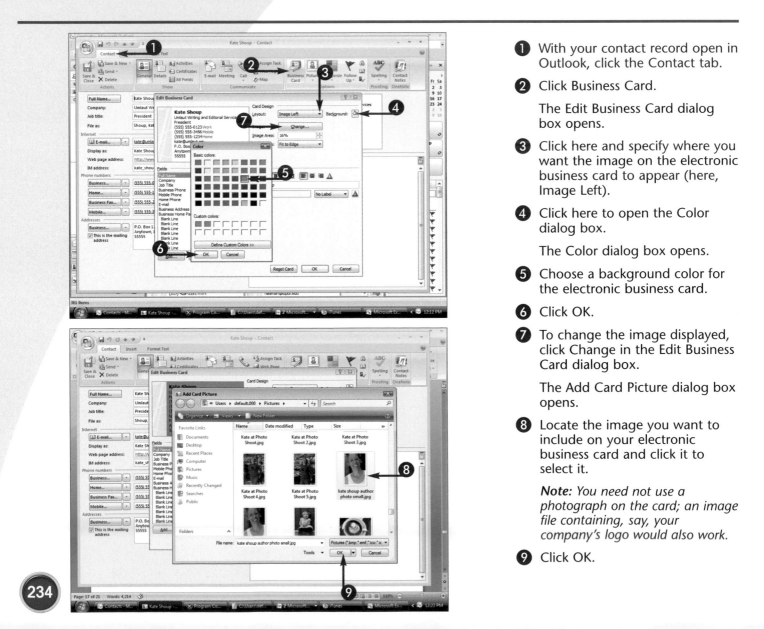

① With your contact record open in Outlook, click the Contact tab.

② Click Business Card.

The Edit Business Card dialog box opens.

③ Click here and specify where you want the image on the electronic business card to appear (here, Image Left).

④ Click here to open the Color dialog box.

The Color dialog box opens.

⑤ Choose a background color for the electronic business card.

⑥ Click OK.

⑦ To change the image displayed, click Change in the Edit Business Card dialog box.

The Add Card Picture dialog box opens.

⑧ Locate the image you want to include on your electronic business card and click it to select it.

Note: You need not use a photograph on the card; an image file containing, say, your company's logo would also work.

⑨ Click OK.

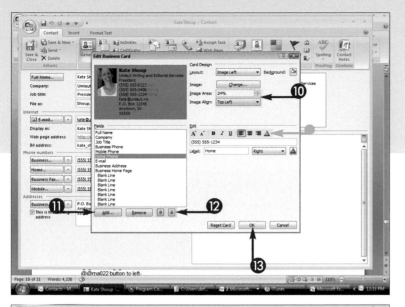

⑩ Select the image size and alignment.

⑪ Click these buttons to add and remove fields from the card.

⑫ To change the order of the fields, click the field you want to move, and then click one of these buttons.

● These buttons enable you to format the font and alignment of the selected field.

⑬ When you finish formatting your business card, click OK.

● The business card is saved in your contact record.

⑭ Click Save & Close.

The contact record closes.

#118

DIFFICULTY LEVEL

Did You Know?

In addition to creating an electronic business card that contains your contact information to share with others, you can configure Outlook to display the contacts it stores in electronic business card form, much the way Rolodexes of old stored paper-based business cards. To view your contact entries as electronic business cards, click Business Cards in the Navigation pane under Current View.

More Options!

Rather than having a separate field for, say, your job title, you might add that information as a label to the Full Name field. To do so, specify in the Edit Business Card dialog box whether the label should appear to the left or the right of the existing text, type the label, and choose the desired font color.

Locate an address with
CONTACT MAPS

If you plan to visit someone listed in Contacts, and if that person's contact record includes an address, you can use Contacts' map feature to pinpoint the person's location.

By default, the Contacts map is displayed in Road view, like a typical map. You can, however, switch to Aerial view, which is a satellite image of the location. In addition, the Contacts map can be displayed in Hybrid view, which combines elements of the Road

and Aerial views. To switch views, click Road, Aerial, or Hybrid in the Zoom slider.

In addition to enabling you to view a map pinpointing the contact's location, you can obtain directions from your location to your destination.

Note: In order to use Contacts' mapping function, you must be online.

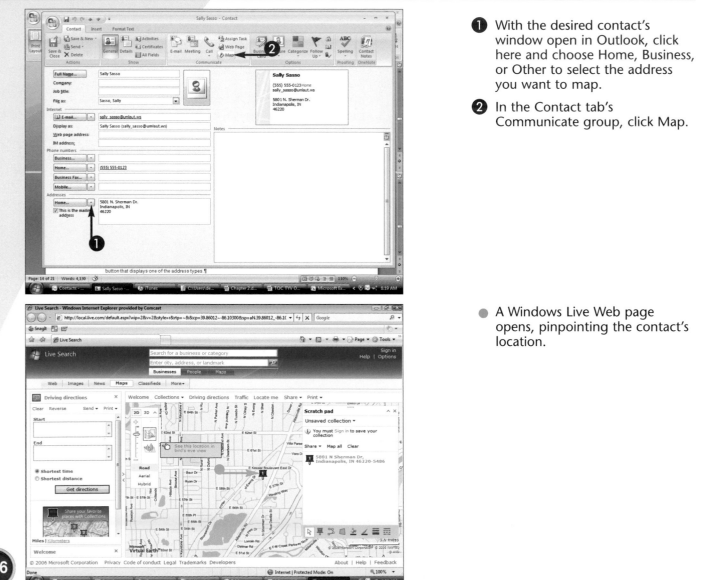

① With the desired contact's window open in Outlook, click here and choose Home, Business, or Other to select the address you want to map.

② In the Contact tab's Communicate group, click Map.

● A Windows Live Web page opens, pinpointing the contact's location.

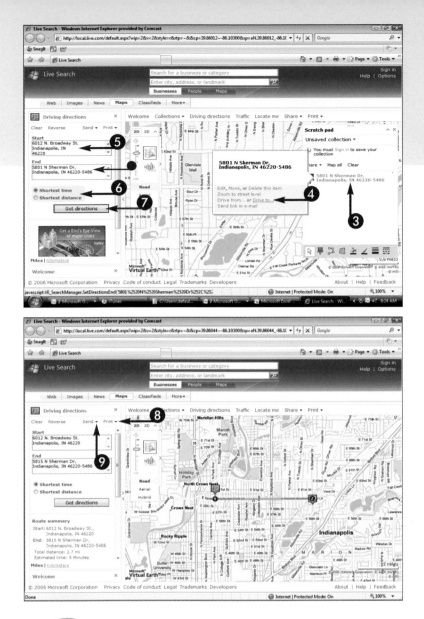

 # 119

DIFFICULTY LEVEL

③ To obtain directions from your location to the contact's, place your cursor over the address link.

④ Click Drive to in the list of options that appears.

● The contact's address is added to the End field in the Driving directions pane.

⑤ Type your starting address in the Start field.

⑥ Specify whether you want the directions provided to be the shortest time or the shortest distance.

⑦ Click Get directions.

The map changes to show your route.

⑧ To print the directions, click here and select whether you want to print the map of the route, text directions, or both.

⑨ To send the directions to your mobile device or via e-mail, click here, choose the appropriate option, and follow the onscreen prompts.

TIP

Try This!

For a better look at the map, regardless of which view you use, you can zoom in and out. To do so, drag the Zoom slider provided on the page.

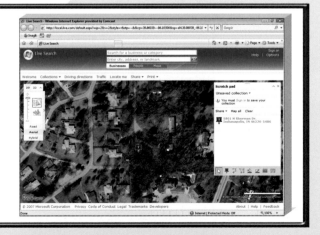

CATEGORIZE
an Outlook item

If several Outlook items pertain to a particular project, company, or what have you, you can create a category for those items. Outlook items in the same category are color-coded. The process for categorizing an Outlook item is essentially the same regardless of what type of item it is.

One of the best things about categorizing Outlook items is that you can then sort them by category. To sort tasks and contacts by category, choose By

Category under Current View in the navigation pane. To sort e-mail messages, click the Arranged By heading at the top of the message list and choose Categories. (Note that Calendar entries cannot be sorted by category.)

To expedite the categorization process, Outlook provides a Quick Click function, which enables you to apply a category to an Outlook item with the click of a button.

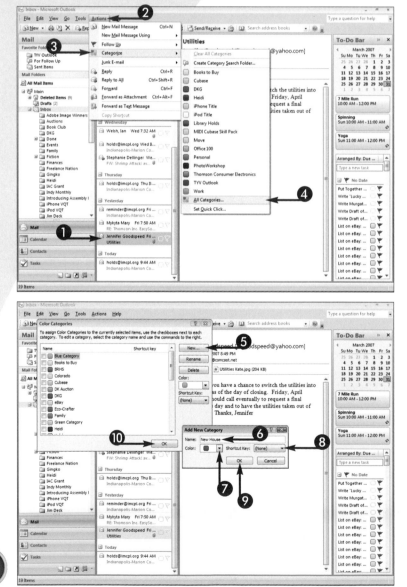

CREATE A NEW CATEGORY

① Click an Outlook item you want to place in a new category.

② Click Actions.

③ Click Categorize.

④ Click All Categories.

The Color Categories dialog box appears.

⑤ Click New.

The Add New Category dialog box appears.

⑥ Type a name for the new category.

⑦ Click here and select the color you want to associate with the category.

⑧ Click here and select a shortcut key to associate with the category.

Note: If you associate a shortcut key with a category, then you can simply press that key combination to apply the category to a selected Outlook item.

⑨ Click OK to close the Add New Category dialog box.

⑩ Click OK to close the Color Categories dialog box.

Outlook creates the new category and applies it to the selected Outlook item.

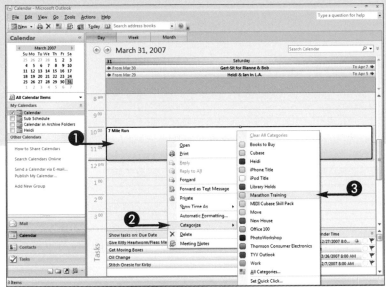

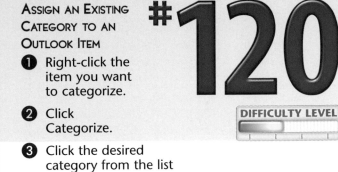

❶ Right-click the item you want to categorize.

❷ Click Categorize.

DIFFICULTY LEVEL

❸ Click the desired category from the list that appears.

● Outlook categorizes and color-codes the selected item.

TIPS

Try This!

If you frequently use the same category, or need to add several items to a category in one sitting, you can use Outlook's Quick Click feature. To do so, choose Set Quick Click in the Categorize submenu and, in the Set Quick Click dialog box, click the down arrow and choose the desired category. Then simply click an Outlook item's Categories column to apply the selected category. To turn off Quick Click, choose No Category in the Set Quick Click dialog box.

Important!

The Categorize submenu contains categories used most recently. If the category you want to apply does not appear in the list, choose All Categories and select the desired category in the Color Categories dialog box that opens.

Forward Outlook information to your
MOBILE PHONE

If you know you will be away from your PC, you can configure Outlook to forward, or *redirect*, Outlook items, including messages, calendar alerts, and more, to your mobile device.

As soon as you are back in the office, you can then instruct Outlook to cease forwarding these items to

your mobile device. To instruct Outlook to stop redirecting items to your mobile device, simply clear the check boxes in the Outlook Mobile Notification dialog box shown in this task and click OK.

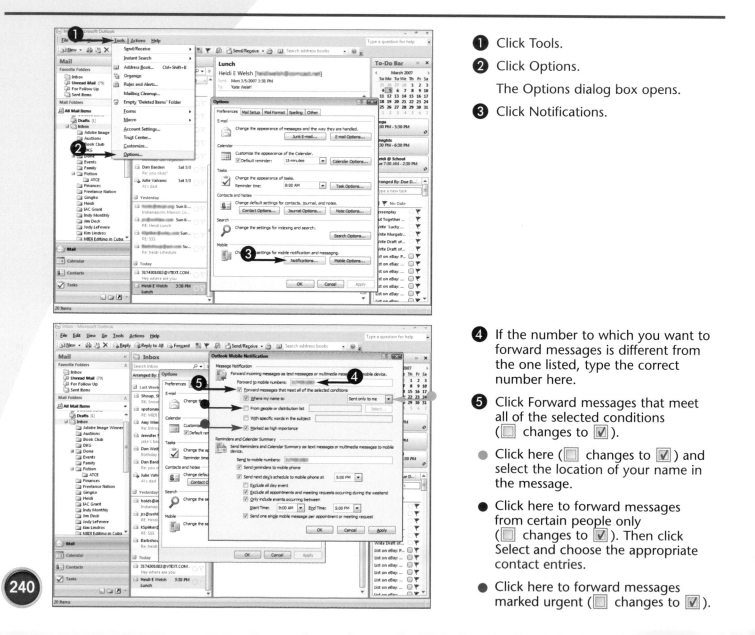

① Click Tools.

② Click Options.

The Options dialog box opens.

③ Click Notifications.

④ If the number to which you want to forward messages is different from the one listed, type the correct number here.

⑤ Click Forward messages that meet all of the selected conditions (☐ changes to ☑).

● Click here (☐ changes to ☑) and select the location of your name in the message.

● Click here to forward messages from certain people only (☐ changes to ☑). Then click Select and choose the appropriate contact entries.

● Click here to forward messages marked urgent (☐ changes to ☑).

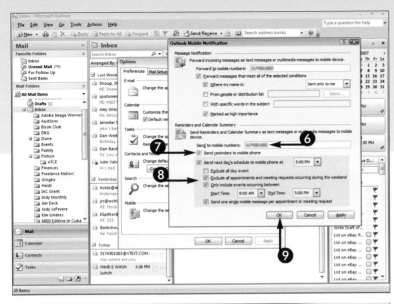

⑥ If the number to which you want to forward reminders and calendar summaries is different from the one listed, type the correct number here.

121

DIFFICULTY LEVEL

⑦ Click here to forward reminders to your mobile phone (☐ changes to ☑).

⑧ Click the desired schedule settings (☐ changes to ☑).

⑨ Click OK to close the Outlook Mobile Notification dialog box.

⑩ Click OK to close the Options dialog box.

TIP

More Options!

Another way to establish redirection settings is to use the Rules Wizard. To do so, click Tools, click Rules and Alerts, and, in the E-mail tab of the Rules and Alerts dialog box, click New Rule. The Rules Wizard starts; choose Send an alert to my mobile device when I get messages from someone, and follow the wizard's onscreen prompts.

Chapter 11: Manage Multiple Priorities with Outlook

241

Send a
CALENDAR SNAPSHOT #122

You can e-mail a calendar snapshot to others — that is, a static view of your calendar as it appears at the moment it is sent. If the recipient of your calendar snapshot also uses Outlook 2007, he or she can drag items from your calendar snapshot into his or her own calendar.

In addition to sending calendar snapshots to others, you can view calendar snapshots sent to you. To do so, click Open This Calendar in the e-mail message containing the snapshot. When prompted, click Yes to confirm that you want to add the snapshot to

Outlook; Outlook displays it side by side with whatever calendar was already displayed. To copy an entry from one calendar to the other, click the entry and drag it.

Note that calendar snapshots are static. When the owner of the calendar makes a change to it, the change is not reflected in the calendar snapshot.

To delete a calendar snapshot — or any of your other calendars — right-click the calendar and choose Delete Calendar Name.

DIFFICULTY LEVEL

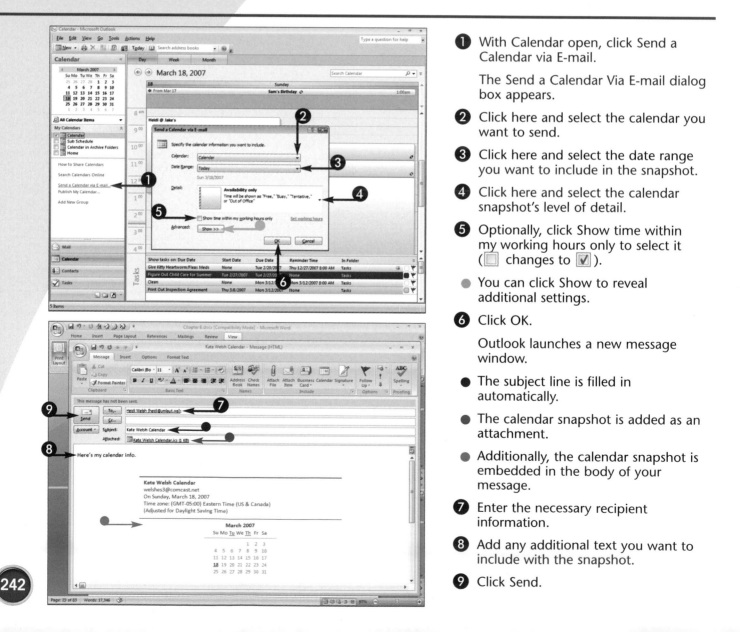

① With Calendar open, click Send a Calendar via E-mail.

The Send a Calendar Via E-mail dialog box appears.

② Click here and select the calendar you want to send.

③ Click here and select the date range you want to include in the snapshot.

④ Click here and select the calendar snapshot's level of detail.

⑤ Optionally, click Show time within my working hours only to select it (☐ changes to ☑).

● You can click Show to reveal additional settings.

⑥ Click OK.

Outlook launches a new message window.

● The subject line is filled in automatically.

● The calendar snapshot is added as an attachment.

● Additionally, the calendar snapshot is embedded in the body of your message.

⑦ Enter the necessary recipient information.

⑧ Add any additional text you want to include with the snapshot.

⑨ Click Send.

View calendars in OVERLAY MODE

#123

DIFFICULTY LEVEL

If you use Outlook to manage multiple calendars — for example, one for work and one for home — you can view those multiple calendars either side by side or in overlay mode. In overlay mode, the calendars appear transparent and stacked, enabling you to see the appointments, events, and meetings in both. If the calendars are displayed in overlay mode, you can revert to side-by-side mode by clicking the arrow button in the tab of either calendar.

Of course, in order to manage multiple calendars, you must first create multiple calendars. To create a calendar in Outlook, click Calendar in the Navigation pane to switch to Calendar mode, click File, and click Calendar. The New Folder dialog box appears; type a name for the new calendar and click OK. You add appointments, events, or meetings to a new calendar just as you would any other calendar.

① With Calendar open, click next to the calendar you want to view in addition to the one that is already open.

You can view as many as 30 calendars at one time.

Outlook displays the selected calendars side by side.

② To view the calendars in overlay mode, click the left arrow in the tab at the top of the calendar on the right.

Outlook displays the calendars in overlay mode.

RECORD JOURNAL ENTRIES automatically

To keep track of your interactions with contacts and other activities, such as the amount of time spent on a particular project, you can use Outlook's Journal feature. Perhaps the most efficient way to use this feature is to configure it to log certain activities automatically.

In addition to configuring Outlook to log journal entries automatically, you can enter them manually. These journal entries can pertain to Outlook items or activities relating to other files on your computer. To manually record an Outlook item, click File, click

New, click Journal Entry, and enter the desired information in the window that appears.

To ensure that your journal entries do not consume more than their fair share of space, Outlook archives them automatically using default archive settings. Clicking the AutoArchive Journal Entries button in the Journal Options dialog box opens the Journal Properties dialog box, where you can change these AutoArchive settings.

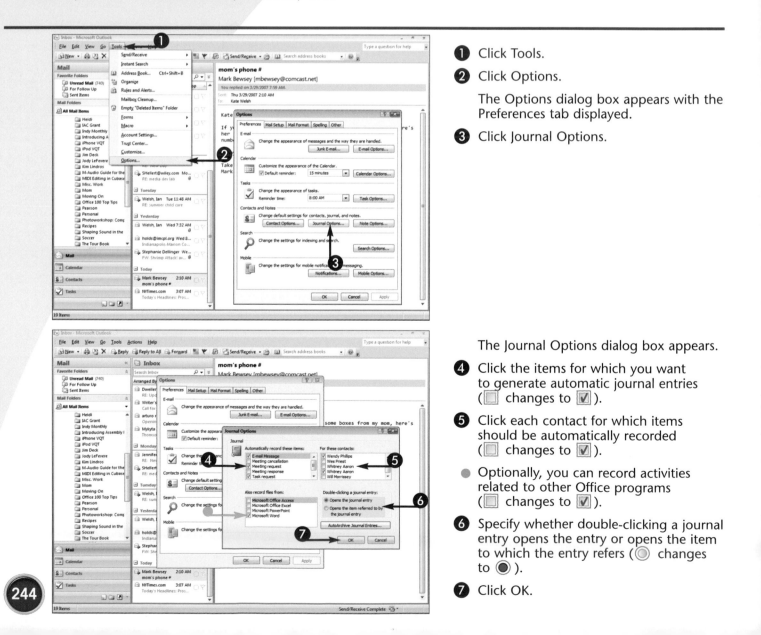

1. Click Tools.
2. Click Options.

   The Options dialog box appears with the Preferences tab displayed.

3. Click Journal Options.

   The Journal Options dialog box appears.

4. Click the items for which you want to generate automatic journal entries (☐ changes to ☑).

5. Click each contact for which items should be automatically recorded (☐ changes to ☑).

● Optionally, you can record activities related to other Office programs (☐ changes to ☑).

6. Specify whether double-clicking a journal entry opens the entry or opens the item to which the entry refers (◉ changes to ◉).

7. Click OK.

DELEGATE
a task

You can delegate a task to another person, who can accept or decline the assignment. When someone accepts a task, that person becomes the task's "owner"; only he or she can make changes to the task. If a task is declined, the person who created the task can revert ownership back to himself.

When the person to whom you delegate a task updates the task, all copies of the task — including the version in your Outlook — are also updated automatically (assuming you

checked Keep an updated copy of this task on my task list). When the person marks the task complete, you are automatically sent a status report notifying you of the task's completion (assuming you checked Send me a status report when this task is complete).

To view tasks that you have delegated to other users, open the View menu while in Task mode, click Current View, and click Assignment.

DIFFICULTY LEVEL

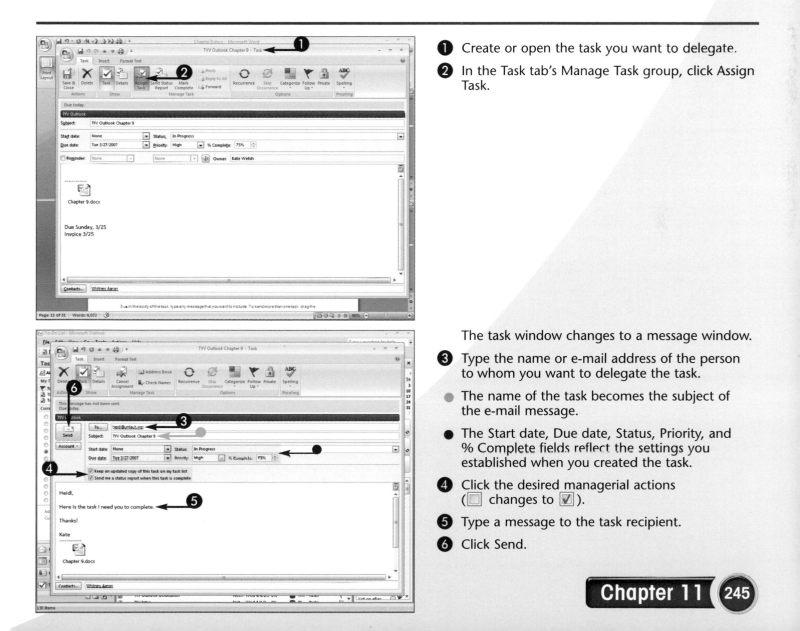

① Create or open the task you want to delegate.

② In the Task tab's Manage Task group, click Assign Task.

The task window changes to a message window.

③ Type the name or e-mail address of the person to whom you want to delegate the task.

● The name of the task becomes the subject of the e-mail message.

● The Start date, Due date, Status, Priority, and % Complete fields reflect the settings you established when you created the task.

④ Click the desired managerial actions (☐ changes to ☑).

⑤ Type a message to the task recipient.

⑥ Click Send.

Chapter 11 **245**

Index

Numbers and Symbols

0 (zero) input mask character reference, 179
9 (nine) input mask character reference, 179
a/A input mask character reference, 179
+ (addition) Excel operator, 83
& (ampersand) input mask character reference, 179
C input mask character reference, 179
/ (division) Excel operator, 83
<> (does not equal) Excel operator, 83
^ (exponent) Excel operator, 83
> (greater than) Excel operator, 83
>= (greater than or equal to) Excel operator, 83
L input mask character reference, 179
< (less than) Excel operator, 83
<= (less than or equal to) Excel operator, 83
* (multiplication) Excel operator, 83
% (percent) Excel operator, 83
# (pound) input mask character reference, 179
? (question mark) input mask character reference, 179
– (subtraction/negation) Excel operator, 83

A

a/A input mask character reference, 179
Accept or Reject Changes dialog box (Excel), 81
Access
    adding pictures to forms, 202–203
    applying input masks, 178–179
    attaching files to records, 182–183
    auto-formatting forms, 198
    auto-formatting reports, 200
    AutoFormat feature, 198
    AutoFormat Wizard, 200
    automating tasks with macros, 194–195
    changing tab order of forms, 199
    collecting data with Outlook, 170–173
    conditional formatting, 204–205
    creating mailing labels, 192–193
    data-collection tools, 170–171
    default values, 175
    displaying summary statistics, 187
    document databases, 189
    exporting reports to Word, 190–191
    Expression Builder, 180
    importing contacts from Outlook, 174
    importing data from Excel, 167–169
    Input Mask Character Reference, 179
    inserting OLE objects, 184–185
    Label Wizard, 192–193
    Macro Builder, 194–195
    making a field required, 176
    Object Dependencies feature, 188
    Object Dependencies task pane, 188
    PivotChart, 208–209
    PivotTable, 206–207
    running filter queries, 186
    saving filters as queries, 186
    saving reports as Web pages, 201
    setting data-validation rules, 180–181
    setting a field caption, 177
    templates, 166
    viewing object dependencies, 188
Account Settings dialog box (Outlook), 230
action buttons (PowerPoint), 132
Action Settings dialog box (PowerPoint), 132
+ (addition) Excel operator, 83
Add Card Picture dialog box (Outlook), 234–235
Add Constraint dialog box (Excel), 93
add-ins, 30
Add-ins dialog box (Word), 32
Add New Category dialog box (Outlook), 238
Add Scenario dialog box (Excel), 88
adding. *See also* inserting
    background color in Excel, 108–109
    captions to photo album PowerPoint presentations, 163
    citations in Word, 50
    commands to the Quick Access toolbar, 22–23
    cross-references in Word, 62
    custom properties, 10
    emphasis with borders in Excel, 107
    field labels in Excel, 94
    images in Excel, 108–109
    line numbers to Word documents, 70–71
    patterns in Excel, 108–109
    pictures to Access forms, 202–203
    pictures to PowerPoint presentations, 154–155
    records using data forms (Excel), 96–97
    sound to PowerPoint presentations, 158–159
    video to PowerPoint presentations, 158–159
    watermarks in Word, 66–67
Advanced Filter dialog box (Excel), 99
aligning cell data (Excel), 118–119
American Psychological Association (APA), 50
& (ampersand) input mask character reference, 179
animating
    PowerPoint slides, 160–161
    SmartArt graphics in PowerPoint, 156
APA (American Psychological Association), 50
applying
    color themes in PowerPoint, 150
    font themes in PowerPoint, 150
    footers at section breaks in Word, 31
    headers at section breaks in Word, 31
    input masks in Access, 178–179
    transition effects in PowerPoint, 129
    workbook themes in Excel, 106
archiving Outlook e-mails, 228
arguments, 84
attaching
    files to records in Access, 182–183
    templates to Word documents, 32
Attachments dialog box (Access), 182
Audio Video Interleave (AVI), 158
auditing Excel worksheets, 86–87
authenticating Office documents, 16–17
author name, 27
auto-formatting
    Access forms, 198
    Access reports, 200

Index

Index

features
AutoFill (Excel), 74–75
AutoFormat (Access), 198
Comments (Word), 41
Drop Cap (Word), 63
Error Checking (Excel), 86–87
Object Dependencies (Access), 188
Photo Album (PowerPoint), 162–163
PickList (Excel), 95
Quick Click (Outlook), 239
Slide Timing (PowerPoint), 128–129
Text Wrapping (Excel), 120
Track Changes (Excel), 80–81
Track Changes (Word), 38–39
Translation ScreenTip (Word), 43
feed post, 231
field labels, 94
files
attaching to records in Access, 182–183
combining Word, 41
HTML (hypertext markup language), 6
filtering
Excel records, 98–99
junk e-mail in Outlook, 226–227
PivotTables in Access, 207
filters (Access), 186
finding synonyms (Word), 44
flagged document properties, 13
font
embedding information, 27
theme, 150
footer building blocks, 30–31
Footnote and Endnote dialog box (Word), 53
footnotes
defined, 52
deleting, 52
inserting, 52–53
viewing, 53
Format Cells dialog box (Excel), 107–108, 111, 119
Format Trendline dialog box (Excel), 117
formatting
building block paragraphs in Word, 33
conditioning in Excel, 110–111
mailing labels in Access, 192–193
forms
adding pictures to Access, 202–203
auto-formatting Access, 198
changing tab order in Access, 199
InfoPath (Access), 171
Formula Auditing tools (Excel), 86–87
formulas (Excel), 82–83
forwarding Outlook information to mobile phones, 240–241
frequency of auto-saving, 26
function Arguments dialog box (Excel), 84–85
functions (Excel), 84–85

gallery
building blocks, 30–31
saving custom cover pages to, 57
generating
indexes in Word, 58–61
table of contents (TOC) in Word, 54–55
Get a Digital ID dialog box (Office), 17
Get External Data - Excel Spreadsheet dialog box (Access), 167
Goal Seek dialog box (Excel), 91
Goal Seek (Excel), 90–91
Goal Seek Status dialog box (Excel), 91
graphics
animating SmartArt (PowerPoint), 160–161
inserting (PowerPoint), 69
>= (greater than or equal to) Excel operator, 83
> (greater than) Excel operator, 83
gridlines (Excel), 121
grouping entries in Access PivotTables, 207
growth trend projections (Excel), 76–77

handouts (PowerPoint), 137
header building blocks (Word), 30–31
headings
displaying in the Word Document Map, 34–35
style text (Word), 54
HighBeam Research, 44
Highlight Changes dialog box (Excel), 80–81
HTML (hypertext markup language) files, 6
HTML Output Options dialog box (Access), 201
hyperlinks (PowerPoint), 133

image (Excel), 108–109
Import and Export Wizard (Outlook), 229
Import Spreadsheet Wizard (Excel), 167
importing
contacts from Outlook to Access, 174
data to Access from Excel, 167–169
Word documents into PowerPoint, 124
index
custom layout, 61
customizing layouts, 61
generating, 58–61
updating, 6
Index dialog box (Word), 60
index entry
deleting, 61
editing, 60
index entry (XE), 58

Index

Index

Index

Read Less–Learn More®

Visual®

There's a Visual book for every learning level...

Simplified®

The place to start if you're new to computers. Full color.

- Computers
- Creating Web Pages
- Mac OS
- Office
- Windows

Teach Yourself VISUALLY™

Get beginning to intermediate-level training in a variety of topics. Full color.

- Access
- Bridge
- Chess
- Computers
- Crocheting
- Digital Photography
- Dog training
- Dreamweaver
- Excel
- Flash
- Golf
- Guitar
- Handspinning
- HTML
- Jewelry Making & Beading
- Knitting
- Mac OS
- Office
- Photoshop
- Photoshop Elements
- Piano
- Poker
- PowerPoint
- Quilting
- Scrapbooking
- Sewing
- Windows
- Wireless Networking
- Word

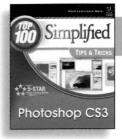

Top 100 Simplified® Tips & Tricks

Tips and techniques to take your skills beyond the basics. Full color.

- Digital Photography
- eBay
- Excel
- Google
- Internet
- Mac OS
- Office
- Photoshop
- Photoshop Elements
- PowerPoint
- Windows

...all designed for visual learners—just like you!

Master VISUALLY®

Your complete visual reference. Two-color interior.

- 3ds Max
- Creating Web Pages
- Dreamweaver and Flash
- Excel
- Excel VBA Programming
- iPod and iTunes
- Mac OS
- Office
- Optimizing PC Performance
- Photoshop Elements
- QuickBooks
- Quicken
- Windows
- Windows Mobile
- Windows Server

Visual Blueprint™

Where to go for professional-level programming instruction. Two-color interior.

- Ajax
- ASP.NET 2.0
- Excel Data Analysis
- Excel Pivot Tables
- Excel Programming
- HTML
- JavaScript
- Mambo
- PHP & MySQL
- SEO
- Vista Sidebar
- Visual Basic
- XML

Visual Encyclopedia™

Your A to Z reference of tools and techniques. Full color.

- Dreamweaver
- Excel
- Mac OS
- Photoshop
- Windows

Visual Quick Tips

Shortcuts, tricks, and techniques for getting more done in less time. Full color.

- Crochet
- Digital Photography
- Excel
- iPod & iTunes
- Knitting
- MySpace
- Office
- PowerPoint
- Windows
- Wireless Networking

For a complete listing of Visual books, go to wiley.com/go/visual